Not by Schools Alone

NOT BY SCHOOLS ALONE

Sharing Responsibility for America's Education Reform

Sandra A. Waddock

PRAEGER

Westport, Connecticut
London

Library of Congress Cataloging-in-Publication Data

Waddock, Sandra A.
     Not by schools alone : sharing responsibility for America's
education reform / Sandra A. Waddock.
          p.   cm.
     Includes bibliographical references and index.
     ISBN 0–275–94790– 4 (alk. paper)
          1. Educational change—United States.   2. Public schools—United
     States.   3. School management and organization—United States.
     4. Education—Social aspects—United States.   I. Title.
     LA217.2.W33   1995
     37000'.973—dc20   94–33259

British Library Cataloguing in Publication Data is available.

Library of Congress Catalog Card Number: 94–33259
ISBN: 0–275–94790– 4

First published in 1995

Praeger Publishers, 88 Post Road West, Westport, CT 06881
An imprint of Greenwood Publishing Group, Inc.

Printed in the United States of America

The paper used in this book complies with the
Permanent Paper Standard issued by the National
Information Standards Organization (Z39.48–1984).

10 9 8 7 6 5 4 3 2 1

"Goodbye," said the fox. "And now here is my secret, a very simple secret: It is only with the heart that one can see rightly; what is essential is invisible to the eye.". . .

"Men have forgotten this truth," said the fox. "But you must not forget it. You become responsible, forever, for what you have tamed. You are responsible for your rose . . ."

"I am responsible for my rose," the little prince repeated, so that he would be sure to remember.

The Little Prince Antoine de Saint Exupéry

So. Would you be proud?

Contents

Preface

This is a book about responsibilities—responsibilities that we sometimes do not like to acknowledge that we have. In particular, it is a book about responsibility for education. For too long we in the United States have attempted to shift the burden of responsibility for children and for their education to someone else, anyone else. Responsibility has shifted off the shoulders of parents, away from extended families and communities, outside of churches and social institutions, out of government's hands. As a result, the burden has fallen solely on the schools. Then, when our children fail to live up to global standards of educational achievement, we have an appropriate target to blame: the schools.

The primary responsibility for education is, of course, rightly placed squarely on the shoulders of educators. Only schools can take charge of the educational system. They need to better understand the dynamics, goals, and organizational characteristics of education. Schools themselves need to restructure the system of education to meet the needs of the global society in which we now live. Schools are in fact responsible for the content and methods of education and for these they need to assume responsibility. So this book is also about the structural and systemic reforms that schools can make to convert themselves into organizations whose members, students, teachers, and administrators alike, continue to grow and learn.

Our society has systematically compounded the difficulties with which schools must contend in recent years by asking schools to resolve various kinds of social problems for which no other institution has been willing or able to bear responsibility. In too many instances families, churches, government, and community organizations have abrogated or not understood fully their own responsibilities for children, families, and education. Schools have not been fully up to the tasks laid at their doorsteps. Teachers and principals have neither the training nor, in many cases, the inclination to assume responsibilities for social problems. Schools are not organized to deal with social problems, yet deal with them they must. Thus, this book is also about finding new ways to organize schools that shift some of the social burdens into more appropriate hands.

The other side of this argument is that although they must take charge of education, schools cannot assume the responsibilities of education alone. They need to request, to demand if necessary, that others accept their own fair share of the responsibilities for education. These responsibilities are far broader than we typically conceive. They relate to our families, our communities, our national ideology and attitudes, to our public policies and the governmental structures that support those policies. They relate to awareness and to the way in which education is portrayed in the media and directly to our values. They relate to developing and maintaining an on-going public dialogue about the responsibilities that we all must assume for the betterment of our communities and, ultimately, our society.

Perhaps paradoxically then, this book is also about the responsibilities that many others bear for education. These others include businesses and families, in particular, but also civic organizations, churches, institutions of higher education, eleemosynary institutions, and government. None of us, not one, can or should escape our own fundamental responsibilities for education.

This book will make an argument that, whatever their inclinations, schools *must* accept the central responsibility for dealing with some of these ills. They are the only institution through which all children must pass. Probably this argument will be contested by the many interest groups and bureaucracies in whose self-interest it is to maintain the status quo. Yet there are strong arguments being made that the quality of education our children attain is central to our survival as a society. We need to acknowledge that centrality. We need to encourage, even demand, that our educational institutions develop their own visions, strategies, and goals for their educational enterprise. For educational leaders, including teachers, this is a national imperative if they are to change the attitudes that have too long placed them in a relatively powerless and neglected position. School leaders cannot expect anyone else to undertake this difficult restructuring process: transformation must come from within, however difficult it is.

For business leaders, fostering a sound educational system is an economic imperative. It is becoming increasingly clear that only nations that have a highly skilled, empowered, and intellectually capable workforce will make significant progress in the next century. But this means that significant changes must be made in businesses themselves, so that they support families, children, and schools. For our changing and troubled families, education is also an imperative. Families need help from schools in understanding their own responsibilities as with respect to education. And families also need to help schools by assuming parental responsibilities that have been too frequently neglected. Only then will children come to school with the attitudes, preparation, and discipline that is so necessary to learning.

For government, civic and community organizations, and churches, the imperative is more difficult because turf and political issues are involved. But it is just as important. As the shapers of public policy and the debates about what is valuable in our society, they are the focal points for creating a new conversation about education and for fostering action.

Over the past decade or so, the public discourse about schools has been heated, but blame for the failures of education has been placed primarily on the schools. Ignored too often are the disruptions in family life, the economic conditions in which many communities exist, and the struggles that individuals and families have to provide balance in their own lives. Ignored is the impact of an almost anti-intellectual attitude, an attitude that ability and not hard work is what matters. Ignored is the impact of an ideology of self-interest and gain, of consumption, and of selfishness. The public conversation about education ultimately shapes institutional and public policies and behaviors. It provides the ideological and attitudinal basis for the educational endeavors of our children and their schools. And the focus of the conversation needs to be shifted away from placing blame and toward working together to effect change.

Our public, civic, community, and religious organizations do more than create the public dialogue about the value, values, and potential of education. Through their own activities and the ways in which they conduct their business, they create the social infrastructure that shapes communities and society as a whole. If they approach social problems as if they were easily isolated into narrow tracks, then bigger problems that are aptly called "messes" will ultimately be left unsolved. Thus, the responsibility of these institutions to change in ways that support education is also an imperative.

Ultimately, this is a prescriptive book about organizational and social change. It is about power sharing and empowering those who have been left too often without power. It is about understanding the dynamics of schools as systems embedded within a larger social system. With this understanding, schools can become organizations in which students and teachers, as learners, can take responsibility for their own education and simultaneously gain appropriate and necessary support from others in society.

This book is not intended as a "how to" handbook, since its prescriptions will have to be applied uniquely to each setting. But it is intended to be a guide for what might be done if only we have the courage, the wisdom, the will, and the leadership to make the necessary changes.

Acknowledgments

This book was harder to write than I would have believed possible when I started, because it speaks to issues of responsibility and the caring that is associated with responsibilities. It was written at a time when both care and responsibility bore heavy weight for me. In acknowledgment of the caring that has been shown me as the book progressed, there are a few special people and institutions that I need to thank.

First, I would like to thank the Spencer Foundation for taking a chance on me by supporting some of the research that underlies this book. The National Alliance of Business, and in particular, Sandra Byrne, project director, also provided support and access to their "Compact Cities." This data proved a useful source of information. To all of those who sat through lengthy telephone interviews or squired me around during site visits, too numerous to recall without leaving out key people, so names best go unmentioned, I also thank you. And to Boston College's Carroll School of Management, which granted a sabbatical leave so the book could be written, also gratitude.

There are always significant people who show that they care when it matters in projects such as this one. Some read early drafts or proposals, others helped push ideas along, still others simply provided general support. While mentioning everyone is impossible, there are a few people that I want to single out for thanks, in particular: Laurie Pant of Suffolk University, who helped me struggle through some of these ideas and made suggestions that pushed me unwillingly toward a far clearer statement of what I meant to say. Jack Neuhauser, dean of Boston College, tried to teach me patience because, as Jim Post of Boston University and now the Conference Board always says, some things, like this book and acts too often neglected, take time. And for Jim, too, who always does take the time even when he is overwhelmed, my thanks. My Boston College colleagues Peter Kugel, Judy Gordon, Joe Raelin, and Sam Graves also provided needed support and critical comments at important junctures.

Karen Coskren, my research assistant and MBA student at Boston College, provided valuable assistance with the manuscript. I thank my sister Eileen Peterson for just being there when it was important and my son, Benjamin, who makes it all worthwhile.

I would like to thank *The International Journal of Value-Based Management* for permission to use material from my article "The Business Role in School Reform: From Feeling Good to System Change" (5[2]: 105–126), and *Business Horizons* for the use of ideas from my article "The Spider's Web: Influences on School Performance" (September-October 1993: 39–48).

Introduction

Consider the school of the late twentieth century.[1] It has not changed a whole lot in the last fifty years or so. Isolated from the rest of the world except for one or two school-business partnerships. Working at the edges of the school, these partnerships attempt to provide students with some insight into the working world or give some marginal discretionary resources for the principal to use. The resources are used on one of a multitude of unrelated programs that the school has set up to cope with the problems that society has dumped on the schools since World War II. Despite the partnerships, schools are failing badly in the United States, so says the common wisdom. But consider: little Johnny or Janey is sometimes left alone on the playground of the school as early as 7:00 or 7:30 A.M. because both Mom and Dad have to be at work. Maybe Mom and Dad are fighting and Janey is afraid that they, like many of her friends' parents, will soon divorce. When everyone finally gets home in the evening, making dinner and television take the place of extended conversation and attention to homework.

The school itself has created barriers that shelter and isolate it from the work of the world that goes on around it. The technological innovations that are pervasive in the business world have yet to penetrate the classrooms, except for a single computer in each classroom that the teacher barely knows how to use. Few businesspeople, even the partners, ever come to the school; those who do are shocked by the conditions they find and by the discipline problems with which teachers must contend. Still, they are comforted by the fact that school feels pretty much like it did when they went to school.

In the school, teachers still lecture to their classes most of the time. Students still sit at their desks trying to absorb what is being said and remember it long enough to repeat it on a test. Workbooks in math, spelling, reading, and social studies are common. Quiet in the classroom, or at least efforts to achieve quiet, bespeak a successful teacher. The teacher is still queen or king of the classroom, separated all day from his or her peers except for lunch breaks when discussion centers around personal rather than school-related issues. Staff meetings are devoted to adminis-trivia, not pedagogy, though periodically there is an "in-service" activity in which teachers are expected to learn something new.

Facilities at the school are deteriorating because of resource constraints and taxpayer revolts that have restricted funding. And every summer about a quarter of the teachers receive notice that they will be laid off, only to be rehired just before school starts. Morale is low, especially since the local newspaper has been paying lots of negative attention to falling test scores. The principal feels battered by complaints from parents about the scores, yet few parents bother to show up at Parent Teacher Association (PTA) meetings.

Simultaneous with a broad back-to-basics movement, the curriculum has expanded to deal with numerous social problems. The district is teaching sex education and passing out condoms at the high school, and not incidentally getting buffeted by the controversy that the decision to do so generated. Environmental education, AIDS education, drug aware-ness and resistance education, understanding handicaps, bicycling safety, and dealing with peer pressure's potential abuse, are only a few of the new curricular demands that have been placed on the school in recent years. None of the old curriculum has been removed or restruc-tured. Yet the school day and year are the same as they were thirty years ago. No time has been added. At 180 days a year, children in this suburb go to school a full forty or more days fewer than most of their interna-tional counterparts.

Drugs and violence are ever-present threats. Although this is a suburban school and there are no police or metal detectors at the door as there are in some urban schools, the principal is ever watchful for strangers near the playground who might be peddling drugs. Discipline is a problem, because the children, even from these middle-class families, have not been social-ized by their stressed-out parents to behave civilly. A majority of the children live in dual-career (dual job), single-parent, or step families, adding to the stress in their lives. Too much of these children's free time is spent in front of the television, though many are pushed into a variety of lessons and other extracurricular activities of various kinds.

With the possible exception of visiting speakers and artists, few members of the local community ever wander through the school doors. Representatives of local businesses, health care organizations, the police, and human service agencies appear in the school infrequently at best. Most of the teachers have little knowledge of the so-called real world, its standards of performance, or its expectations of its employees. A few have been invited in as summer interns by local business partners, but they have not been able to translate their new knowledge into a curriculum that affects more than the students in their own classes.

The school, in effect, is isolated from the rest of the community that surrounds it, except for the buffeting it takes from increasing demands on the curriculum, increased parental and school board pressure for better test performance, and more solving of problems that the rest of these groups and organizations refuse to deal with themselves. The doors are, after all, closed at three and the school does not seem particularly inviting to the general public. Once in a while a public event is held at the school, but that requires paying the janitors exorbitant overtime rates, so such events are infrequent.

Teachers spend the bulk of their days in their own classrooms, dealing with between fifteen and thirty students. Little or no time is available for staff development or discussion of teaching methods. The overall curriculum is generally handed down by state or local authorities to be implemented individually by each teacher. Teachers' contracts specify their working conditions and hours. For some teachers, those specifications represent the limits of the work they will do; for others, they provide merely a floor. Since teachers are in the classroom during most of the day, scheduling meetings is tough, without finding substitutes to take over so teachers can be free to meet. Summers, vacation time, and after the bell rings, after all, are time for personal fulfillment and cannot be infringed upon for work, unless of course, extra pay is involved. A few of the teachers send home periodic newsletters, but for most, the contact with parents takes place primarily at report-card and conference time. Some parents, too often those of the children with the most problems, can't manage to make it to conferences at all.

Many parents are too busy with the difficulties of single parenthood or two-earner families to spend a great deal of time in the schools. When they get home at night it's all they can do to get supper on the table, never mind ensuring that the children's homework is done or finding out much about what went on in school today. Although some parents volunteer at the school, other parents are too busy or too intimidated by their own memories of school to venture into the classroom. Past failures in school, memories of being sent to the principal's office, or the fact that they didn't graduate themselves serve as an intimidating barrier to certain of the parents. Meetings with teachers are difficult to schedule and often just plain difficult because they are dealing with performance, expectations, or problems, and getting bad news is never pleasant. For poor, less well educated, or foreign-born parents, there are the more subtle barriers of language, culture, and professional status that make approaching the school's staff as an equal problematic.

Even for well-educated parents of good students, life is hectic and the school is relatively inaccessible. There are significant barriers to overcome: taking time off from work, for example, for a parent-teacher conference or to attend a big event scheduled at school. Some parents, typically those in managerial or professional positions, can rearrange their schedules to accommodate these events, though the culture of most of their businesses does not provide a great deal of support for parenting time off. Taking time off, even by professionals and managers, is subtly frowned upon. Parents with less flexibility in their jobs, often find themselves missing events they might otherwise like to attend because scheduling time off is impossible without risking their jobs. For women, the problem is particularly acute, since there is both the social expectation that they will be at the school to deal with their children's needs and the expectation that they will work at least as hard as the men in their organizations if they hope to succeed. Teachers, many of whom are themselves working parents, have nonetheless been heard to proclaim, "If they really loved their kids, they'd stay home from work to be with them."

The parent-teacher organization serves primarily as fund raiser, using bake sales, auctions, and other fund raisers to obtain a little extra money so that principal and teacher can implement some of a multitude of school programs. Run by a few dedicated volunteers, the PTA recently attempted to work closely with school staff to develop a set of core values that could pervade the school and refocus the teachers' and children's energies. The need to do this came both from the district, which established the program, and from a crisis that the school dealt with in the previous year resulting from falling test scores. Everyone was optimistic about the potential for this program last year, but turnover in the PTA officers and a "work to rule" action by the teachers, because their contract has not been renewed, have diminished attention to the implementation plan.

As mentioned, the school has a variety of programs, some developed by the staff, some supported and even implemented by the PTA, and some sponsored by the district. Each program has its own specific set of purposes: to improve reading or expose students to the classics, to bring in a poet in residence, to provide drug-awareness education, to help counsel teens at risk (of dropping out or pregnancy), to provide jobs for a few students, to visit a local worksite, as examples. Few of these programs are coordinated with each other. Each one is overlaid on what already exists, with little thought to how they relate to each other or to the needs of the students as people, learners, or family members. Each program is noble in its objectives and has good will behind it. But each one done during the school day takes time away from teaching. There is no real forum, particularly with the seemingly endless job action, for discussing how these programs might be coordinated or what should be kept and what dropped. None of the programs is sufficient to deal with the students' life problems or get them into shape to learn.

The community itself, while well off, has been struggling in recent years with tax restrictions that have affected the schools, police, and fire departments in particular. There are many more parents already un-employed or worrying about becoming unemployed than in past years. Even the business partners are finding it hard to spare the slack resources that used to help out the principal. Other organizations in the community, the local Y, a range of churches and synagogues, nonprofit and human service organizations, and local health organizations, have little to do with the schools at all. Each operates well within its own sphere, tending to its own business.

This school is hypothetical, but the problems described—its isolation from the rest of the community, the fragmentation of curriculum, the relative stability and inflexibility of its structure—these are problems that characterize many schools today. It is dealing with these issues that this book is about.

NOTE

1. The images created here are a composite of many schools that I am familiar with, having visited or participated in them during the course of this research as well as from the many books and articles that are cited in the reference list. Probably not all of these conditions apply to any one school though, and of course, the problems that children in the inner city, where family disintegration and economic circumstances are far worse than in the suburbs, make the task of education even more difficult than described here.

Chapter 1 _____

A Context of Change

Change is an imperative in the social, technological, and global world that educators, businesspeople, communities, and public leaders face today. Turbulence, chaos, and competition intensified by technological innovation and increased capacity for communication are shaping this new world. Businesses have been and are being transformed. Public institutions and government agencies are being reinvented.[1] Community and social activists along with public policy makers are shaping new means to achieve their goals. These means rely simultaneously upon the incentives of the market, the mandate of policy, regulation, and law, and collaboration among sectors to act in the interest of the broader community. In the face of this turmoil and change, one institution has remained fairly stable, despite significant efforts at reform: the public school.[2]

The stability of schools as organizations stands in marked contrast to the dramatic changes in structure that many of our other social institutions, at least those that have been successful, have been going through for about twenty years.[3] Business organizations, in particular, have found that the pressures of global competition and the technological advances posed by the computer have reshaped the way that the most successful among them conduct and organize themselves. Flattened hierarchies, decentralized decision making, shared power, and renegotiated relationships between management and other employees have become the norm in companies that are on the frontiers of their industries. Progressive companies have discovered that such structures are necessary if they are to be able to adapt successfully to the chaotic conditions in which they find themselves. Even the highly bureaucratized agencies of government are increasingly being subjected to reinvention[4] so that they can achieve greater economies and more efficiency through using the types of incentives that we normally think of as more suited to the private sector.

Since the issuance of *A Nation at Risk* in 1983, U.S. schools have been faced with ever exacerbating public criticism in leading popular, education, and business periodicals. Teacher morale has suffered under the sometimes vitriolic public rhetoric on the crisis in education. These criticisms have resulted in numerous reports, conferences, editorials, and public attention to the quality of schools. Many books and articles have been published suggesting revisions, reforms, and (in the current terminology) restructuring. Most of this attention has suggested that schools are failing. Despite the attention, schools have not changed very much.

Highly centralized bureaucracies, rigidly structured union work rules and constraints, isolation of teachers in classrooms with little opportunity to communicate with colleagues, and few staff or organization development opportunities characterize most schools.[5] Most schools still lack much direct contact with parents, businesses, or social service and community agencies, which tends to increase their isolation. Much curriculum is still premised on lectures taught to passive students by teachers serving as founts of wisdom pouring knowledge into waiting and empty heads.

Despite numerous efforts at reform, calls to arms, and tens of thousands of partnerships between schools and businesses started in the past fifteen years, most schools continue to use outmoded teaching strategies. Their organizing structures are geared more to a mass production economy than the technologically sophisticated society that is rapidly becoming reality.[6] Governance bodies are too frequently dominated by political rather than educational concerns, and schools are plagued by failures of funding resulting in part from taxpayers' unwillingness to fund schools they perceive to be failing.

Principals are too often constrained by teachers' tenure, union rules, or simple lack of real managerial authority from using even the simplest managerial devices to foster improvement or provide incentives. Education schools are criticized for low-admission criteria as well as failing to provide sufficient academic rigor and depth of knowledge to prospective teachers, leaving them unprepared to teach academically rigorous topics. Too frequently, textbooks and school equipment are outdated; physical facilities are run down; computers are too few and teachers ill-trained at knowing how to use them even when they are available.[7]

These are only a few of the problems of organizing that characterize U.S. schools today. This catalog does not even begin to account for the social problems that are plaguing schools, which must be dealt with before the job of education can be adequately addressed. If, in the words of *A Nation at Risk*, the United States was faced in 1983, with a "rising tide of mediocrity,"[8] then as the twenty-first century draws nearer, the tide continues to rise.

WHY NO RESPONSE?

Why haven't schools responded to the demands of the global village by changing their own structures, decision making, and curricula? Why have schools been able to remain relatively isolated not only from the technological and organizational changes that are currently driving society (not always positively[9]) while being severely buffeted by the social changes? To understand the situation of schools, we need to understand the historical context in which modern-day schools developed, the systems under which schools operate, and the macrosystems in which they are embedded. We need to understand better the influences, responsibilities, and structures of external institutions that affect schools and their performance, yet are beyond the direct control of schools. And we need to better understand the responsibilities for their own transformation that schools themselves must assume.

Most importantly, we need to understand far more about responsibility for education than we currently do. The widespread perception that U.S. public schools are failing has resulted in a plethora of blame. The schools are to blame for low expectations, failure to respond to the changes in society around them, and for falling scores on standardized tests, among a multitude of other sins. In assigning blame for these failures, we make two assumptions. First, we assume that "if only" schools would understand some simple reform or institute some new state-of-the-art program or other, the schools would improve. If only they could be more like Japanese, German, or Swedish schools, then our students would surely perform up to international standards. If only they would implement choice, the market would solve their ills. Second, we assume that responsibility for education rests solely or certainly primarily with the schools. Both of these assumptions are severely flawed.

As the complexities of education reform that will be outlined in coming chapters indicate, there really is no simple or short-term answer to the problem of school reform or restructuring. There is no panacea, despite the American penchant for seeking one.[10] The problems of schools are simply too complex to hope that any single program or proposed solution, such as choice, partnerships with business, school-to-work transition programs, or imitating other nations, will solve the problems. The solutions that will work, have, in the end, to deal with the structural, organizational, and systemic constraints and opportunities that schools have or can create. Each school must ultimately find its own way of organizing and operating, since each situation is unique. Yet by better understanding the dynamics of organizing and schools' relationships to important external constituencies, it may be possible to provide a framework that can help many schools figure out their own paths to reform. The hope of a simple solution has again and again proved an elusive dream because of the very complexity involved with education. The assignment of responsibility for education is equally complex, especially since we have tended to shift more and more of the burden, not just of education, but also for many social problems, to schools in recent years.

Fundamentally, the responsibility for restructuring schools does in fact rest squarely on the shoulders of those in charge of day-to-day operations: school people—administrators, teachers, and even students. There can be no doubt about the need for school officials, teachers, and students to assume this responsibility. But, and this is a critical but, many others also need to assume relevant and important responsibilities for education. Both types of responsibilities have been neglected in recent years.

Although infrequently acknowledged, it is the broader social system in which a school exists that influences its ultimate performance. Lack of recognition of the scope of these responsibilities and the influence of outside organizations and institutions on schools has resulted in many responsibilities for education being abrogated by important constituencies. Families, businesses, communities, churches, governmental agencies and others must begin to recognize and assume appropriate responsibility for education.

Through the next chapters we will begin to explore the obstacles to change, the responsibilities of key constituencies, and the ways in which rethinking the structure, responsibilities, and relationships among these constituencies might enhance prospects for truly improved education in the United States. Before we begin this exploration, it is important to understand where U.S. public schools stand now as a result of their development in the context of a democratic society. In particular, schools' relationships with external constituencies or stakeholders will be explored, especially as those relationships shifted during the latter part of the twentieth century.

THE PROBLEMS OF EDUCATION: AN OVERVIEW

The industrial revolution had a profound impact on the development of schools in the United States, although many educators would hate to admit it. While schools have retained a calendar based on an agrarian society, the methods, structures, and curricula they have adopted have been largely aimed at an industrial society, members of which are well enough educated to take their places in the assembly line.[11] Under this design, students or workers could perform tedious, repetitive tasks, that required little real thought, but did demand the ability to follow orders, be disciplined, and tolerate boredom. Children learned these skills in schools. Those who persisted through graduation also learned to deal with rote memorization, disciplined and structured days, and tedious and repetitive tasks very similar to the types of unskilled or semiskilled jobs they would face later on at work.

With the emergence of Frederick Taylor's principles of scientific management in the early 1900s, the theme of efficiency began to dominate industry. This same theme spread into the schools through the early 1900s, as an assembly-line approach to educating the masses was adopted.[12] The structure of industry and the structures that schools, as well as the unions to which their teachers now belong, developed along remarkably parallel lines. Hierarchically structured industrial organizations were based on a command-and-control mentality. Command and control assumed that top management had all the answers and the workers were merely cogs in the great industrial wheel, exchangeable, easily replaceable, and tool-like.

Perhaps unwittingly, schools too developed a command-and-control mentality, placing teachers in the role of expert in the classroom and administrators in the role of authority with few bridges in between. In the case of schools, the command-and-control mentality was implemented through lesson plans, relatively rigid (albeit locally controlled) curricula, and fairly strict lines of authority from teachers to principals to superintendents to school boards or committees.

Through the end of the nineteenth and into the twentieth century, public schools had to deal with educating masses of immigrants, most of whom did not complete high school. Problems of educating a wide diversity of children to the same standard were highlighted by the desegregation movement, which had begun officially with the Supreme Court's *Brown vs. Board of Education* decision in 1954, but gained momentum during the 1970s.[13] Throughout the 1970s and into the 1980s, schools struggled with issues of desegregation, not always successfully. Busing was introduced in the 1970s in attempts to equalize education.

One unintended consequence of busing, particularly in urban areas, was the phenomenon known as "white flight."[14] Middle-class whites, and frequently middle-class people of color as well, left cities in droves. In many cases they were simply following middle-class jobs, which were rapidly being relocated to the suburbs. Too often, however, this flight of the middle class left schools even more segregated than they had been and class lines even more sharply drawn, because those left were too poor to escape. As we shall see later on, the social problems resulting from the poverty, familial disintegration, and lack of economic opportunities has created significant problems for inner-city schools. Too infrequently acknowledged in public policy are both the racial and class-based implications of these problems.

Concerns about educating all of America's children are not new. In the late 1940s, the United States was educating less than 50 percent of the population to the high-school graduation level. Neither are dropout or literacy rates worse today than they were thirty or forty years ago.[15] Indeed, as a nation we are, in fact, educating a greater percentage of students than in the past. The history of graduation rates shows evidence of steady growth until the mid-1960s when graduation rates stabilized. In 1870 only 2 percent of the population graduated from high school. By 1900 that number had risen only to 6.4 percent. Slightly over 50 percent of the population was graduating from high school by 1940, with that rate gradually creeping up to 59 percent by 1950. In the 1950s about 62 percent of eligible students graduated on average, with that number stabilizing somewhat under 75 percent on average since the 1960s. Graduation rates peaked at 77.1 percent in 1969, however they have generally ranged between 72 and 75 percent since then.

Part of the impetus for increased graduation rates during the late 1950s and 1960s may have been the intense competition between the U.S. and the USSR spawned by the cold war. The U.S. educational system received a severe shock with the launching of Sputnik by the USSR in 1957, since Sputnik symbolized America's loss of leadership, particularly in science and mathematics. The Sputnik shock and the rhetoric surrounding it triggered a sense of crisis in public schools, which were perceived not to be teaching these topics adequately. To deal with this crisis, science and math programs were beefed up. In fact, schools themselves changed very little. Problems remained but were less visible to the general public, at least until 1967 when Jonathan Kozol published *Death at an Early Age*. Along with others, this book sent shock waves through the educational establishment.[16]

Schools were subjected to other shocks, some of them less immediately observable, but which had long-term consequences for performance. One shock, the impact of which was not realized until much later, was the women's liberation movement, which began in the 1960s. The women's movement made it possible for talented women to enter professions other than those traditionally reserved for them, one of the most important of which was teaching. While providing many benefits to women in increased career opportunities, this movement made it increasingly difficult to recruit talented individuals to teaching. Combined with the already low status and relatively low pay of the teaching profession, the public perception that teachers were underqualified began to grow. Scholastic Aptitude Test (SAT) scores of students entering into schools of education slipped even more than those of the general student population during the 1960s and 1970s, only beginning to climb again in the late 1980s as standards began to tighten.

Another shock, which had long-term and relatively insidious effects on the schools, was the taxpayer revolt. Although some argue that investments in schools went up during the 1980s and into the 1990s as teachers' salaries improved marginally, clear disparities existed and still exist among communities. Because schools depend largely on property taxes, the potential for funding differences is great and is, in fact, frequently large among districts. School funding is political because it is based on property taxes, and it was on property tax issues that taxpayers tended to revolt first: in California with Proposition 13 and in Massachusetts with Proposition 2 1/2. Both of these propositions limited the amount of revenue that local communities could raise and, as a by-product, how much could be spent on schools.

Herman "Dutch" Leonard studied Massachusetts in the ten years after Proposition 2 1/2 was passed. Proposition 2 1/2 limited total property taxes to 2 1/2 percent of market value and, more insidiously, limited the increase each year to 2 1/2 percent of the total tax. To override these restrictions required a popular referendum. The results of Leonard's study suggest some of the harm that the taxpayer revolt has done to the schools. Although the spending per student in Massachusetts remained above the national average during the ten-year period from 1979 to 1989 (after Proposition 2 1/2 was passed), "the emphasis Massachusetts placed on per student operating spending for elementary and secondary education dropped significantly."[17] This effect is magnified when higher cost-of-living rates in Massachusetts are taken into consideration. Leonard concludes that there was a fairly significant shift in the relative priority that the state placed upon education during the ten-year period of the study—and that shift did not bode well for schools, which were systematically squeezed. Taxpayers' anger at the slowness of reforms may have similarly affected other states.

Spending on schools has in fact increased over the years, but partly because an increasing percentage of students now remain in schools longer. Schools also have been asked to take on more responsibilities over the past thirty years. Curriculum demands increased, simultaneously with a demand to return-to-basics, and children with special needs have been integrated into mainstream classrooms or provided with many new and frequently costly services.[18] State spending increased during the 1980s, while federal spending decreased. But overall as a percent of gross national product, school spending in 1987 was below that in 1970. Teacher-pupil ratios have dropped in the past twenty years, but, as will become evident in the next chapter, the problems with which children are coming to school and the tasks that schools have been asked to assume, have increased dramatically in that same time period.[19]

Also, during the 1960s, unions began to gain bargaining power in education. Unions provided many benefits to teachers, including a strong unified voice with which to deal with management, advocacy for better working conditions, and greater recognition by the public and management. The conditions of schooling, however, were already relatively isolating and fairly rigidly structured. Unions served to increase the distance by their emphasis on professionalism, rigidity through the establishment of job standards, and lack of flexibility through emphasis on what teachers could and could not do under their contracts.

As attempts to foster professionalism increased, schools further distanced themselves from the business community, which some believed had had too great an influence in the early part of the century.[20] Schools also, perhaps inadvertently, distanced themselves from parents in their role of education expert, implicitly suggesting that in all matters educational, they knew better than parents. For many parents, this stance erected virtual barriers between school and parent. The problem was particularly severe for less well educated parents, for those who did not finish school themselves, or for parents who had had trouble during their own schooling. These parents were more likely to be intimidated by the barrier of professionalism and the implications that they, as parents, did not have much to offer to their children's educations. As more and more women began taking full- or part-time employment during the 1970s and 1980s, some as much because of economic necessity as for career reasons, time available to participate in or oversee children's education also diminished.

Increasing suburbanization also meant a loss of extended family to help raise children, and a resulting greater reliance on professional advice with respect to childrearing. Since much education in earlier times had actually been done through the role modeling provided by nuclear and extended families,[21] the loss of family control over many aspects of children's education left schools more completely responsible for that education. The long-term process of industrialization had also had a similar effect by creating a situation in which most men's work was done largely outside the home, away from the children, reducing opportunities for informal education and role modeling.[22]

The mentality of professionalism was reinforced by unions, which attempted to raise salaries and improve working conditions for teachers.[23] While trying to improve teaching as a profession, unions had the paradoxical effect of further imposing rigid work rules, occasional nasty and very public strikes, and other constraints on teachers' activities. Both of the major teachers' unions, the American Federation of Teachers and the National Education Association, have in the past adamantly opposed merit pay proposals, which might provide school administrators with some management leverage over what goes on in the classroom. Instead of merit pay, unions promote reliance on credentials and seniority, believing that these are more objective performance indicators.[24]

These constraints have somewhat ironically inhibited teachers' efforts to be accepted as professionals. They reflected in large part the types of very real organizational constrictors under which teachers already operated in their schools.[25] Unfortunately for any attempts at managing or structuring schools differently, these strictures provide a rationale for stability and lack of change rather than encouraging adaptive responses to changing internal or external conditions. Unions are, in their own structures, products of the same command-and-control mentality that bureaucratically constrains most schools. Indeed, one union official has argued that when schools themselves change structures and incentives, unions will also have to change both in attitude and in the types and orientation of constraints they present to administrators.[26]

Despite all of these shocks and much rhetoric about the problems of schools, little changed in schools structurally. Classrooms still retained their structure as isolated entities with teachers at their head. Attempts at educational innovation, such as discovery learning advocated by Jerome Bruner, placed emphasis on equality and mainstreaming of the disadvantaged, different, and disabled, and child-centered approaches developed during the 1970s. These initiatives have been labeled by at least one observer as an "era of softness."[27] This era of softness stands in contrast to the obverse, "era of hardness," which followed. Built upon the concepts of essentials of learning prominent during the 1940s and 1950s, the era of hardness gave attention to a back-to-basics movement that emphasized the three "Rs" of reading, 'riting, and 'rithmetic, frequently to the exclusion of other important skills and areas of knowledge.[28] Neither hard nor soft approaches, however, did much to improve the performance of schools, in part because little changed structurally, attitudinally, or in content inside schools or at the classroom level.

FRAMING THE EDUCATION DEBATE IN THE LATE TWENTIETH CENTURY: BUSINESS IS MOBILIZED

In 1983, the public debate entered a new era that raised consciousness about some of the major failures of education. Sparked by the publication of *A Nation at Risk*, the public's attention to education was galvanized by phrases such as "mediocre educational performance," and "an act of unthinking, unilateral, educational disarmament." The report, in combination with a general movement toward more public-private sector interaction,[29] set the stage for a re-entry of business leaders, as well as leaders in other sectors and parents, into the public policy debate about education. Despite great interest in and participation in educational governance throughout the early twentieth century, business had largely taken a back seat to community activists and parents in educational governance over the previous twenty years.[30]

Through the rest of the 1980s, the reawakened business community involved itself directly in the public debate about education and also became directly involved in education in many instances. There were two streams to business involvement: the partnership stream, which dominated certain aspects of the education reform debate, and school choice, which was a product of a market-driven ideology.

School choice was spearheaded most vocally by Chubb and Moe of the Brookings Institution.[31] Chubb and Moe advocated school choice by parents as a market mechanism that would, by itself, foster improved schools, that is, as a panacea despite their own proclaimed lack of panaceas. In a general ideological climate during the 1980s in which the market was viewed by many as supreme, notions of using parental choice seemed to offer a potential solution to school performance problems. By subjecting schools to market pressures, local governments could foster improvements, since schools that did not perform up to standard would be deselected, lose money, and presumably eventually go out of business. In part, this emphasis on choice was an attempt to foster "excellence" in education. By the mid 1980s, excellence as a goal for education had partially replaced the long-term goal of equity, especially as the public attention was increasingly drawn to the need to educate all children to some global standard and not just an elite few.[32]

To the dismay of many educators, this pattern of using market incentives to achieve public goals followed a significant trend in the business environment without a whole lot of input from educators. Additionally implementation of choice plans in various cities and states imposed severe constraints upon less successful schools, particularly those in disadvantaged communities, without necessarily recognizing the difficulties they were facing. Further, at least one author seriously criticized the premises on which the Chubb and Moe study rested, suggesting that their analysis was, at best, flawed.[33] Always controversial because of its tendency to leave the worst schools in place and the most defenseless children behind, the school choice movement nonetheless gained substantial ground during this period.

The partnership stream took an altogether different tack, focusing on the need for both a systemic and collaborative approach to education reform. Thousands of school-business partnerships were formed during the 1980s and early 1990s on a one-to-one basis with schools or school systems. Indeed, by at least one count more than 140,000 such partnerships were established during the 1980s.[34] The growth in collaboration between schools and businesses during this era highlights some of the activity that was taking place. By 1991 the National Association of Partners in Education (NAPE) estimated that more than half (51 percent) of America's 16,000 school districts were actively involved in partnership programs. These programs were estimated to include some 2.6 million volunteers and to reach as many as 29.7 million students, or 65 percent of the total number of students attending schools where there were active partnerships.[35]

NAPE also estimated that as many as 65 percent of districts with partnerships included improving achievement as a program objective, and 37 percent included better career awareness and 39 percent incorporated career-related activities. Further, some 41 percent of all districts with partnerships were estimated to be providing tutoring as one of their elementary school activities. Partnership programs with public schools encompassed pre-schools, elementary schools, middle schools, and high schools. NAPE estimated that the combined dollar value of the goods and services contributed by partners was nearly a billion dollars in total.[36]

Content areas for these partnerships could be categorized into four main areas: curriculum and instruction (33 percent), direct student support (31 percent), professional development (14 percent), and districtwide policy and program initiatives (22 percent).[37] Despite the progress in direct business involvement in education, which tended to increase over the years, some critics still believed that business-education partnerships were working mainly at the margins.[38]

While most such partnership initiatives are well intended, they tend to tap into the inclination of schools to build new program after new program, without doing anything to alter the organizational structure or the overall system of educating students. The result, probably for most partnerships, despite some movement toward a more truly collaborative approach that did attack systemic issues, was that little changed in the schools or for the children or teachers. The Boston Compact's experience perhaps best symbolizes the difficulties that such collaborations have had in achieving systemic changes within schools. Lessons from efforts to replicate the Boston Compact also provide some insights into potential future directions, on which the premises of this book rest.

Begun in 1982, the Boston Compact was certainly a, if not the, pioneer of public-private partnerships in education (as well as in many other arenas).[39] The original impetus for the Compact derived in part from the Job Training Partnership Act (JTPA), which replaced the Comprehensive Employment and Training Act (CETA). JTPA mandated collaboration between the public sector and businesses for purposes of job training for the disadvantaged and created Private Industry Councils (PIC) to administer federal funds for job training. These PICs consisted of representatives of business, government, and communities and, in theory, were granted real decision-making power in the job-training arena.

In Boston, the PIC was established in the late 1970s apart from, and in fact served as the model for, JTPA's PICs. Boston's PIC consisted of powerful business leaders, as well as others from community and government agencies. A variety of circumstances in Boston led the PIC to focus on the problems of Boston schools. PIC leadership recognized the importance of education in creating a competitive workforce and developed the notion of a compact or bargain between the business community and the schools. Signed in 1982, the Boston Compact provided that the business community would grant priority hiring for graduates of the Boston Public Schools in exchange for specified and measurable improvements in the schools' performance. Measures included attendance, graduation rates, and test performance; the reward for improved student and school performance was to be access to jobs. In effect, the Compact was a jobs program held out as a carrot to inner-city students so they would be motivated to improve their education.

When the Compact came up for renewal five years later, it ran into trouble. Although the business community had been reasonably good at fulfilling its end of the bargain, not much had changed in the schools, including performance. The Compact was ultimately renewed (now twice) with reemphasis on the importance of improved school performance. To date, however, there have been few efforts at systemic reform emerging from the Boston Compact in the Boston Public Schools. Although intentions were the best, the Compact proved to be "yet another program" for many school people (possibly because they had not been deeply involved in the planning efforts).

Despite the limited actual success of the Boston Compact in significantly changing the way schools operated, the Compact did receive a great deal of public attention during the 1980s. Certainly for many cities it served as an example of how collaboration between business, schools, and government might develop. In 1986, the Boston Compact became the basis for a twelve-city demonstration project by the National Alliance of Business (NAB).[40] Using the incentive of jobs after graduation or part-time during school years, NAB attempted to replicate the Boston Compact in cities throughout the country. Creators of projects in the twelve cities soon realized that they needed to develop projects specific to their local needs and that ultimately a simple school-to-work transition program, such as the Compact represented, would be unlikely to effect much significant change in the schools themselves or the performance of students.

Although a great deal was learned in some of the demonstration cities about the process of intersector collaboration, the other major learning was that education reform was neither quick nor simple. Slowly, in some of these cities, as well as in other cities around the nation where businesses had begun collaborating with schools, the recognition began to dawn in the business community that schools would need to change radically if performance were to improve. Slowly, school officials and business leaders alike began to become aware of the systemic and societal nature of their problems. Slowly, the term systemic reform, that is, reform that dealt with the fundamentals of the way schools were organized and structured, their relationships with external organizations and with families of their students, and the ways that teachers were trained, began to enter the policy debate about school reform.

Some of this new language of restructuring derived from the business community's own experiences with global competition and the restructurings that were caused by the need to regain competitiveness. Some came from the frustrations of public officials and businesses who thought they were pouring in resources to schools and seeing so little change. In line with the developing notions of systemic change, the business establishment also took another potentially more potent tack in attempting to fuel and shape the public debate about schools: advocacy for public policy change.

Powerful business organizations, such as the Business Roundtable, the Committee for Economic Development, the Conference Board, and the National Alliance of Business, focused their energies on education and its reform. At least at the leadership level, business executives had begun to recognize the centrality of education as a workforce issue. Report after report was issued, new centers on education emerged, and conferences were held to discuss the risks that the nation faced from a failing education system.

Among the most visible business organizations that became committed to education reform was the Committee for Economic Development (CED). CED, an independent research and educational organization with membership of 200 business executives and educators, issued a series of important reports and held a variety of symposiums on education. CED's position on education helped to frame the public debate in a new way, by beginning to focus on education as an investment in the future rather than simply as a current expense. In establishing this framing, CED picked up on one of the themes made explicit in *A Nation at Risk*, that U.S. economic competitiveness was directly linked to the quality of public school education.

With reports bearing such titles as "Investing in Our Children" (1985); "Children in Need: Investment Strategies for the Educationally Disadvantaged" (1987); "The Unfinished Agenda: A New Vision for Child Development and Education" (1991); and "Business Impact on Education and Child Development Reform" (1991, authored by P. Michael Timpane and Laurie Miller McNeill), the CED took a prominent and very public role in framing the debate about education as one of investment in the future. This debate and the emerging focus on linkages between public education and competitiveness, about which some business leaders were becoming increasingly concerned, was intensified in 1987. In that year, Johnston and Packer published *Workforce 2000: Work and Workers for the Twenty-first Century*.[41] This seminal publication of the Hudson Institute explicitly linked significant demographic changes, industrial and economic competitiveness, and public education.

By identifying trends in workforce demography and then pointing out that historically less well educated groups would be a greater percentage of the workforce in the future, Johnston and Packer hit a public nerve. Their book made explicit what had been quite unspoken in the past—that if the U.S. economy was to compete successfully with the economies of other nations, and if our standard of living were to be maintained, more effort would have to be focused on educating historically undereducated groups: people of color and women, in particular. Development of what the National Center on Education and the Economy was later to call the "high skills" workplace[42] depended on the availability of high-skilled rather than low-skilled workers. A low-skilled economy, so said the commission, would be a low-wage economy, and the nation's standard of living, already perceived by some to be slipping, would slip still further.

Other business organizations, like the National Alliance of Business, also had become directly involved with education reform following publication of *A Nation at Risk*, attempting in many cases to play a catalytic role. Based on some of its learning from its twelve-city Compact Project,[43] NAB ultimately joined forces with the Business Roundtable to articulate a broad-based position on education reform for the business community. The Business Roundtable (BRT), perhaps the nation's most important business group, made a ten-year commitment to systemic education reform in 1990. With the issuance of its own report, "The Business Role in State Education Reform," the BRT fostered a major commitment by its members to work toward reform of public education through the public policy process at the state level over a ten-year period. Local and national Chambers of Commerce and the Conference Board led similar reform efforts as well.

All of these activities by the business community, supplemented by many others, focused public attention on education and the "crisis" that education faced in America. To some extent, however, these efforts were perceived by educators to be those of outsiders attempting to interfere with organizations already being run professionally. The isolation of the school from the business community, as well as the parental and general communities in which they existed, generally continued. The prevalence of partnerships with businesses and community organizations combined with an increasing recognition of the importance of parental involvement in education[44] had begun to break down some of the barriers by the end of the 1980s.

There are hints that a shift toward systems and away from the typical fragmented thinking is beginning to penetrate public policy and strategic thinking around school reform. Since the issuance of *A Nation at Risk*, businesses, schools, and policy makers have struggled to meet the demands posed by that report, largely by implementing new programs aimed at one or another aspect of the educational problem. With the continued frustration produced by the relative lack of positive results for all of these innovations, a new type of thinking began developing in the early 1990s. For the first time under the banner of America 2000's educational goals (now GOALS 2000: Educate America), the U.S. government articulated a set of national goals that have the potential to begin the long-term process of shaping a common vision about education. The goals represent a small movement toward common understanding about what is needed to reform education and what some of the underlying issues are for schools.

In fact, the national education goals themselves may be less important than the processes which are being undertaken to try to implement them. These implementation strategies represent a fundamental shift not only in the role of DOE, but also in the direct involvement of key players within each local community. Behind GOALS 2000 lies a basic shift in thinking about what it will take for schools to perform up to par: the emerging perspective is that all of those parties that affect students, schools, and families need to be brought together to discuss the roles of schools. Hence a first step in becoming a GOALS 2000 community is to bring together key business leaders, community and church leaders, school officials, the media, and others who have an interest in education to begin to engage in a dialogue about what needs to be done to improve schools.[45] While the federal government supplies few resources for communities to begin this dialogue, the striking thing is that this perspective has emerged at all.

Accompanying the conversations that are beginning in some communities is recognition that schools alone are not responsible for education. The African saying, "It takes a village to raise a child," is becoming more widely understood and accepted locally as well as nationally. One example of the shift in thinking that is taking place comes out of the Department of Labor's Secretary's Commission on Achieving Necessary Skills (SCANS) reports, focusing on the educational skills and competencies identified within those reports. Called the "missing link between business and schools" by *Business Week*,[46] SCANS identified those academic skills and personal competencies necessary for individuals to be successful in the workplace. The SCANS report[47] proposes a vastly different agenda for schools in the interest of "reinventing K–12 education." Among other ideas that SCANS draws from attempts over the past ten years to improve school performance is one critical lesson: "the entire community must be involved." This is a very different statement than saying "schools must improve," the more typical assessment of what needs to be done.

Business managers played a critically important role in helping to define the SCANS skills and competencies. Interestingly, those very skills and competencies are far closer to the types of skills and competencies needed to run a representative democracy than the types of skills previously demanded of its workforce by businesses, which enabled people to work in routine, mass production types of jobs. SCANS suggests that future workers will need competencies in allocating resources, interpersonal skills, information management, systems thinking, and technology. These competencies need to be built on a foundation of basic academic skills (reading, writing, arithmetic and mathematics, speaking, and listening), thinking skills, and personal qualities of responsibility, self-esteem, and integrity, among others. Recent research by the Committee for Economic Development indicates that many employers strongly believe that these types of skills are missing in recent high-school graduates.[48]

As businesses begin to better understand their own needs for a highly skilled workforce if they are to remain globally competitive, they will also need to understand that as part of the larger system into which graduates will go, they too need to change. Articulating the "know-how" of a high-performance workplace suggests that there will, in fact, be high-performance workplaces by which highly skilled graduates are employed. Although there is some sense of chicken and egg in the problematic thus posed, it is clear that both schools and businesses must "up the ante" on what is expected of workers and employment opportunities must, in fact, be available. The dialogues that are starting in many communities around education, if they are not to be "empty collaboration,"[49] have the potential to make inroads in both school and business arenas because they will foster recognition of the interdependence of schools, businesses, and other community organizations for building strong communities and businesses.

Collaboration among government agencies to achieve common objectives is as new to U.S. governmental agencies as it is to schools, yet is being reflected in the thinking of both the education and labor departments. In fact, in some places, representatives from both agencies have gone together to help communities begin the local dialogue on improving education. Notable, however, is the fact that little has been heard from the federal agency that represents social services involved in the village-making that helps raise successful children, the Department of Health and Human Services.

THE ARGUMENT FOR THIS BOOK

Here is the crux of the matter and the central focus of this book. The problems that education faces today are systemic problems. They are deeply embedded within the structures under which schools operate. They are deeply embedded in family and social problems. They have to do with the other systems that operate in the broader environment in which schools themselves exist, what we can call the macroenvironment. Schools cannot change through programs or partnerships alone. They can change only if they take charge of themselves and begin to rethink their systems, their internal operating procedures, and the ways in which they relate to those constituencies that they once considered "outside."

Schools thus themselves have to assume responsibility for these reforms. While outsiders can attempt to persuade educators to change, while incentives and advice can be offered, and while criticism for lack of change can rage, the only ones capable of effecting real change are those inside the school. Change has to happen not only at the classroom level, but also in the ways in which schools themselves are organized.

Further, change has to happen in the ways in which schools relate to outside constituencies. The boundaries that have been built up so high around schools need to be broken down and communication needs to be established so that mutual responsibilities can be articulated and action plans created. As will be seen in the next chapters, the problems of schools are far from simple. Simple solutions won't work. For anything at all to work, society itself needs to accept responsibility for the welfare and well-being of children, for discipline and guidance, and for creating policies that provide a reasonable start toward gaining an education.

NOTES

1. See D. W. Osborne and T. Gaebler's (1992), *Reinventing Government: How the Entrepreneurial Spirit is Transforming the Public Sector* (Reading, MA: Addison-Wesley).

2. Many observers have commented on the lack of significant change in public schools in the United States, despite the many criticisms of schools. See, for example, R. S. Barth (1991), *Improving Schools from Within: Teachers, Parents, and Principals Can Make the Difference* (San Francisco: Jossey-Bass); R. D. Van Scotter (1991), *Public Schooling in America: A Reference Handbook* (Santa Barbara, CA: ABC-CLIO); D. Perkins (1992), *Smart Schools: From Training Memories to Educating Minds* (New York: Free Press); P. A. Graham (1992), *SOS: Sustain Our Schools* (New York: Hill & Wang).

3. The term "institutions" is being used here to reflect a wide range of organized entities, including the family as well as more formally structured organizations. This usage follows that of R. Bellah and colleagues in (1991), *The Good Society* (New York: Alfred A. Knopf).

4. See Osborne and Gabler (1992).

5. For example Barth (1991), Perkins (1992); and Woodring (1983), *The Persistent Problems of Education* (Bloomington, IN: Phi Delta Kappa Educational Foundation).

6. R. B. Reich (1990), "Who Is Us?" *Harvard Business Review* January–February: 53–64; C. Handy (1989), *The Age of Unreason* (Boston: Harvard Business School Press);

and M. B. Katz (1987), *Reconstructing American Education* (Boston: Presidents and Fellows of Harvard College).

7. This is especially true of inner-city schools, as J. Kozol so aptly points out in (1991) *Savage Inequalities: Children in America's Schools* (New York: Crown).

8. National Commission on Excellence in Education (1983), *A Nation at Risk: The Imperative for Educational Reform* (Washington, D.C.: U.S. Government Printing Office).

9. See N. Postman (1992), *Technopoly: The Surrender of Culture to Technology* (New York: Alfred A. Knopf) for a wonderful critique of the impact of technology on society.

10. Even Chubb and Moe, who claim there is no panacea, ultimately propose choice as a panacea, but this is too limited a position for so complex a problem. See J. E. Chubb and T. M. Moe (1990), *Politics, Markets, and America's Schools* (Washington, D.C.: The Brookings Institution).

11. Van Scotter (1991); Woodring (1983); Graham (1992); Reich (1991b); Handy (1989); Katz (1987) as well as R. B. Reich (1991a), *The Work of Nations: Preparing Ourselves for Twenty-first Century Capitalism* (New York: Alfred A. Knopf) all discuss this phenomenon.

12. See Katz (1987) for an interesting analysis of the history of education. Also L. A. Cremin (1990), *Popular Education and Its Discontents* (New York: Harper & Row), provides a comprehensive history.

13. Van Scotter (1991), again, is helpful here.

14. See Van Scotter (1991), 23–24; and P. Woodring (1983), 72–76, for discussions of white flight and busing as initiatives to achieve integration.

15. Katz (1987).

16. See Van Scotter (1991) for a helpful synopsis of the development of educational thought through this period.

17. H. B. Leonard (1992), *By Choice or By Chance? Tracking the Values in Massachusetts Public Spending* (Boston: Pioneer Institute for Public Policy Research).

18. See Van Scotter (1991), 129.

19. Data are reported in Van Scotter (1991), 128–156.

20. C. Crossen provides an excellent summary of business involvement in education in (1990), "Getting Down to Business," *The Wall Street Journal* February 9: R30.

21. See J. Schor (1991), *The Overworked American: The Unexpected Decline of Leisure* (New York: Basic Books), for an interesting analysis of some of these shifts.

22. See D. A. Hamburg (1992), *Today's Children: Creating a Future for a Generation in Crisis* (New York: Times Books).

23. See Woodring (1983), 86.

24. See Woodring (1983), 83.

25. Gary Watts of the National Center on Educational Innovation of the National Education Association made this useful observation.

26. Gary Watts, NEA, personal communication.

27. See Van Scotter (1991), 6–9.

28. See Van Scotter (1991), 9–13.

29. This movement was begun during the same time period and was formalized in law in the Job Training Partnership Act, which established mandatory public-private partnerships in job training for the disadvantaged arena. Some of these, most notably that

in Boston, focused directly on the educational system, recognizing that the quality of the educational system was directly linked to the ultimate quality of the workforce. See S. A. Waddock (1989a) "Understanding Social Partnerships: An Evolutionary Model of Partnership Organizations" *Administration and Society* 21(1): 78–100.

30. See Crossen (1990).

31. See J. E. Chubb and T. M. Moe (1990); and (1988), "No School is an Island: Politics, Markets, and Education," in W. L. Boyd and C. T. Kerchner (Eds.), *The Politics of Excellence and Choice in Education: 1987 Yearbook of the Politics of Education Association* (New York: The Falmer Press). Other articles in this volume also provide a useful perspective on the choice debate.

32. See W. L. Boyd and C. T. Kerchner (1987), "Introduction and Overview: Education and the Politics of Excellence and Choice," in their edited volume *The Politics of Excellence and Choice in Education: 1987 Yearbook of the Politics of Education Association*. See also L. Iannoccone (1988), "From Equity to Excellence: Political Context and Dynamics," in the same volume; and P. A. Graham (1992), *SOS: Sustain Our Schools* (New York: Hill & Wang).

33. D. Hogan (1992), "School Organization and Student Achievement: A Review Essay," *Educational Theory* 42(1): 83–105.

34. National Alliance of Business (1989c), *A Blueprint for Business on Restructuring Education* (Washington, D.C.: National Alliance of Business).

35. National Association of Partners in Education, (NAPE) Inc. (1991) *National School District Partnership Survey: Statistical Report 1991*, November (Alexandria, VA: National Association of Partners in Education, Inc.).

36. NAPE (1991): 9–13.

37. NAPE (1991): 14–15.

38. For example, see T. Kolderie (1987), "Education that Works: The Right Role for Business." *Harvard Business Review* 65(5): 56–62; National Alliance of Business (1989c); and S. A. Waddock (1993a), "Lessons from the National Alliance of Business Compact Project, *Human Relations* 46(7).

39. See S. A. Waddock (1989a) and (1986), "Public-Private Partnership as Product and Process," in James E. Post (Ed.), *Research in Corporate Social Performance and Policy*, 7 (Greenwich, CT: JAI Press), for more comprehensive treatment of the Boston Compact as well as the theoretical issues surrounding the development of collaborations between sectors.

40. For complete analysis of what was learned in the Compact Project, see S. A. Waddock (1993b) "The National Alliance of Business Compact Project: Business Involvement in Public Education," in James E. Post (Ed.), *Research in Corporate Social Performance and Policy*, 13; and (1993a).

41. W. B. Johnston and A. H. Packer (1987), *Workforce 2000: Work and Workers for the Twenty-first Century* (Indianapolis, IN: Hudson Institute).

42. The Commission on the Skills of the American Workforce (1990), chaired by Ira Magaziner, published a report, *America's Choice: High Skills or Low Wages!* (Rochester, NY: National Center on Education and the Economy).

43. Among its other publications, NAB published the following directly on education reform: (1989a), *The Compact Project: School-Business Partnerships for Improving Education*, Washington, D.C.: National Alliance of Business; (1989d), *America's Leaders Speak Out on Business-Education Partnerships*, Washington, D.C.: National Alliance of

Business; (1989c); (1990b), *Business Strategies that Work: A Planning Guide for Educational Restructuring*; and (1991), *The Compact Project: Final Report*, Washington, D.C.: National Alliance of Business. See also Waddock (1993a) and (1993b).

44. The work of J. P. Comer of Yale University, in particular, had highlighted the centrality of parents in education. See, for example, (1989), "Child Development and Education," *Journal of Negro Education* 58(2): 125–139; (1988), "Educating Poor Minority Children," *Scientific American* 259(5): 42–48; (1984), "Home-School Relations as They Affect the Academic Success of Children," *Education and Urban Society* 16(3): 294–337; and (1987), "Our National Dilemma: Building Quality Relationships," *EDRS*, November: 40.

45. R. E. Freeman and J. Liedtka discuss the need for dialogue in (1991), "Corporate Social Responsibility: A Critical Approach," *Business Horizons*, July–August: 92–98; see also F. E. Bird and J. A. Waters (1989), "The Moral Muteness of Managers," *California Management Review*, Fall: 73–88.

46. A. Bernstein (1992), "This is the Missing Link Between Business and Schools," *Business Week*, April 20: 42–43.

47. See the Secretary's Commission on Achieving Necessary Skills (1992), *Learning a Living: A Blueprint for High Performance, A SCANS Report for America 2000*, (Washington, D.C.: U.S. Department of Labor).

48. See the Louis Harris Study Sponsored by the Committee for Economic Development (ca. 1992), *An Assessment of American Education: The View of Employers, Higher Educators, The Public, Recent Students, and Their Parents*, New York, Committee for Economic Development.

49. Alan Melchior of the Center for Human Resources, Brandeis University, suggests this phrase for some of the numerous partnerships between business and schools in which little is actually happening.

Chapter 2

The Social Fabric of Education

Although we tend to think of them as separate from other institutions,[1] such as the family, the community, and local businesses, schools actually operate within a network—a social fabric—of these other institutions. The interrelationships, status, stability, and policies of these institutions, which comprise a system or macrosystem, can have both positive and negative impacts on schools. Unfortunately, because we have tended to view schools as separated and separable from other institutions, the struggles that schools face in dealing with obstacles and opportunities presented by external institutions have been too seldom acknowledged in ways that might help school professionals deal with those obstacles and opportunities. The last chapter outlined some of the developments that public education in America has undergone during the twentieth century and particularly during the latter part of the twentieth century as businesses and other groups were galvanized into action about school performance. This historical context suggests that although there has been a great deal of finger-pointing and blame laying about school performance, schools have actually changed very little.

In addition, every society has a prevailing ideology or set of shared values that shape attitudes, opinions, policies, and structures for that society.[2] The ways in which the ideology or indeed the society itself affects schools are seldom articulated explicitly. Combined, the social fabric and ideology create a set of attitudes and social context that deeply influence schools and their ability to perform their educational tasks. This social fabric presents schools with some of their most intractable difficulties. As an embedded institution itself, a school cannot necessarily completely influence the texture of the social fabric that is created around it. The social fabric, however, can be altered by responsible action both on schools' and other institutions' parts. It is to this social context, to the influences of families, communities, and attitudes and ideology on the school that we now turn. In the next chapter, we will explore how other formal institutions outside the school influence the performance of schools.

THE FAMILY IN FLUX

Profound shifts have taken place in the American family over the past thirty years. These shifts have caused great destruction to the immediate social fabric that surrounds children and that might shield them from many negative forces. These shifts have made the emerging goal of education for all[3] more difficult to achieve than is generally realized because the stresses that children are experiencing directly influence their ability to learn, their attitude toward education, and their willingness to work hard. Family structures inherently support or do not support the goals of schools through the preparation, attitudes, and home-based support for education they provide to children. The relative stability, economic status, and social character of the family thus has important implications for children's readiness to learn when they actually pass through the doors of the school building. A quick assessment of some of the statistics surrounding family life in modern-day America will highlight some of the issues with which teachers and their young charges today must contend.

First, being married is far less common today than it was thirty years ago, with relevant implications for family stability. Census Bureau data indicate that married-couple households represented about 57 percent of all households in 1988 versus about 75 percent in 1960 (and about 61 percent as recently as 1980). The most precipitous drop occurred in the married with children category, which declined from 44.2 percent in 1960 to 27.0 percent in 1988. One implication of this drop is that the population with an interest in paying taxes to support schools, that is, families with children, has dropped dramatically in the past thirty years. When taxpayer revolts hit, it is clear from these statistics, the political base with a potential bias toward school support has been substantially eroded.

The declining rate of married with children is closely associated with the drop in family stability that has resulted from a very high divorce rate. The divorce rate, while declining slightly from a peak in the late 1970s, still hovers near 40 percent. Concurrently, the percentage of one-parent families has increased dramatically since 1970, accounting for 27 percent of family groups with children under eighteen in 1988 versus about 13 percent in 1970. There is strong evidence that the stresses of divorce and single parenting lead to less effective parenting for a fairly substantial period of time after divorce.[4] Additionally, children themselves suffer from the aftermath of divorce;[5] the stress of divorce can make schoolwork that much more difficult to attend to during the school day as well as at homework time.

In addition to the normal stresses of single parenthood, single-parent families tend to be more economically disadvantaged than two-parent families and are far more likely to be living in poverty. Some 16 percent of all families live in poverty, but only 8 percent of these are two-parent families; about 60 percent of black and Hispanic single mothers live in poverty. The Census Bureau also estimates that although about 25 percent of children are currently living with only one parent, as many as 60 percent of children will spend some portion of their lives with only one parent. Nearly 16 percent of children already live in stepfamilies and 20 percent of all children in the United States now live in poverty. Each one of these factors adds significant stress to a child's life.

Further, significant upward shifts have occurred in the participation of women in the labor force, with almost 66 percent of married women with children under eighteen now working. Shifts in workforce participation among married women since 1960 are dramatic. In 1960 only about 30 percent of married women were employed versus nearly 58 percent in 1989. Currently 66 percent of wives with children under eighteen are employed, while as recently as 1975, the rate was only 45 percent. Many of these working women have entered the labor force because two incomes are now needed to support the family, not solely for the purpose of pursuing careers. Despite their increased workforce participation, women continue to carry most of the responsibility for running the household and raising the children.[6]

As the evidence presented above suggests, the nuclear family in the United States is in trouble. Perhaps just as serious as the deterioration of nuclear and extended family structure fostered by divorce, single parenting, and the stresses of two careers is the slide into poverty and other economic difficulties faced by a great many families with young children. Also notable is both an increasing gap in the earnings of low- and high-income families and an increase in the poverty rate especially among children during the 1980s.

Consider the following data. First, overall income growth during the 1980s was minimal.[7] Further, there was a growing disparity between the incomes of the very rich and the rest of society, with the richest 1 percent gaining the most and the bottom 40 percent of the income distribution experiencing declining income. During the 1980s, the old saw that the "rich get richer while the poor get poorer" held true and, as well, the number of people classified as poor also grew. The gap (in 1989 dollars) between the richest 5 percent and the bottom 80 percent shifted from $48,344 in 1947, to $83,212 in 1973, to $119,848 in 1989.[8] The largest actual drop in income occurred in families headed by someone under twenty-five; minorities are more likely to be poor than whites; and women are more likely to be poor than men.[9] Any number of studies, including those of conservative analyst Kevin Phillips, suggest that this gap between rich and poor is real.[10]

Even more disturbing are the statistics for children, a group among which poverty has been growing faster than among the population at large since 1969. Nearly 20 percent, or one-fifth, of children in the United States, the richest country in the world, now live in poverty. Among female-headed households the poverty rate for children is even more stunning: in 1989, 42.8 percent of white children, 62.9 percent of black children, and 65 percent of Hispanic children in these households lived in poverty.[11]

Associated with the increase in the poverty rate is a decline in government benefits—the safety net—that used to help support families in need. The reality of government assistance is that during the 1980s, the number of families who were lifted out of poverty through government aid dropped, and for young families, the drop is dramatic. In 1979 39.7 percent of female-headed families were assisted out of poverty-level living through governmental programs; by 1988 the rate had dropped to 22.8 percent. For married-couple families during the same time frame, the rate dropped from 33 percent to 24.4 percent.[12]

Even more material for education, what little progress in income was made came from a combination of more hours and more people working. Most women with small children now work outside the home, in many cases because they have to maintain family income because real wages are being squeezed; indeed, nearly all of the 7.5 percent rise in total family income during the 1980s can be attributed to increased earning by wives. Of course, the entry of more women into the labor force compounds the problem of finding both early childhood and middle childhood day- and after-school care, which is already in short supply. And when there are two earners in a family, expenses associated with working, for example, expenses for child care, commuting, clothing, and food, also go up.[13]

Free or leisure time has been significantly eroded in the years since World War II and, in particular, since 1969.[14] By one measure both men and women in families with two children have added 132 and 113 hours more to their annual work (or about three weeks of work per year) since 1969.[15] That leaves nearly three weeks less time for parents to spend with their children (or for themselves) each year. This time might have been spent playing with children, attending to their needs, instilling values, or simply having the time to be a parent without dealing with the many stresses of modern life. Instead, it is spent trying to maintain income or quality of life through working more hours.

All of these shifts in the structure of the family have placed tremendous burdens on family life and on the ability of parents to provide a supportive environment that encourages children to perform well in school. Particularly with respect to jobs and family-related policies, businesses may have a major role to play in helping schools, although to date these shifting family structures have received little attention from business. Each of these situations poses a stressful situation for a family, making integration of work, family, and school life difficult. Arguably, then, these shifts in the status of the family can be linked both directly and indirectly to the problematic performance of schools.

While I do not mean to suggest that poverty, dual-career families, single parenthood, divorce, or working harder in and of themselves contribute to educational problems, the decay of inner cities, rural poverty, and the lack of attention to their children by some extremely busy parents certainly make the job of educators more difficult. Because families and communities represent social systems, the conditions of both affect other things they touch, including the schools. For example, there is a great deal of evidence to suggest that children from better-off families or families that value education highly and place high expectations for performance on their children achieve more in school than when parents pay little attention to their children's educational or other needs or when education is itself devalued. Loss of hope, lack of opportunity, and failures of vision all contribute to a weakening of the "demand" for education that can place these high expectations upon children and that contribute positively to the life of the schools.

Even among better-off families, however, there may have been some significant abandonment of parental duties, toward letting the schools pick up education for moral responsibility, values, sex education, and the panoply of other curricular elements now foisted onto the schools. When I asked my son's second-grade teacher whether he had seen any change in the children he was teaching in our suburban, well-off community, over the past twenty-five years, he responded something like, "Yes, some of these children are barely civil. They seldom eat a meal with their parents, and they know little of what we used to know as family life."

Poverty, unemployment, lack of adequate health care, lack of taxpayer support for education, lack of role models all contribute to the development of children who see little reason to work hard in school, for it is the family on which both the readiness for education and ultimately for citizenship rests. Without models in the family who help children balance their needs to meet goals of self-interest and individualism with those of sharing and community, it is hard for children to understand that they must, in the final analysis, take responsibility for themselves. Children without security or safety, with no role models who work, who experience violence and abuse, are not in much of a position to learn.

COMMUNITY INFRASTRUCTURE

The shifts in family life documented above suggest that children today are being brought up considerably differently than in the past. Gone for far too many children are the strong sense of community and family that once provided a structure, value system, and set of restraints on behavior (because someone knew you and would tell your parents if you mis-behaved) beyond the immediate family. Mobility, suburbanization, and the loss of extended family have all taken their toll on the ability of families to provide structure and stability to children. Two-career or -job families make childrearing even more difficult than it is otherwise, since time for dealing with children is limited, parents are tired, and may be preoccupied with their own affairs. The great mobility of our society means that there are fewer families today than in the past that have aunts, uncles, grand-parents, and cousins nearby to fill in for the times that parents are at work.

The result of these changes is that there has been a breakdown of what one participant in my research termed the "invisible community," that is, the unpaid support network that used to exist in communities where women were available to serve in largely volunteer capacities when needed. Along with the disappearance of the extended family and the support it once provided, the dominance of two-earner and single-parent families has thus eroded the community infrastructure. The invisible community used to provide mostly voluntary services when needed, for example community members might bring soup to the sick, provide baskets of food to the poor, be there to help out when a helping hand was needed, or simply be around to provide security, safety, and support to neighborhood children (and others) when parents are unavailable. Neighbors once knew who children were and provided both guidance and support for them.

Today in many suburban and especially in urban communities neigh-bors barely know each other. They seldom have time to interact because they are either at work, running errands, or sitting at home watching television. Because nearly 70 percent of women are now working, because many neighbors do not know each other, and because in some areas the streets outside the home are dangerous, this support network has largely disappeared.

In addition, the entry of women into the workplace has resulted in a diminishment of what author Suzanne Gordon terms the "caring society."[16] As women have assumed more of what used to be predominantly male jobs, they have tended to leave the caring professions of teaching, nursing, and social service and adopt what were once male roles, along with male attitudes toward achievement, success, and "women's work." The caring professions and volunteer activities, in particular, have suffered from the lack of availability of qualified people, particularly women, with the time or inclination to devote to activities that once provided a broad and supportive social infrastructure within communities. Caring itself has become less acceptable to women, Gordon documents, as women themselves have adopted male models of what success is and have become subject to a dominant corporate culture that virtually prohibits much if any attention to the caring functions.[17]

Also diminishing is a meaning of entertainment that primarily involves face-to-face interactions among people and, for children, simply playing with others—that is, those essentially civilizing experiences of interacting with others within a community with a common purpose in mind.[18] Such interactions arguably form the basis for an informal infrastructure of friendship among people in a community. Through this infrastructure, people knew and understood each other and were able to provide support when needed. Today, children are as likely to be watching television or playing with a video or computer game as they are to be playing with each other. These are activities that are typically done alone rather than in interaction with others, although I have noted that my son and his friends manage to work together on certain of the computer games. Still, the primary modality of the computer game or the television broadcast is an individual absorbing what is going on on the screen, making sense of the images, and not really becoming involved with others.

Additionally, because many parents are so busy, some children spend much of their childhood in organized or adult-structured activities—or worse, in front of the television. At least the lucky ones whose parents can afford adequate childcare for them have these structured lives. Running from activity to activity, some of these children have little time to really play on their own with the attention or direct supervision of adults. Yet it is in playing that children really learn to model the behaviors of familiar adults that will ultimately develop the children themselves into successful adults.[19]

Other children, not so fortunate, find themselves learning street smarts in sometimes almost wholly unsupervised activities that lead to the type of violence and destruction so eloquently described by Alex Kotlowitz in *There Are No Children Here*.[20] These children are living in decaying inner cities characterized by poverty, drugs, violence, abuse, and unemployment among adults. For them, as Kotlowitz suggests, there are few successful male role models, mothers are frequently on welfare and, when they work, it is in subsistence-level jobs that are barely adequate to shelter, feed, and clothe the family.

The formal safety net, the one that President Reagan spoke of in the early 1980s, has also been seriously damaged by twelve years of withdrawal of federal and squeezed state financial resources. Although the tax burden in the United States is still relatively low compared to that of other industrialized nations (in 1987, the United States had the lowest tax burden of any industrialized country except Turkey),[21] the taxpayer revolts of the early 1980s have left many communities and, in particular, many school systems squeezed.

Further, during the 1980s, the distribution of federal dollars has shifted toward favoring the very rich, away from investment in what can broadly be termed community infrastructure or what President Reagan called the safety net. States and local communities have been forced to pick up services that the federal government has dropped, typically with taxes, such as sales taxes, property taxes, and nontax revenues including fines and fees, which are more regressive than income taxes.[22]

Television itself has had an impact on the community as it provides a means of entertainment that can be achieved without benefit of interaction with others.[23] For some children, television is a primary babysitter and purveyor of values as well as of education itself.[24] As babysitter, the medium of television is largely passive, providing entertainment, a wide perspective on the world, and access to a great deal of potentially educational material. But, with some notable exceptions, most TV programs today are hardly structured for educational purposes and are sorry substitutes for hands-on activities, active involvement with parents and other children, and simply playing either independently or with other children.

More critically, the value messages that television conveys to children are not necessarily those that a strong and supportive family would convey. The primary values conveyed on television are those of materialism, self-interest, and immediacy, rather than responsibility, caring, or delayed gratification.[25] Nor are the family and community values important to our society always obvious in the violence or values of many television shows and of the advertising that permeates those shows. These values combined with both the passivity that television engenders and the short attention span it fosters make the job of educator, whose responsibility it is to instill a longer-term work-oriented ethic, all the more difficult. And, as we shall see in the next section, public attitudes and expectations about education don't help much to instill an ethic of hard work in today's child.

ATTITUDES AND EXPECTATIONS

Changes in family structure, discipline, and stability apart, the United States has an attitude problem when it comes to education. This attitude problem manifests itself in several ways. First, schools and teachers have relatively low status in the United States especially when compared to the status of their counterparts in other nations. Second, the United States tends to have an anti-intellectual bias that makes it difficult for some people to believe in the value of education. Third, the general attitude toward education in the United States seems to be that aptitude matters more than hard work in becoming an educated person. Fourth, despite all the recent rhetoric about the "crisis" in American schools, there is still a pervasive public perception that the problem of education really lies in someone else's schools or in the inner-city schools, but that the crisis does not affect local (read "my children's") schools. Finally, the individualistic American ideology plays an important role in fostering independence of action for schools, but may be partially responsible for a prevailing sense that schools have to solve their problems single-handedly and for lack of a commonly accepted set of goals for education. These issues will be discussed in more detail below.

Pervasive cries of "crisis" in the schools have been accepted as reality by many policy makers, educational and business leaders, and academics who are familiar with international comparisons of academic performance. This awareness has, however, yet to penetrate very deeply into the consciousness of most people. Even in businesses that are engaged in school-business partnerships, the awareness of the realities and problems of education typically does not penetrate into the ranks of middle- and lower-level management, or to employees who may not be directly involved in the partnerships.

In fact, the rhetoric about education contrasts rather sharply with public attitudes as those measured in a series of important studies reported in the prestigious journal *Science*. These studies compared United States, Japanese, and Chinese students' actual performance in mathematics and science in 1980, 1984, and again in 1990, tested their general knowledge, and assessed the attitudes of both student and their parents toward their educational achievement.[26] Not only did American students make a poor showing in math and science with respect to their Japanese and Chinese counterparts in first and fifth grades in 1980, but these differences were stable over the ensuing four-year period.

When retests took place again in 1990, few differences from the earlier results could be found. The U.S. students consistently underperformed the Asian students in math and reading by a wide margin. In fact, the average math score of eleventh graders in vocational high schools in Taipei exceeded that of the average math score for all American students. Only in general information, that is, knowledge learned outside the school curriculum, did U.S. students outperform Japanese and Chinese students.

The relative performance of U.S. versus Japanese and Chinese students is discouraging enough in its own right, and is consistent with other measures of international academic achievement, in which U.S. students consistently score at or near the bottom.[27] Even more discouraging, however, may be the attitude about education that these researchers discovered both in their 1980 and 1990 studies. When asked in 1980 how satisfied they were with their children's academic achievement, more than 40 percent of U.S. mothers were very satisfied, compared to about 5 percent of both Japanese and Chinese mothers. The authors hypothesized that one reason for this attitude may have been lack of information about the relative standing of U.S. children versus children of other nations.

Since at least 1983, however, the U.S. public has been bombarded with articles and news reports about the so-called crisis in the schools, which in theory might have resulted in less satisfaction. Disturbingly, these researchers conclude, "If anything, somewhat more American mothers say they were 'very satisfied' with their children's performance in 1980 compared with 1990," even though they were aware of U.S. children's relatively low comparative status.[28] This finding pervades public attitudes in America. Garrison Keillor has termed such thinking the Lake Woebegon effect,[29] because in the mythical Lake Woebegon everyone's children are above average. Opinion surveys consistently find that the American public hates Congress but believes that its own congressman (or woman) is doing just fine. So too with schools. Public opinion polls consistently show that U.S. respondents rate their own children's schools at a much higher level than they do the public schools in general or rate themselves at being good in school despite evidence to the contrary.[30]

One disturbing recent study conducted for the Committee for Economic Development (CED) by the Louis Harris Group evaluated high-school graduates' performance along a wide range of measures. Measures included ability to work cooperatively, attitude, reading, motivation, writing, discipline, math, and complex problem solving, among others. On all measures both parents and students rated the level of educational preparation of high-school graduates a good deal higher than did either employers or educators.[31] This study concludes that there is "reality gap," a big difference between how students and parents view educational attainment and the ways in which those who deal with high-school graduates after they graduate perceive them. The CED observes: "the current crop of students and their parents are deluding themselves. This points up the real necessity of enlisting and informing America's parents about what employers and higher education institutions expect. It also means . . . that students and their schools need to be made aware of what standards are demanded."[32]

Perhaps even more problematic than the Lake Woebegon effect are the low expectations that American parents have for their children regarding their education. Related to a pervasive anti-intellectualism in the nation, in the *Science* studies parents were asked about their expectations of their children's performance. Unlike the Chinese and Japanese, who would be satisfied only with a higher score than they expected their child to receive, the Americans claimed that they would be satisfied with the score they expected.[33] This attitude suggests that there is a great deal of complacency about performance levels and a lack of recognition among American parents of the need for higher levels of achievement across the board.

Chester Finn puts the matter most baldly in asking why the nation hasn't made greater progress in educational reform: "Perhaps the biggest reason is that people aren't changing their actual behavior at the 'retail' level of education. Although parents acknowledge that we have a very serious national education problem, they are reasonably content with their children's education and with their local schools. The nation may be at risk but 'I'm all right.' "[34]

This attitude also reflects what David Perkins has termed the "trivial pursuit" theory of learning in which an accumulation of a lot of facts is accepted as what learning ought to be.[35] In contrast Perkins offers "theory one," which relies on clear information, thoughtful practice, informative feedback, and strong intrinsic or extrinsic motivation.[36] The trivial pursuit theory of knowledge combines well with another attitude that is pervasive in U.S. culture, that is, that ability matters more than effort in academic achievement.[37] Under this line of thinking, children are not expected to work hard to achieve academically, but rather are expected to either "get it" the first time because they have the native intelligence to do so or are not expected to be able to get it at all.

Only 27 percent of students surveyed in one study believed that studying hard would be the most important factor in influencing their math performance. This contrasts with their counterparts in Japan and China where most students and parents alike believe that "studying hard" is the most important factor in school achievement. This attitude is also apparently pervasive among teachers, for when asked the same question 93 percent of Japanese and only 26 percent of U.S. teachers responded studying hard, versus having a good teacher, innate intelligence, home environment.[38]

It seems that the notoriety that schools have received has penetrated very little into the public's real understanding of the status of the schools. The purported crisis in American schools is seemingly just that—purported—in most people's eyes; it just doesn't seem real. The schools with which most people are familiar, which are operating in many of the same ways that they did when parents themselves were in school, seem OK. Since parents are generally satisfied with their own children's and their children's schools' performance, there is little real incentive for schools to change. In fact, really significant restructuring might engender even more public attacks on schools, since the lack of change is apparently comforting to parents, who can recognize their own experience in school in what they see their children going through.

After all, since everyone has been through school him- or herself, everyone knows how school should be: it should be exactly like it was when I was there. This attitude also means that most people think, whether they have any expertise about schools, children, or organizations, that they know what needs to be done to make the schools better. Mostly these prescriptions have to do with returning-to-basics, working harder on drills, or generally making schools look more like they used to, except that computers should be introduced.

This complacency and attitude of "I know how to reform the schools" suggests that parents and the general public alike are unfamiliar with the changed conditions of the family, changed social influences on children and their behavior, and the economic, social, and political realities of the world into which students will graduate. Still, this attitude of relative complacency with the status quo of schools contrasts starkly with the rhetoric surrounding schools. Yet it is arguably the same lack of change in structure, content, and the process of education that is so bothersome when the realities of schools today are explored.

There is another aspect to the attitude problem that characterizes American education: education is viewed typically as an expense rather than an investment in the future. A wiser course might be to follow the suggestion of the Committee for Economic Development,[39] and begin to view education not as an expense but as an investment. To the extent that businesses and taxpayers view education as a cost to themselves, they will tend to make short-sighted decisions that pare away resources that schools need to develop the ability to deal with the multitude of problems now dropped at their doorsteps.

No one would expect a business to be able to restructure itself without significant investments in human resource development, training, technology, and new equipment that brings the company into the future. Yet schools are consistently asked to "do more with less," which works only until the creative energies of teachers and administrators are strained to the breaking point. Respect, value for, and dialogue with educators about what they are attempting to do, the conditions they actually contend with, and where they need help, can begin to expand everyone's vision about real solutions to the manifold problems of educating America's youth adequately.

Education, viewed as a long-term investment, has the potential to help make U.S. society competitive internationally, providing a high-skilled workforce[40] that is capable of governing itself in a representative democracy. This is particularly true, since it is increasingly clear that more educated individuals have far greater earning power than less well educated individuals. Unfortunately, at least in recent years, the differential in wages is due less to a great increase in the earning power of more highly educated people than to a fall in the real wages of those with less education, whose average earnings have actually deteriorated. Despite the rhetoric about the need for educating all, it is clear that the supply of jobs at living wages—and which provide an incentive for better education—may in fact be questionable in the future. One study concludes "since average real wages for less-educated and low-wage workers have deteriorated, it is unlikely that the skills demanded of those average workers rose in the 1980s. Rather, the increase in the college-to-high-school wage gap reflects a modest increase in the demand for college-educated workers, not an across-the-board, economy-wide trend toward higher skilled and higher wage jobs."[41]

Arguably, without an educated citizenry, more jobs will be lost to offshore sites capable of providing the proper workforce and an increased proportion of our citizenry will land in jails, in drug cultures, or in the growing underclass, diminishing the quality of life for all. The need for less complacency and more recognition of the investment that education is should be particularly apparent when sweeping global and national economic changes are taken into consideration. The next chapter will consider these changes in more detail.

The data about pay and skill level directly contradict much of the argument that has been made around the issue of improving education, arguments that attempt to counteract the complacency of the American public toward its education. They are equally problematic if one assumes that the whole reason for providing education is to prepare people for work. Rather we need to think more broadly as a society about the role of education and the schools, as well as the ways in which businesses can integrate themselves into society's long-term goals. Still, the very complacency about education that has been documented is problematic, whether we view the purpose of education as for citizenry or work or both, as is more reasonable. When the dramatic changes that have taken place in enterprise around the globe are taken into consideration, the need to rearticulate the purposes of and responsibilities for education become even more apparent.

IDEOLOGY

The economic, family, and demographic shifts highlighted above are underpinned in the United States by a guiding ideology that determines our culture, norms, and shared values. An ideology is a set of shared beliefs or values that are explicit or implicit in a society (or organization). Lodge suggests that ideology has five components: (1) relationships between individual and group; (2) institutional guarantees; (3) means of controlling production of goods and services; (4) the role of the state; and (5) the prevailing conception of reality and nature.[42] The United States' ideology is one of individualism and, it will be argued below, this individualism has had significant consequences for the structure and performance of the educational system. Among the dominant characteristics of an individualistic society are individualism or the sense that each individual or very small group should look after itself and let the community take care of itself without intervention, competition, a limited role for government, and specialization and fragmentation.[43]

From a governance perspective, the running of schools in the United States is left to the local level, with some mandates provided at the state level. Consistent with a low-key role for central government, the federal government has traditionally little authority over schools, which is reflected in the lack of national education goals. Only with the passage of the GOALS 2000: Educate America Act in 1994 did a clearer national direction develop at the national level. Still, there are more than 16,000 school districts in the country, each governed by a school board or committee, frequently elected and sometimes appointed by the local political authorities. School boards, guided by the states, which each have their own sets of standards, ostensibly have control over what happens in local schools. States mandate the required number of school days, with the average in the United States about 179 days.[44] All other industrialized nations have more required school days than does the United States, which still operates on an agrarian calendar and for a relatively short day.[45]

Further, unlike other countries that have established national goals for education and have developed a reasonably unified structure, the U.S. educational system is characterized by extreme fragmentation, lack of common goals, and control at the local or state, rather than the national, level. Curriculum tends to be devoted to "covering" topics, sometimes topics mandated at the state level and other times fostered by textbooks that emphasize topical coverage rather than problem-solving skills or more in-depth assessment of areas. These are hardly new problems, yet little has been done to deal with them.[46] Students and teachers alike struggle alone, in relative isolation, except in instances of deliberate partnership programs, to meet their goals.

The governance structure of the U.S. educational system is thus indicative of the ideology of individualism that guides U.S. society.[47] Further, schools are funded primarily at the local level, making them subject to the local policies as well as to the ability of local cities and towns to pay. Since there are fewer families with children in school and less willingness in the past decade or so to pay taxes, funding schools has become problematic for many communities. The U.S. educational system, viewed in its totality, thus reflects some of the extremes of individualism as does the general public attitude toward schools. Based on what has been termed a "collateral systems" model,[48] that is, each institution operating distinctly and largely separate from other systems, we tend to view schools as largely to blame for the failures of their students. We implicitly or explicitly assign each school or school system the responsibility for creating its own curriculum, and each teacher the responsibility for designing what happens in his or her classroom. Little staff development time is built into school schedules, because it has been (until the passage of GOALS 2000) assumed to be unnecessary. Similarly, we assume that each student will study and work largely independently of others. Collaboration in fact is termed cheating, and students are punished for it. In taking this perspective, we assume that each individual student as well as each individual school or school system can operate successfully largely on its own.

Lodge has argued that individualistic societies will have a difficult time competing successfully in a global village in which businesses and governments are cooperating since cooperation changes the tilt of the playing field.[49] Similar arguments can be made about the educational system: defining goals, working collaboratively with others, and providing a holistic conception of education that surrounds a society with a positive attitude toward both the common good and a set of common educational goals would arguably provide a more solid foundation for changing education than our current highly fragmented, individualistic system.

Some authorities have argued for such a structure. One of these is John Goodlad who has devised a set of academic goals that encompass mastery of basic skills and intellectual development, vocational goals (including career skills and work attitudes), social, civic and cultural goals aimed at interpersonal development, and citizenship, focusing on development of cultural and personal values.[50] The lesson from global competitors at the national level suggests that a more collaborative approach that focuses on the common good may be a more appropriate model for a world growing increasingly interdependent.[51]

POLITICAL CLIMATE

Under the auspices of the America 2000 program, the Department of Education did issue six education goals for the year 2000 as the 1990s began. All children should start school ready to learn. The high-school graduation rate should increase to at least 90 percent. Students at grades four, eight, and twelve should demonstrate competency in challenging subjects, including English, math, science, history, and geography, and learn to use their minds so they are prepared for responsible citizenship. U.S. students should be first in the world in science and math by 2000. Every adult should be literate and have adequate citizenship skills. Every school should be free of drugs and violence.

When the GOALS 2000: Educate America Act was signed into law in 1994, it contained two additional goals. One goal focused on continuous improvement of professional skills and knowledge for teachers. The eighth goal emphasized the promotion of partnerships to increase parental involvement in children's social, emotional, and academic growth.

Coming to agreement about even such a general set of goals as the GOALS 2000 goals in our pluralistic and individualistically oriented nation, however, has been difficult and few steps have been taken in most communities to make the significant structural changes necessary to achieve those goals. Interestingly, it was during the market-oriented Bush years in the White House that the nation actually did take its first tentative steps toward articulating a national educational policy. An assumption seems to have been made, however, that by providing parents with "choice" about the schools their children would attend, the structural, funding, and curricular issues associated with schools would magically disappear. To their credit, staff members at the Department of Education attempted to implement these goals by taking a systemic approach that brought various members of local communities together around the problems of education, despite the fact that little funding was allocated for this important process of community development.

Reasonable as these education goals seem, they do require significant structural changes to achieve. The changes required, it will be argued below, have to do with both what goes on within and outside of schools, and they will not be achieved without investment. Arguably, it will not be sufficient to simply change the schools to achieve these goals. A more-systemic approach that recognizes the influence that other elements of society have on schools and that works cooperatively with those other elements to achieve common goals is necessary. Yet because of the independence of each school system and the individualism that characterizes society, bringing communities together with schools for common purpose has been somewhat foreign to the U.S. mind-set.

The political climate during the 1980s and early 1990s was one that fostered a great deal of individualism and self-interest. Gone from the public dialogue was any sense that there might be a greater good beyond individual, company, or organizational gain. One author has termed this an era of "wilding" in which any sense of moral decency, common good, or caring effectively disappeared for a large (if not majority) segment of the population.[52] Combined with these attitudes, deterioration of family structure, and loss of community described above, this political climate in which "getting one's own" seemed to be the primary objective made the task of educating, which by its nature is a long-term struggle to gain (ultimately) wisdom, more difficult.

Since the word responsibility had generally fallen out of the public dialogue (at least until the election of Bill Clinton, when it resurfaced a little), it has become fashionable to suggest that many children and the families are victims: victims of an uncaring society, victims of poverty, victims of abuse or any other injustice. The implication is that because they have been victimized, they are not responsible for their own behaviors, attitudes, or actions. Yet this is a relatively new assumption for Americans whose pioneering spirit conquered what was once known as the wild west despite many obstacles and who placed a man on the moon against many odds.

Arguably, we can make a set of assumptions that places these children in their victim status and absolves them of their responsibility to learn and schools of their responsibility to teach them. Or we can begin by assuming that whatever status one begins in, one is a responsible individual who, provided sufficient support and guidance, can overcome even difficult obstacles. It is the recapturing of that aspect of the American ideology or spirit that has been lacking from our public dialogue and that is so necessary if the conversation about responsibility is to be effective in the long run. Thus, individuals have responsibilities for themselves and their families. As will be seen in later chapters, it is this latter set of assumptions that, I believe, holds the best hope for our public schools.

The families of school children, the communities within which they live, and the values and ideologies they hold, it has been argued in this chapter, fundamentally influence the performance of schools. But there are other social institutions, formal institutions, whose influence must also be taken into account if we are truly to understand where schools are in the social fabric. It is to these institutions that we turn in the next chapter.

NOTES

1. L. E. Preston and J. E. Post (1975), *Private Management and Public Policy: The Principle of Public Responsibility* (Englewood Cliffs, NJ: Prentice-Hall) term this way of thinking about institutions as "collateral systems" thinking because we tend to think of each organization or institution operating independently or collaterally of others. They contrast this perspective with an interpenetrating systems perspective in which "the larger society exists as a macrosystem, but that individual (and particularly large) micro-organizations also constitute separatable systems within themselves, neither completely controlling nor controlled by the social environment" (p. 25).

2. The best work on ideology has been done by George Lodge, whose recent books do an excellent job of comparing what he terms individualistic and communitarian ideologies. These will be discussed in more depth later in the chapter. See G. Lodge (1990) *Perestroika for America: Restructuring Business-Government Relations for World Competitiveness* (Boston: Harvard Business School Press); and G. Lodge and E. Vogel (1987), *Ideology and National Competitiveness: An Analysis of Nine Countries* (Boston: Harvard Business School Press).

3. P. A. Graham (1992), in *SOS: Sustain Our Schools* (New York: Hill & Wang) suggests that educating all is a relatively new goal for the United States.

4. D. A. Hamburg (1992), *Today's Children: Creating a Future for a Generation in Crisis* (New York: Times Books), does a masterful job of detailing the problems of the family and today's children (see p. 179).

5. Hamburg (1992), 179.

6. J. Schor (1991) *The Overworked American: The Unexpected Decline of Leisure* (New York: Basic Books).

7. Data in this section are from L. Mishel and D. M. Frankel (1992), *The State of Working America, 1990–92 Edition* (Armonk, NY: M. E. Sharpe Company).

8. Data extracted from Table 1.6 in Mishel and Frankel (1992).

9. Mishel and Frankel (1992), 13–17, 167–229.

10. See K. Phillips (1990), *The Politics of Rich and Poor: Wealth and the American Electorate in the Reagan Aftermath* (New York: Random House).

11. Mishel and Frankel (1992), 171–177; statistics from 177.

12. Mishel and Frankel (1992), 177.

13. Mishel and Frankel (1992), 39–48.

14. See J. Schor's *The Overworked American*; S. Gordon (1991), *Prisoners of Men's Dreams: Striking Out for a New Feminine Future* (Boston: Little, Brown and Company); and Mishel and Frankel's statistics (1992).

15. Mishel and Frankel (1992), 47.

16. Gordon (1991).

17. See Gordon (1991).

18. See Hamburg (1992), for an insightful discussion of the role of community in childrearing.

19. Hamburg (1992), describes what has happened to children.

20. A. Kotlowitz (1991), *There Are No Children Here: The Story of Two Boys Growing Up in the Other America* (New York: Doubleday).

21. Mishel and Frankel (1992).

22. Mishel and Frankel (1992), 61–63.

23. N. Postman (1979) discusses the role of television in *Teaching as a Conserving Activity* (New York: Delacorte Press).

24. See Postman (1979) and Hamburg (1992), for in-depth discussions of the impact of television on children. L. A. Cremin, as well, discusses the fact that education is derived from many sources, school being only one of them and television being important among the alternatives. See his (1988), *American Education: The Metropolitan Experience, 1876–1980* (New York: Harper & Row).

25. See Postman (1979), for a critique of television.

26. H. W. Stevenson, C. Chen, and S.-Y. Lee (1993), "Mathematics Achievement of Chinese, Japanese, and American Children: Ten Years Later," *Science* 259(1): 53–58; and H. W. Stevenson, S.-Y. Lee, and J. W. Stigler (1986), "Mathematics Achievement of Chinese, Japanese, and American Children," *Science* 231: 693.

27. Tables from the National Assessment of Educational Progress (1989), *A World of Differences, An International Assessment of Mathematics and Science*. Reported in Richard D. Van Scotter (1991), *Public Schooling in America: A Reference Handbook* (Santa Barbara, CA: ABC-CLIO).

28. C. Stevenson, and Lee (1993), 55.

29. This phrase can be attributed to Garrison Keillor of National Public Radio fame.

30. Reported in R. D. Van Scotter (1991), *Public Schooling in America: A Reference Handbook* (Santa Barbara, CA: ABC-CLIO); and C. E. Finn, Jr. (1992), "Up From Mediocrity: What Next in School Reform," *Policy Review* Summer: 80–83; Committee for Economic Development (ca. 1992), *An Assessment of American Education*, A Louis Harris Study (New York: Committee for Economic Development).

31. CED's Harris Study (ca. 1992).

32. CED's Harris Study (ca. 1992), 12.

33. Stevenson, Chen, and Lee (1993), 56–57.

34. Finn, Jr. (1992).

35. D. Perkins (1992). *Smart Schools: From Training Memories to Educating Minds* (New York: Free Press).

36. Perkins (1992), 43–72.

37. Stevenson and colleagues (1993), 57; and Perkins (1992), 34–37.

38. Stevenson and colleagues (1993), 57.

39. Committee for Economic Development reports: (1985), *Investing In Our Children: Business and the Public Schools* (New York: Committee for Economic Development); (1987), *Children in Need: Investment Strategies of the Educationally Disadvantaged* (New York: Committee for Economic Development); (1990), *An America That Works: The Life-Cycle Approach to a Competitive Work Force* (New York: Committee for Economic Development); and (ca. 1992), *An Assessment of American Education*, A Louis Harris Study (New York: Committee for Economic Development).

40. National Center on Education and the Economy's Commission on the Skills of the American Workforce (1990), *America's Choice: High Skill or Low Wages!* (Rochester, NY: U.S. Department of Education).

41. Mishel and Frankel (1992), 93–95.

42. See above, particularly Lodge and Vogel (1987), 9.

43. Lodge and Vogel (1987), 12.

44. M. J. Barrett (1990), "The Case for More School Days." *Atlantic* 266(5): 90–91.

45. Barrett (1990).

46. See J. I. Goodlad (1976). *Facing the Future: Issues in Education and Schooling*, ed. J. S. Golub (New York: McGraw-Hill).

47. See Lodge (1990); and Lodge and Vogel (1987).

48. See Preston and Post (1975).

49. Lodge (1990); Lodge and Vogel (1987).

50. See Goodlad (1976).

51. Lodge terms this approach "communitarianism," to be distinguished from "communism." It emphasizes the common good, a holistic approach to community concerns, and responsibilities as well as rights, among other characteristics.

52. C. Derber (1992), *Money, Murder, and the American Dream: Wilding from Wall Street to Main Street* (Boston: Faber and Faber).

Chapter 3 _____

The Institutional Fabric of Education

Major forces in society, such as economic conditions and demographic trends change the structure, shape, and demands upon schools. By understanding these trends, we can better understand why schools are currently perceived to be failing so badly. Also, we live in a context of institutions,[1] both formal and informal, and other forces including economic and demographic forces. Formal institutions and the policies, programs, and practices they generate influence the ability of schools to do their jobs because these institutions are all inherently interconnected and interdependent with each other and the ways in which they interact ultimately affect the performance of schools. Formal institutions include schools, businesses, governmental and social service agencies, teachers' unions, and schools of education.

Despite the interconnectedness, we have tended in the past to operate, in effect, as if each institution were essentially distinct from the others. Some of this tendency derives from the fundamental individualism embedded within the U.S. character, which has already been discussed. Yet, if we carefully consider the societal system as a whole and the relationship of our own system to the global village, we can begin to draw out important connections. By doing this type of analysis, we can better understand the potential that schools may have for transforming themselves through their relationships with others. It is on developing this understanding of the broader institutional fabric of trends and formal institutions to which this chapter turns.

TRENDS AND FORCES

This section will look at two important types of trends, economic and demographic, and the ways in which those trends relate to schools, those occurring in the global and domestic economy and demographic trends that increasingly affect our ability or our willingness to educate our children.

Economic Changes and Schools

That the complacency of the American public about its schools described in the previous chapter is misplaced can be seen in the economic shifts that have taken place in recent years. No longer is America always in the competitive or economic forefront. Competitive realities have only quite recently begun to be addressed at the public policy level. The existence of competitive problems has been ignored, in part out of complacency for many years. These problems have a sort of "push down" impact on schools that needs to be articulated. In general, we can state that the quality of the workforce bears a direct relationship to competitiveness. In turn, the quality of education received from grades K–12 determines whether or not the workforce is capable of the types of achievements necessary in a globally competitive economy. Further, the availability of jobs, pay levels, and the amount of time individuals have to work determine the extent to which resources are spread equitably or inequitably. Ultimately, the overall quality of life in a society is affected by the combination of education, workforce quality, job type and availability, and pay levels, as well as the culture, norms, and values of that society. This section will explore some of the realities of the global economy that the United States now faces.

The fundamental argument of this section is that what makes educational problems seem more severe today than in the past are convergent sets of social forces, technological advances, and business dynamics that have fundamentally altered the premises on which both schools and businesses operate. Social forces are creating more of an underclass that is difficult to educate,[2] has severe problems with family disintegration, and may experience only intermittent workforce participation in low-skill, low-wage jobs.[3] Even for middle- and upper-income families, finding time to reinforce educational (or any other) goals and values, read, and do homework is problematic because, as noted in the previous chapter, most families now have both parents working or are single-parent families. These realities of family life mean that children too often do not come to school prepared to learn, may not understand the connection between work and school, and may in fact not really value their education as much as they need to.

Technological advances, in particular, demand what Shoshana Zuboff has termed a more literate and "intellective" workforce capable of problem solving using predominantly intellectual rather than physical skills.[4] Global competition has focused attention on the quality of the workforce in other nations, forcing U.S. businesses to pay attention to high value-added products and services to remain competitive.[5] Movement toward high value-added products requires using a more highly skilled workforce to compete. Achieving that highly skilled workforce necessitates improving the general level of education overall.

At the same time, the standards of high performance or what has been termed "high skills" workplaces have upped the educational ante for those organizations on the cutting edge. In 1994 the AFL-CIO Committee on the Evolution of Work issued a report entitled *The New American Workplace: A Labor Perspective*, which was aimed at fundamental changes in the relationship between labor and management due to changing technological and economic conditions. By committing to forming partnerships between unions and management that would create a new system of work organizations, the AFL-CIO hopes eventually to establish what it terms union/management brokered high-performance workplaces.

These workplaces have five characteristics. First, they redistribute decision-making authority from management to workers. Second, in the high-performance workplace, jobs require more skill variety and more responsibility from employees, who are frequently organized into teams that deal with whole production or service processes. Third, the high-performance workplace has a flattened management structure, where the role of manager becomes more facilitative and leading than authoritative. Fourth, operating through unions, workers in the high-performance workplace have more decision-making responsibility, thereby gaining input into strategic decisions that affect their work. Finally, the AFL-CIO expects that rewards from reorganizing work will be distributed equitably between labor and management. At the present time, these characteristics represent long-term goals for workplaces rather than changes that have already taken place, but the issuance of this report by the AFL-CIO, a major union, indicates that significant changes in expectations placed on workers can indeed be foreseen.

Although not all organizations by any means have instituted high-skills workplaces, those that have find it necessary to hire workers who bring a great deal of intellectual and problem-solving capacity to their positions.

Even companies with relatively low-skilled positions sometimes find it hard to recruit entry-level workers with sufficient skills and appropriate attitudes toward work. But companies not pursuing cutting edge status through a value-adding workforce face problems of hiring workers at low enough wage rates to be economically competitive and an employee base that is barely able to sustain itself economically. Simply put, there may not be enough jobs available at an acceptable standard of living unless companies change their strategies so they are competing on the basis of adding value rather than de-skilling work. And, of course, the U.S. educational system at present is hardly capable of producing a workforce that can universally meet such a value-adding standard.

Despite some recognition of these trends, most U.S. businesses still see little need to change their workforce practices or skill levels[6] or even their product mixes. Indeed, there is little expectation that the number of higher-skilled jobs will grow rapidly over the next few years, and some reason to believe that the trend of the 1980s toward more lower-paying, lower-skilled jobs will continue.[7] There is, as a result of these conflicting forces, a paradox in this situation. If businesses choose to ignore the need to upgrade workforce skills and technological sophistication, the societal choice is, as the Commission on the Skills of the American Workforce has put it, one of "high skills or low wages."[8] The competitive choice may be one of low value-added and hence lower competitiveness globally. The individual "choice" is one of low skills, low wages, and all the attendant problems of quality of life. This choice contrasts with a high-skills, high-wages job that enables individuals to contribute to work, society, and their families.

Ultimately, the low-skills and low-wages choice may put the entire U.S. economy at a competitive disadvantage, since many foreign competitors are in fact focusing on high value-added products using a skilled labor force.[9] Most difficult of all may be the growing recognition that low-skill, low-wages jobs are hardly sufficient to support a family, nor do they put pressures on education to improve or children to achieve. At the same time, there may not be enough higher-paying, higher-skilled positions to go around to provide sufficient incentive to really go about the difficult task of improving schools unless both businesses and schools work together toward the common end of developing people's citizenship and work skills to the fullest.

Business Realities: Higher Skills for Added Value

In part, the perceived decline in school performance may really be a matter of increased expectations of what a high school graduate should be able to do. As noted above, these performance expectations will only increase in the future if society itself is to remain competitive. The more usual approach of "de-skilling" jobs is a strategy that is unlikely to provide much of a competitive advantage in a world where value-added is a primary consideration, although many companies do not yet recognize this fact.[10] For astute observers of the global business and economic environment, it is becoming clear that a technologically complex, globally competitive business environment requires constant adaptation to new customer demands that are far different from those required in the mass-production-oriented business climate on which the United States had relied for decades after World War II.

Many business leaders seem to believe that business-as-usual strategies will continue to work,[11] but given competitive conditions that assumption is probably faulty. Increasingly, businesses that compete successfully in the global market will have to rely on the advanced skills, problem-solving capacity, creative energy, and implementation abilities of their workforces, just as foreign competitors are doing.[12] Cheaper labor alone won't solve all of business' future problems because international competitiveness is increasingly premised on a "high-skills" rather than a low-wages workforce.[13] In fact, management guru Peter Drucker has recently argued that "leadership throughout the developed world no longer rests on financial control or traditional cost advantages. It rests on brain power."[14]

Businesses that choose to ignore the need for a more-, not a less-skilled workforce will in the long run find themselves unable to sustain their competitive edge against other companies choosing to hone and upgrade worker skills or able to find a sufficiently qualified workforce. More radically, an America that fails to provide a high-skilled workforce will very likely be unable to compete internationally.[15] Indeed, restructuring, streamlining of staff, automation, and similar company and public sector actions may mean that many fewer jobs overall will be available in the future. The jobs that remain, however, will demand a higher-skilled workforce, necessitating a more-prepared citizenry and workforce than was needed to fill jobs in the past. This skill level is increasingly important because it is the lowest-wage occupations in the United States that have experienced the greatest decrease in real wages in recent years,[16] making it ever more difficult to support a family.

Changing Work: Technology

Zuboff[17] provides evidence that work itself has changed in recent years, at least in industries where high value-added technologies are in use. Technological solutions to problems formerly solved by the brute strength of skilled or unskilled labor are changing the most basic of industries. Work formerly done using "hands on" approaches is now performed by far fewer workers analyzing computer output and ordering computer-based equipment to perform tasks that used to be done by hand. Mechanics working in garages now have to interpret computer output to know what is wrong with cars, and have to understand enough electronics to repair the multitude of computerized functions that are now embedded in every vehicle. Simply running a copy machine or dealing with an answering machine (not to mention a VCR) now takes a certain amount of technological competence.

Even the construction industry, long considered the industry for the brawny, now demands competency in mathematics and computers. As the president of a construction firm, who is heavily involved in educational improvement efforts, puts it, "The construction industry faces a multifaceted problem. The thought has always been, 'Don't worry. You can always drop out and go into construction.' We're a labor-intensive industry, but we've lost high pay for our unsafe, undesirable conditions. As we have to compete for scarce [labor] resources, we'll get what's left if we don't do something. . . . And today, without algebra, geometry, trigonometry, you won't make a good carpenter. There's a saying in the industry, 'How would you like to build a smart building with dumb people?'"

As this executive indicates, the reality is that the construction industry has evolved along with the rest of the world: there are few large construction sites today that are not equipped with computers to manage the workflow. People on the site have to be able to interpret the data on the screen, place orders when necessary, assure materials flow and work processing, and perform the myriad other tasks associated with building complex structures. Similar technological advances are taking place in most industries with significant implications that require a workforce capable of dealing with advanced technology, on-the-spot decision making, and working in teams.

Global Demands

Construction is a local business, but the types of demands now being placed on construction workers are hardly local. Progressive competitors have realized that leaps in competitive strength can be gained by applying advanced technology, decentralized information housed in personal computers, and new workforce strategies to even such "brute strength" industries as construction. Some companies have responded to competitive pressures in the past by "de-skilling" jobs and finding cheap labor in low-wage parts of the world. De-skilling can be only a temporary strategy if competitors are enhancing skills and adding more value through intellective capability as many global competitors are. Enhanced skills enable competitors to compete more efficiently or effectively, provide services that better meet clients' needs, or produce products with higher levels of quality.[18] In effect, enhanced skills provide a greater potential for value-added and, from a competitive perspective, increasing the chances of global competitiveness through production of higher quality goods and services.

Outsourcing Jobs

Outsourcing is a tactic similar to de-skilling, which has typically involved sending low-skilled jobs to cheap-labor regions. As Cohen and Zysman[19] have argued, however, with the outsourced low-skilled jobs, eventually go the higher-skilled (e.g., R&D) and related service jobs as well. It is on the linkages between high-skilled, high-paying jobs in manufacturing, the skilled positions that go with services that support manufacturing, and the preparedness of the workforce to cope with such positions that the quality of life ultimately depends. As the number of manufacturing jobs requiring only unskilled labor shrinks, the demand for individuals with higher-order skills to fill what jobs are available grows correspondingly.

The United States cannot afford to lose all of its low-skilled jobs, nor can people live on the poverty wages that companies find necessary if they are to price competitively. This situation creates a dilemma for the nation and for companies who want to continue to do business in the United States. People cannot live on subsistence wages; companies cannot afford to pay more. Outsourcing jobs means fewer jobs available, and the only way for local economies, individuals, and companies themselves to stay competitive may be adding higher value-adding jobs. And these jobs require more education and higher skill levels on the part of workers. All of this pushes up the demand for improved education, while simultaneously suggesting to workers who have low skills that their services are less needed than ever. Simultaneously, as Juliet Schor points out, many companies are working their employees far harder, with 50- to 60-hour weeks becoming increasingly common, while few companies are willing or perhaps able to split up those hours into more adequately paying jobs.[20]

Service Jobs

With the decline in the number of individuals working in the manufacturing sector has come the growth of the proportion of employed working in services. It is the nature of service positions that they require immediate action: the customer expects the bank teller to deal with his or her concerns without a lot of bureaucratic red tape or having to "ask the boss"; the salesperson in a retail store who succeeds in a competitive environment has outstanding skills in dealing with people, knows the merchandise, and can access the computer system to determine where a requested item can be found if it is not in the store.

Even lower-skilled service jobs, for example, typically require strong interpersonal and communication skills, the ability to work well with others, and, increasingly, the ability to interpret complex data to solve problems on the spot. These demands are only likely to accelerate in the future. Service jobs that are relatively low skilled are also, as Robert Reich[21] points out, relatively low paying, making supporting a family difficult, thus making the dilemma described in the previous section even more intractable.

Increased Interdependence

Even the higher-skilled jobs may be outsourced if the need for a skilled workforce becomes more intense[22] and cannot be met domestically. Countries with an inadequately skilled labor force and school systems that fail to graduate literate individuals able to work competently in teams that add value will increasingly find themselves a poor second choice to those with higher-skilled and higher-paid labor forces.[23] These new realities[24] for business mean that businesses must recognize their increased dependence on the adequacy of the systems that support the growth and development of the populations in countries in which they are located. In the United States, businesses have traditionally thought themselves to be quite separate from government, social agencies, and schools. As the impact of these forces becomes clearer, however, these lines of separation have become less distinct.

The foregoing suggests that there are two different problems. First is the inability of businesses (and public policy makers) to recognize the need to invest sufficiently in all human resources so that adequate skill levels are present in the workforce, that is, lack of real school reform. Second is a lack of recognition of the need for a major strategic shift in the nation's industries toward higher value-added, less resource-dependent technologies that can actually use the skilled labor presumably to be produced by schools. These problems are confounded by a third reality: increasing workforce diversity.

Demographic Realities: Increased Diversity

Demographic shifts are also forcing companies to reconsider their relationships with other institutions in society. In many cities so-called "minority" groups are becoming the majority. Certainly, demographic trends do not favor the continued dominance of white males, as the Towers Perrin and Hudson Institute's Workforce 2000[25] was among the first to forcefully point out. By the year 2000, white males will become an increasingly smaller proportion of the working population, as women, blacks, and Hispanics become a greater proportion of the employable. Since these groups, especially the so-called minorities, historically have received the least-sound and most-problematic schooling, their education clearly demands attention. Though historically least educationally qualified to take on jobs demanding higher skills, they are yet the very labor force on whom business, government, and ultimately society must depend for its future quality of life.

"Workforce diversity" has become a euphemism covering up the underlying issues of race and class that have kept our nation from having the political and social will to educate large groups of children. Where other nations, such as Japan and Korea, have functional literacy rates as high as or higher than 97 percent of their population, the United States seems to have assumed, if not overtly then through actions, that many children are not educable—or, perhaps, not worth educating. The United States has, as a result, been saddled with functional illiteracy rates estimated to be as high as 40 percent. Functional literacy is sufficient to enable a worker or citizen to function effectively and the level of achievement differs according to the particular demands being made upon a person.

That many of the children left behind in the educational system belong to minority or poor families is frequently overlooked or ignored. The evidence of such neglect can be seen in the dilapidated ruins of school buildings, outdated textbooks, the poor status of teaching as a profession, and lack of attention to educational improvement except rhetorically that characterizes inner-city schools in particular.[26] Sadly, the devaluing of education for some population groups seems now to be rapidly spreading to all children, as the noose of resource constraints for schools has become tighter and tighter, with taxpayer revolts fueling a public willingness to support schools only marginally, and too many families under enough stress that they are unable to provide basic attentions to their children.

The risk of a successful educational policy, also an unstated, largely indiscussible, fundamentally ethical issue, is that with education comes advancement and power for those who command the intellectual and competency-based resources that a solid education provides. And with increased demographic diversity, that advancement and power will inevitably devolve to groups and individuals formerly in the ranks of the historically less powerful.[27] Education for all means that people—all people—can cope with the value-adding workplace realities described above. Between the economic and demographic realities of the nation are some difficult decisions to be made about the ways in which education is structured and how achievement is to be gained so that the explicit goals of education for all can actually be achieved.

INSTITUTIONAL SPIDER'S WEB

Institutions or formal organizations make up the bulk of the spider's web of social fabric in which schools are embedded (see Figure 3.1). Because we think of schools as largely independent of other institutions, we sometimes forget that what other institutions do (or don't do) has a great deal of influence on how well schools can do their own jobs. The following sections will explore the impact of some of the most important external institutions on schools. These formal institutions, combined with family and community, make up the significant strands of the web.

Human Services: Social Service Organizations and Government Agencies

Human services, as provided by formal institutions outside the family, are delivered primarily through social service agencies and governmental agencies. Social service organizations include all of those organizations whose stated mission is to better the lives of individuals, families, or communities, and that operate as distinct entities from governmental organizations. These agencies, frequently funded by government grants or by donations, comprise part of the so-called safety net that keeps families in need afloat and helps them satisfy basic needs. The relative strength of these organizations enhances the governmental safety net for families struggling with various types of social problems, such as lack of adequate housing, unemployment, illness, or other problems.

Another related group of institutions that create the safety net are agencies of the government. Government agencies, like social service agencies, operate in what Benson has called policy sectors or "arenas in which public policies are decided and implemented."[28] In practice, government agencies operate in programs, that is, agencies develop programs

Figure 3.1
The Spider's Web of Influences on School Performance

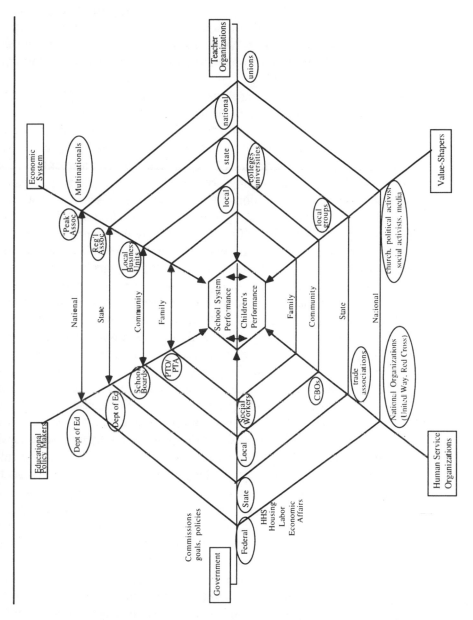

intended to deal with one or more aspects of the problems the agency was created to resolve within a policy sector. Each policy sector deals with a different type of problem, such as housing, welfare, employment, defense, environment, and, of course, education. Through the years many government initiatives have developed into highly rigid bureaucracies, each of which develops its own sets of rules and regulations to guide decision making.[29]

Of thirteen cabinet-level agencies, four other than the Department of Education are concerned with developing policies and programs that inherently affect families and children. These include the Departments of Health and Human Services, the Department of Housing and Urban Development, the Department of Labor, and the Department of Commerce. Thus, there are housing policies, health provisions, job-training programs, economic development programs, social services, and child-welfare agencies. Unfortunately, until the recent Clinton Administration took office, there were few efforts to coordinate the programs of different agencies or governmental departments around more holistic social goals, the Department of Labor's work on SCANS (Secretary's Commission on Achieving Necessary Skills) being the most notable exception. Instead, each agency or department historically develops its own goals, programs, and foci. Undoubtedly, the individualism and independence that characterizes American operating styles will continue to dominate attempts to coordinate among agencies, even should there be attempts to do so.

Bureaucratic rigidity and compartmentalization by program and focus frequently result in turf battles. Each human service or governmental agency attempts to gain and keep control over its specific policy domain without much regard for how issues or problems within that domain relate to issues or problems in other related domains. In too many instances what becomes important is gaining more resources or program money rather than finding innovative ways to help clients. This lack of interaction among government agencies in the mix of key policy sectors whose programs and policies affect family welfare, economic conditions, and community status can also be cited as one of the dominant institutional influences on school performance, particularly in the recent era in which services have been withdrawn.

Programs developed by human service organizations have similar problems in failing to deal with whole individuals, families, or systems, but rather tackle each problem in piecemeal fashion.[30] For example, a family might need housing assistance, job assistance, food stamps, and employment training, each of which is delivered by a different agency. Disadvantaged recipients of agencies' services are typically shunted from agency to agency depending on what that agency does and what the current program offerings are.[31] This shunting creates even more difficulties in the lives of people whose lives are already enormously burdened and who may have few coping mechanisms. Because social and governmental services are not coordinated and because all children pass through schools, the burden of this lack of coordination falls primarily upon the schools, which are ill-equipped to contend with it.

This fragmentation of services, which occurs, nationally, statewide, and locally, makes it difficult for schools, which have to deal with students and the panoply of problems that they may bring to school with them (of course, too many schools are not student oriented). Complicating the schools' situations is the fact that many of the social problems that used to be handled in other forums, particularly by communities, families, churches, and community organizations, are now handed to schools for resolution.

One recent study concludes that "American children may have lower average skills in mathematics and science partly because more of them are poor."[32] As resources for social service organizations have been squeezed, the ability of these agencies to help families in need has also been reduced. The impact of these resource constraints is that increasing numbers of children fall into conditions of poverty that are unrelieved by either community or social service supports. The study, for example, shows that while 44 percent of children in the lower fourth quadrant of testing in mathematics and reading and 42 percent in science were from disadvantaged groups, the numbers are reversed for the advantaged group. In the advantaged group 48.5 percent scored in the upper fourth in math, 46 percent in reading, and 42.5 percent in science. The high correlation between poverty and lower scores highlights the difficulties students in disadvantaged conditions face in attempting to achieve at higher levels.

It is not that disadvantaged students cannot achieve scholastically (8 percent score in the upper fourth quadrant in math and reading, and 9 percent in science, for example), but that for children in these conditions, such achievement comes with much more difficulty, and they need more support than children from more advantaged backgrounds, whose families may be able to supplement educational institutions. This is where social service and other civic institutions may be able to step in, by providing access to their services and, for museums and other cultural organizations, by potentially helping expose all of these students to a broader world.

The principal of an urban school discussed the impact of the combination of poverty and abandonment of community-oriented goals by society on schools: "Schools are required to do more than public education was ever intended to do. Schools have become the answer to social problems, to the ills of society. But we were not intended to take the place of churches regarding moral and ethical training. We are not the solution to crime and drug problems. There's been an overreaction to the handicapped. We have to deal with all the social problems; schools are expected, asked, forced to try all sorts of things. This takes away from quality education."

Because the safety net is failing for many children, schools have become, in effect, substitutes for secure, loving families and social service agencies have not been able to fill in. Urban and probably rural poverty make the situation particularly acute. One teacher in Cincinnati stated, "School is home for a lot of children. We have to do everything we can to make school productive. . . . If we are allowed to educate children, we'll need a component to educate parents. If alternative programs are to succeed, parents need to be involved in the schools and have relationships with teachers. They need to respect the teachers and have working relationships with them. As counselors, teachers are doing a lot of parenting action. They are also counseling parents who don't know where to turn. Schools have become social service agencies. They can't turn parents away because what's done with the parents helps the child." And, unfortunately, the constraints on resources for social service agencies and the general fragmentation of services they provide mean that schools are the one central factor in some families and, in particular, most children's lives.

The impact of the fragmentation of services is thus that each human services agency tends to operate in much the same way that it has been suggested earlier in this book that schools do, that is, as if they were operating in isolation from the rest of society. Coordination of services and collaboration among agencies, while potentially desirable goals, go much against the grain of American ideology and have largely been structurally embedded in our governmental, as well as our school, system. At the same time, the changing characteristics of the social problems facing the nation and its communities have forced schools to assume some of the responsibilities for providing what can only be called social services, for example, feeding hungry kids, initiating health and safety programs, AIDS education, environmental education, dealing with drug, social, emotional, and physical abuse, providing before- and after-school care, trying to quell violence and deal with trauma.

The tragedy is that all of these issues must be dealt with whether or not school personnel have the resources or training needed. Schools are forced to contend with these problems because they must otherwise deal with their consequences for children who have not received these services. That gap in what can only be called parenting and community support for education makes educating children next to impossible since a hungry, abused, scared, or neglected child is focused on more fundamental needs than education.

The fragmentation of programs and services that might help families and children in need thus represents a gap in direct influence—an influence characterized by lack of support and lack of coordination and lack of holistic thinking. It is a gap that affects the schools significantly. Rather than forming a positive network of supportive services that can easily be tapped by schools when needed, each agency—and school—operates in its own domain or policy sector with little regard for what is happening in other domains. In the relative isolation from other institutions that results, schools are left with the responsibilities and challenges of dealing with many problems that detract from their primary focus of education, particularly when the rest of society decides, as it seems to have done, to abandon much semblance of caring and community.[33]

Teachers' Unions

Another institution that both directly and indirectly impacts the quality of education is the unions and other organizations to which teachers belong. At the present time there are two main teachers' unions, the National Education Association and the American Federation of Teachers. Although both unions have been strongly behind efforts to professionalize teaching over the years, they have also been intensely involved in behaviors that work directly against true professionalization. Unions have sometimes fostered adversarial teacher-management relationships, set up barriers to entry into the profession, and taken teachers out on debilitating strikes. At the same time, they have pushed hard to assure the professional status of teachers, improve working conditions, pay, and status, and provide a mechanism for communicating with teachers throughout the nation. Union structures exist at the national, state, local, and building levels and, depending on the attitudes and stances taken by members, can greatly affect the ways in which teachers do their jobs, interact with administrators and students, and organize themselves. As a result of this pervasiveness, the impact of unions on the teaching profession has been quite strong.

While unions may resist changes that many observers perceive to be necessary to improved education, representatives of both the American Federation of Teachers and the National Education Association in interviews recognized the need for significant changes in the teaching profession. One sign of movement is a recent effort to consolidate the two teachers' unions, which have historically had different foci. In other areas, key union leaders have been speaking out in favor of radical change. For example, Rochester, New York's Adam Urbanski is an outspoken national figure advocating structural changes in the relationships between schools and teachers and in performance standards for teachers.

Although Urbanski is probably not typical of union leaders, he suggests the need for significant change through the unions, "Our agenda is simple: more children need to learn better. That's really the foremost priority for me. I want the teachers to do better only if the kids do, not if the kids don't. That takes repositioning of the union. The union model is structured in an industrialized unionism, which served a useful purpose, for parity with management, dealing with a spectrum of unilateral capriciousness, and providing dignity to workers. Few of my colleagues realize that that was a phase. . . . I would marry the roots of unionism with the best example of modern unionism, Solidarity in Poland."

In discussing what the unions need to do today, Urbanski suggests, "We are the conscience of society. Dignity, self-determination, and fair play are the values. We need to take these into consideration and mix in professionalism. A union that strives for autonomy over both the conditions of work and the knowledge base necessary for work does not back away from due process and fair play, and does not back away from guarding against excesses. That union knows that if business goes down, so does the union. I am startled that people miss this lesson. They're playing by old rules in a new game. It's a changed game, not just increasingly sophisticated. Change is inevitable and growth is optional. You atrophy and die if you don't change. If the union does not change, it will be left in the dust."

Teachers' unions, according to Gary Watts of the National Education Association, currently have structures that mirror or shadow the hierarchical systems used by school systems. This argument is similar to that made by Urbanski. Many union contracts impose relatively rigid rules on teachers, on their expectations about work, and what they will and will not be expected to do. Unions have simultaneously attempted to help teachers develop a sense of professionalism by erecting barriers around the teaching profession and have diminished teachers' status as professionals by imposing the types of work rules, standards for performance, and inflexible systems that have kept blue collar workers in other unionized situations from more creatively working in alliance with managements.

Those union representatives interviewed for this study suggested that unions and schools, when they change, need to join in partnership with schools and others involved in the school reform process. But as Urbanski says, the partnership must be real, not just in name: "This union won't play an advisory role. If you want us as partners, you have to accept us as full partners in decision making or there's no parity among equals. Unions are really struggling for some kind of status and teachers are too. Our argument is fairly good. We have a shared perspective here, we want to work collaboratively, not adversarially. We can sabotage any effort by doing nothing. If management pretends to know all the answers, we'll pretend they do too."

Urbanski's agenda has to do with empowering the teacher at the classroom level, where education takes place. But despite progress by unions in some domains such as working conditions and pay, unions have, if anything, imposed greater restrictions on what teachers can and cannot do with respect to their teaching assignments. There are rules and restrictions relating to preparation, out-of-class work, working with management and administration, and many other aspects of teachers' working lives with which other professionals do not have to contend. These restrictions create a double bind for many teachers, who on the one hand wish to be considered professional and on the other hand act like factory laborers in their demands and in their attitudes toward work.

Even Urbanski whose union in Rochester, New York, is progressive and has been actively working for change with school and city administrators, admits, "The jury is still out on whether these changes will work. We are not in favor of collaboration except in parity. Managers in most districts are willing to go only so far. There's an increasing amount of involvement, increasingly more input. . . . One block is centuries of weight on their disinclination to change. The district is still the boss, still pays the bills. And they say, 'What do you mean a 50/50 relationship?' We're not begrudging to parents, teachers, but we need dignity: we need a fair, level playing field." It is on the availability of this level playing field that, arguably, improved education will rest, as we shall see later on.

Teacher Education

Another subject of much criticism has been the colleges of education that train future teachers. Often criticized for irrelevance and lack of rigor, colleges of education are beginning to respond to increasingly demanding challenges. Some of these changes are the direct result of changing state statutes that require more liberal arts or subject-matter education for future teachers. In Massachusetts, for example, the undergraduate education degree has been eliminated in favor of a major in the liberal arts or sciences with education courses as a supplement. The relatively low regard in which teaching as a profession is held by U.S. society, combined with the opening up of other professional opportunities for women over the past twenty-five years, have further eroded the profession's ability to attract the most qualified individuals into teaching.

Like school districts and local school boards, schools of education are themselves decentralized and highly independent of each other. Although they respond to state mandates regarding curriculum, it is difficult to mandate significant changes because of the political resistance to change that is generally encountered. Colleges of education and the universities within which they reside in effect set important standards for the teaching profession (and ultimately for its status in society) through their admission requirements, the level of academic achievement of their students, and their curricula. The recent history of colleges of education in these regards has not been auspicious. Until quite recently when some reforms (some mandated at the state level) began to take effect, colleges of education have been widely considered to have low admission standards, weak students, and uninspiring curricula. And this is not a new phenomenon. Over the years, many studies have documented the problems of colleges of education in trying to attract and retain highly qualified individuals. The low status and relatively low pay of teachers have placed further downward pressures on admission and graduation standards. The complacency about education's real performance discussed above combines with families' and teachers' desire to maintain their free time to make significant school restructuring difficult.

Only recently have state standards regarding what curriculum education students should follow begun to become more rigorous. Most curricula in colleges of education are far from standardized, although one observer suggests that there are (or should be) some common elements, such as understanding the meaning, purpose, and problems of universal public education, the nature of the learner and the learning process, the methods and materials of instruction, and the practice of teaching.[34] Despite this agreement, complaints of duplication of content, uninspiring content, low quality of teaching, lack of direct contact with or knowledge of schools by college professors, and low standards in colleges of education persist. In addition, one of the most persistent problems has been the low quality of students entering the professional colleges of education, students whose SAT scores are substantially below those entering other majors.

Further, as noted earlier, the women's movement has had a deleterious effect on teacher education, as many talented women who used to go into teaching turned to higher-paying and higher-status jobs when they began to open up. The many problems with which education has been beset in the 1980s and 1990s, the faltering resource and public support base, and the difficulties of the children themselves have done little to make teaching a more attractive profession. This is not to suggest, of course, that women or anyone else ought to be relegated to low-paying, low-status positions. Rather, it is to suggest that as a society we need to reconsider the status, pay, and performance criteria of teaching in a real way so that teaching becomes a profession that is inherently attractive to bright and capable people of both genders and all ethnic backgrounds.

There is some evidence that change is under way. Many states have begun to look at requirements for entering the teaching profession, and some colleges of education are more tightly linking their curricula into the liberal arts and sciences to provide a more solid academic base for future teachers. As with public schools themselves, the constraints under which education colleges have operated for many years have become so tight that there is increasing recognition that something dramatic needs to change if the situation is to improve.

Colleges and Universities

One of the institutions that certainly ought to place value on the quality of schooling that young people receive is certainly our colleges and universities. Institutions of higher education have as their central mission educating people to take leadership, professional, and informed citizenship roles in society. In theory then, colleges and universities should maintain relatively high admission standards as an important criterion that places significant value on the education that has taken place at an earlier stage of a student's life as well as to ensure their own academic integrity. One aspect of such a stance would be that high admission standards would provide an incentive for aspiring high-school students to work hard, achieve good grades, and gain a solid foundation.

In practice the situation in the United States is quite different. While certain universities and colleges have high standards, others are quite willing to admit almost any student capable of paying the bills or, in some cases, simply filling a seat in the classroom. The United States has a vast proliferation of colleges, far beyond what any other nation can offer. This access to higher education is, in one respect, a valued aspect of American life. It provides an opportunity for many college students to fulfill their version of the American dream, Horatio Alger style, by gaining an advanced level of education. There is thus a great tension between providing a wide array of educational opportunities to individuals of varying ability and willingness to work hard and the desire to maintain high standards at the university, a standard that filters down to the schools in the form of incentives to work hard in high school.

One union representative put it this way: "Institutions of higher education are more interested in keeping up enrollments than producing a quality product. They have great variation in their admission and graduation requirements. It seems that students can get into college no matter what, so where's the incentive to do better?" While this problem applies to all majors in colleges and universities, it is particularly acute for colleges of education, which have generally lower admission standards than many other colleges.

Educational Policy Makers

One of the predominant and most direct influences on education is educational policy, which is created at four levels, locally through school administration and school boards and committees, at the state level through state departments of education, and nationally through the policies of the federal Department of Education. Although the educational policy system is part of government, its influence on schools is central to school performance. At the national level, the Department of Education sets federal policies and, more recently, goals for education. In the United States, however, the federal government has historically had relatively little direct influence on schools, which are run by local school boards under the auspices of state education agencies. The federal government role until quite recently has largely been one of assuring civil rights around educational issues, disbursing grants and loans primarily for higher education, and administering the funding for disadvantaged youth.

With the promulgation of the national goals for education by the Bush Administration and their mandate into law by GOALS 2000: Educate America, the U.S. Department of Education attempted to assume a more proactive role in setting a national education agenda. But because the primary responsibility for education constitutionally belongs to states and local communities, the Education Department must attempt to achieve its goals by trying to persuade local communities and states to accept and endorse the goals, rather than by direct action. Nonetheless, whatever their limitations, the national goals at least set a target for schools to attempt to achieve against which their actual achievement can be measured.

State boards or departments of education are primarily responsible for setting state educational policies for all of the local school districts that fall within their domains. They may provide funding support, determine funding policies in general (e.g., use of property vs. other taxes), or choose textbooks (in some states) for the entire state. Teacher contracts may be negotiated at the state level, although most are negotiated at the district level.

Education in the United States is a $425 billion business.[35] The common wisdom is that the United States spends more per pupil on education than do many other nations, however, the reality is different. Not only are there more children living in poverty in the United States than in most other industrialized nations, spending on grades K–12 as a percent of gross domestic product (GDP) is less in the United States than in every country other than Australia and Ireland. For example, while Sweden spends 7.0 percent of GDP on education, Austria 5.9 percent, Switzerland 5.8 percent, Japan 4.8 percent, Canada 4.7 percent, and West Germany (before integration with East Germany) and France 4.6 percent, the United States spends only 4.1 percent.[36]

The reason that U.S. expenditures on education are typically considered higher is that higher education expenditures are frequently included with K–12 and U.S. spending is proportionately higher for more advanced education than in other countries. In 1991–1992, the United States expended $425.2 billion on education at all levels, of which $261.1 billion or 61.4 percent was spent on elementary and secondary education. The other 38.6 percent was spent on colleges and universities. Some 57 percent of total expenditures for K–12 was spent on public schools (with another 5 percent on private schools). Of total federal expenditures for education of $61.4 billion only 46 percent or $28.3 billion is spent on elementary and secondary education.[37]

In addition to the differences that exist at the country level, there are dramatic differences in spending on a state-by-state basis. For example, 1988–1989 spending in the highest ten states ranged from $4,888 in Wisconsin to $5,723 in New York per pupil adjusted for cost-of-living differences. In contrast, spending in the lowest ten states ranged from $2,680 in Utah to $3,400 in Tennessee. Overall, the United States spent $4,246 per pupil in 1989 suggesting that even when the cost of living is taken into account, there are great differences in the amount that the public is willing or perhaps able to spend for education, depending on the particular state one lives in. And even though there is a great deal of truth in statements that schools need to work smarter not just demand more resources, there is a clear relationship between the funding level of schools (at least when those funds are not wasted on superfluous administration) and the quality or performance of schools.

At the community level, local school boards, more than 16,000 in the United States, hold primary responsibility for the delivery of educational services, for local school policies and procedures, for staffing, and for direct service delivery. These boards exercise the most potent and direct control over school policies, curriculum, teacher and principal assignments and other staffing issues, as well as local funding decisions, in conjunction with other local authorities. To the extent that school boards work in the interest of children and the schools, they can be effective political and governance advocates for schools. To the extent that they are embroiled in local politics and focus their attention on minutiae (micromanagement), they may actually impede schools' educational missions.

In turn, at the family level parents can become involved to some (typically small) extent in school policies by working together with teachers and principals in parent-teacher associations or organizations (PTA/PTO). In recent years, many schools have responded to pressures for improvements by establishing policies of site-based or decentralized management, frequently engaging interested parents in advisory and even governing boards that directly influence individual school policies, programs, and procedures. These types of mechanisms and other similar mechanisms permit parents' voice in the affairs of schools. Until quite recently in some schools and still on-going in most schools, this voice has been limited, at least as far as curricular or school policy matters go. PTA/PTOs have generally done more fund-raising activities that help schools primarily at the margins than focusing on policy-setting and many advisory or governing boards including parents have had difficulties in establishing real power over school policies.

Further, during the Reagan and Bush Administrations education was largely neglected fiscally. The prevailing mentality developed during this era that you can have it all for nothing or for very little that characterized the 1980s resulted in serious fiscal constraints for many schools. The unwillingness of the public to pay for education resulted from a widespread perception that it was possible to have a good education system without spending much money on it or that there was a great deal of waste within the current system. Although changes may be under way, the task of changing this perception is a difficult and potentially long-term one that requires a refocusing on community and social welfare.

Textbook Publishers

One less well recognized set of influences on the quality of education that is delivered are the textbook publishers and the textbooks that they produce. In some states, where there is statewide adoption of texts, much material has been watered down or eliminated so that little of controversy (or interest) remains in the texts. In many cases, teachers and administrators may have little choice about the texts they will use, as these decisions are made at the district or state level. The "dumbing down" of textbooks that has taken place to accommodate the plurality of interests means that in too many instances students are not being exposed to materials that challenge their thinking or, literally, that take the students themselves seriously as learners.

Institutions that Shape Values

Values in America crystalized in the 1980s by focusing ever-more attention on individualism, materialism, and self-interest than had been traditional in our society. At least one observer, sociologist Charles Derber, has termed this trend "wilding" and suggested that the loss of community-based values evident especially during the latter half of the 1980s and into the 1990s has made for a society that may be or soon will be incapable of taking care of its own.[38] Derber describes the case of the Ik, a tribe that lost all capacity to care for others, eroding its moral center and destroying any sense whatsoever of the common good. So uncaring did the Ik become in the interest of each individual filling his or her own stomach, that some parents threw their own children out to starve, others stole food from the dying or buried the dying while they were still alive. In short, the loss of a sense of common good, community, and caring absolutely destroyed the Ik's capacity for showing moral concern for the other. Derber suggests that during the past decade or so, the American public has become much like the Ik, with caring and community being lost to the ravages of self-interest and greed.

The attitudes and values that a society holds are presumably shaped in a variety of ways, including the religious and moral training that children receive, the relative strength of cultural and religious institutions, and the impact that those institutions have on people's lives, as well as the national ideology, and the values promulgated by the media and shaped in law and general public policy by the political or public policy processes. Among these factors are the lack of the political will in the nation to change the educational system radically, which means that resources for change are difficult to find. This lack of will is bolstered in part by a very real anti-intellectual tradition that places little real value on education despite rhetoric to the contrary.

In addition to families, there are other, more formally organized institutions such as the media, churches, public policies, and political organizations that also play a significant role in shaping values. Political organizations at the national, state, and local levels help shape attitudes and values related to participation in a representative democracy and in a capitalistic economy. Political organizations and the political process shape the general ideology of a nation. The diversity of values inherent to the American system is both a benefit and a problem in this respect.

In countries where there is more homogeneity of ethnic backgrounds and religious values, such as Japan, Korea, or Germany, it seems easier to place a value on education and have most of the people in the nation agree with the importance of that value. In the United States where ethnic diversity is much greater, coming to an agreement about the value of education is far more difficult. For some cultural groups, education is in general valued less than for others. Some groups believe that schools ought to do the primary work of educating children, while others think that parents and others play a significant role. The diverse values at play, as well as the mixed goals that education in the United States has historically had of educating for a job versus educating for citizenship, combine with the lack of public discourse over the past couple of decades about what the goals and characteristics of education should be. As Bellah and his colleagues pointed out, there are few public forums available in the United States for such important dialogues and as a result our sense of community as a nation, as well as more locally, has eroded.[39]

The media are important in creating values and impacting education in several ways. One influence is that of advertisements, a second is through the types of articles and programs that the media presents to the public, and a third is through the role of creating and producing programs about public issues for general consumption. In all of these activities, the media serves as either the mirror of public values or actually generates those values through what is chosen and what is not chosen to be presented to the public.

Not all of the media's influence around values is positive. Much of it, in fact, is either self-serving, materialistic, or oriented toward promoting even more individualistic behaviors aimed at consumption. Children in schools are exposed to a great deal of media influence through the television they watch and the ads and billboards they see each day. A great deal of programming on television, even that aimed directly at children, promotes violence as well and a lack of concern for human life. Children incorporate these values through their viewing and often without an adult present to counteract or even discuss what is happening.

The Institutional Network Created by the Spider's Web

This chapter has explored the institutional network within which schools exist. The strands of the web play a vital, if often unrecognized, role in determining how well schools can perform their jobs. If these institutions are working well and if the incentives they provide work to positive effect on the schools, then schools and children will benefit. If these institutions are fragmented or thoughtless in their policies and values with respect to education, as unfortunately they too often have been, then schools will suffer.

Our "each boat on its own bottom" individualism might cause us to suggest that schools ought to pick up the slack, filling in where these institutions leave off. Indeed, schools have been trying, often heroically, to do just that. But the reality is that schools and their spokes, the other institutions, are a system of interdependencies. The failures of one will become the failures of all in the long run. By beginning to recognize these interdependencies and the ways that they influence each other more clearly, we can move toward a new set of relationships among all of these important institutions.

NOTES

1. R. N. Bellah, R. Madsen, W. M. Sullivan, A. Swidler, and S. M. Tipton (1991), *The Good Society* (New York: Alfred A. Knopf).

2. R. B. Reich (1990), "Who Is Us?" *Harvard Business Review* January–February: 53–64.

3. C. Handy (1989), *The Age of Unreason* (Boston, MA: Harvard Business School Press).

4. S. Zuboff (1988), *In the Age of the Smart Machine: The Future of Work and Power* (New York: Basic Books).

5. I. Magaziner and M. Patinkin (1989), *The Silent War: Inside the Global Business Battles Shaping America's Future* (New York: Random House).

6. National Center on Education and the Economy's Commission on the Skills of the American Workforce (1990), *America's Choice: High Skill or Low Wages!* (Rochester, NY: U.S. Department of Education).

7. L. Mishel and D. M. Frankel (1992), *The State of Working America, 1990–91 Edition.* (Armonk, NY: M. E. Sharpe Company), p. 71.

8. See National Center on Education and the Economy's Commission on the Skills of the American Workforce (1990).

9. I. Magaziner and M. Patinkin (1989), C. Handy (1989), R. B. Reich (1990), and M. E. Porter (1990b), *The Competitive Advantage of Nations* (New York: Macmillan).

10. See National Center on Education and Economy's Commission on the Skills of the American Workforce (1990).

11. Two useful citations here are I. Magaziner and M. Patinkin (1989), and National Center on Education and the Economy's Commission on the Skills of the American Workforce (1990).

12. C. Handy (1989).

13. I. Magaziner and M. Patinkin (1989).

14. See P. F. Drucker (1991), "Japan: New Strategies for a New Reality," *The Wall Street Journal* October 2.

15. Two important works in this area focusing on management issues are M. E. Porter (1990a). "The Competitive Advantage of Nations," *Harvard Business Review* March–April: 73–93; and R. B. Reich (1990). See also Porter (1990b); and R. B. Reich (1991a), *The Work of Nations: Preparing Ourselves for Twenty-first-Century Capitalism* (New York: Alfred A. Knopf).

16. L. Mishel and D. M. Frankel (1992), 71–82.

17. See S. Zuboff (1988).

18. I. Magaziner and M. Patinkin (1989), make this argument strongly.

19. S. S. Cohen and J. Zysman (1989). "Why Manufacturing Matters: The Myth of the Post-Industrial Economy," *California Management Review* 29(3): 9–26.

20. J. Schor (1991). *The Overworked American: The Unexpected Decline of Leisure* (New York: Basic Books).

21. See R. B. Reich (1991a).

22. See Reich (1991a), and I. Magaziner and M. Patinkin (1989).

23. See M. E. Porter (1990b); and I. Magaziner and M. Patinkin (1989).

24. The term comes from P. F. Drucker (1989), *The New Realities: In Government and Politics / In Economics and Business / In Society and World View* (New York: Harper & Row).

25. The work that drew attention to shifting demography most explicitly is William B. Johnston, & A. H. Packer (1987), *Workforce 2000: Work and Workers for the Twenty-first Century* (Indianapolis, IN: Hudson Institute).

26. One place where these ideas are stated is J. Kozol's (1991) compelling book *Savage Inequalities: Children in America's Schools* (New York: Crown).

27. See Kozol (1991), for an elaboration.

28. J. K. Benson (1982), "A Framework for Policy Analysis," in D. L. Rogel, D. A. Whetten, and associates (Eds.), *Interorganizational Coordination: Theory, Research, and Implementation* (Ames, Iowa: Iowa State University Press), 147.

29. See D. E. Osborne and T. Gaebler's (1992) *Reinventing Government: How the Entrepreneurial Spirit is Transforming the Public Sector* (Reading, MA: Addison-Wesley).

30. Osborne and Gaebler (1992).

31. One important work that highlights the structure of government while proposing significant changes to it is that of D. E. Osborne and T. Gaebler (1992).

32. L. Mishel and D. M. Frankel (1992).

33. See S. Gordon (1991), *Prisoners of Men's Dreams: Striking Out for a New Feminine Future* (Boston: Little, Brown and Company).

34. See P. Woodring (1983), *The Persistent Problems of Education* (Bloomington, IN: Phi Delta Kappa Educational Foundation), 90–91.

35. National Center for Education Statistics (1992), *Digest of Education Statistics*. U.S. Department of Education, Office of Educational Research and Improvement.

36. Data are for the year 1985 and reported in L. Mishel and D. M. Frankel (1992), 246.

37. National Center for Education Statistics (1992).

38. C. Derber (1992), *Money, Murder, and the American Dream: Wilding from Wall Street to Main Street* (Boston: Faber and Faber).

39. Bellah et al., in their first book (1985) *Habits of the Heart: Individualism and Commitment in American Life*. New York: Harper & Row, discuss the loss of community to the forces of individualism and self-interest. In their second book (1991), *The Good Society* they push the argument further to suggest institutional failings as well as the lack of public discourse on important topics.

Chapter 4 _____

The Realities and Responsibilities of Education

Schools today face significantly different issues than they did twenty or thirty years ago.[1] Curriculum demands have shifted dramatically, sometimes in diametrically opposed ways. Resources are more constrained and expectations for performance are much higher than in the past, at least rhetorically. Strong family structures have deteriorated, with the result that today's children are very different in the amount of discipline they receive, which shows in their values, their attention spans, and their knowledge base. In effect, many children today may be less prepared to learn than they were in the past. Communities have become less cohesive through interrelated processes of suburbanization, inner-city decay, and busy, stressful lives. Television and other broadcast media now play more prominent roles in most people's lives than in earlier eras, resulting in more isolation and, for many, less community involvement.[2]

"Society"[3] has tended in the past fifty years to dump many of its problems on the schools, as if hoping thereby to avoid dealing with them through costly or difficult public policy decisions. The truth is, however, that most teachers and school administrators are ill prepared and in some cases rightly unwilling to tackle all the problems that society wishes to dump upon them. Yet to this point they have had few alternatives but to tackle those problems or live with the consequences of not doing so.

Many educators have the attitude that they know best about education, though they may understand relatively little of the work world or the realities of their students' lives. The result of these attitudes is that barriers are erected between what goes on in the outside world and what goes on in school, despite the fact that external pressures are buffeting the schools' ability to live up to social expectations. But, because each community (or nation) constitutes a system in which elements interact with each other and are interdependent, schools cannot afford to maintain this oasis in a desert attitude any longer. Nor can other institutions continue to operate as if their actions had little or no impact on the schools. Too much change is taking place externally that *does* inherently affect the schools for the isolationist structure to be effective.

The last two chapters explored the ways in which the social fabric in which schools are embedded has changed in recent years. This chapter will explore the ways in which social problems arising out of the decaying social fabric impact the schools. It is unreasonable to expect that any one institution can cope with all of these demands, yet that is the expectation that we have set upon the schools. Although many articulate observers have pointed out that social problems are being dumped on the schools, it is not at all clear that most parents, businesspeople, civic leaders, or government officials really understand what has happened to schools as a consequence. This analysis will provide a basis for arguing later on that responsibility for some of these problems must begin to be picked up outside schools so that schools can get on with their primary task of education.

PERSISTENT PROBLEMS OF EDUCATION

Long-time observers of education point to serious internal structural problems that impede the ability of schools to adapt to the changed external environment in which they operate. Consider the structure of the school day as a starting point. While many businesses and even some government agencies are slimming down, eliminating management layers, and focusing on customer needs and quality improvements through the empowerment of employees at local levels, schools have remained largely unchanged structurally. In part, I believe, this is because teachers and administrators know little about the ways in which organizational structure operates as either a barrier or enhancement to an organization's achievement of its goals.

Part of the problem is simply lack of time, for planning, for conversations about teaching, for working together. Teachers' days are chock-full with classroom activities and individual planning activities. Few schools have built-in adequate staff development, strategic planning, or other developmental time and too few command the teachers' attention once the school day has ended, since union contracts in general spell out the amount of commitment teachers have to make. Too many expect teachers to serve all of the emotional, psychological, health, and nurturing needs of their young charges as well as their educational needs.

In the typical school, teachers still work in isolated classrooms with between twenty and thirty-five students. Their day, in most instances, is highly structured, broken into forty-five- to sixty-minute periods (at least at the middle-school and high-school levels). During these periods, at least at higher levels, the teacher generally lectures to students about a specific topic. Then, when one topic is over, students move on to the next topic. The isolation for teachers is not just from each other around issues related to education. Teachers are too often unfamiliar with the world around them, a world that they presumably are teaching their students about, a world their students increasingly need to know more about. One principal interviewed admitted, "Educators get into a box. They don't know much about the outside world. You need a broad background for working with children that many educators don't have."

Students are still expected in most schools to be passive, disciplined receptacles of the information and facts that the teacher is conveying. Indeed, the expectation is that the students will become *knowers*, that is, that they will memorize the facts and information conveyed,[4] rather than that they will necessarily understand the meaning and use of those facts in a broader context—that is, that they will become learners. In elementary school classrooms, the structure of the day may be somewhat more fluid, but the emphasis is still on acquisition of facts. In this picture, the teacher is the active participant in the classroom, while students are largely passive.

Although there is more active learning at lower grade levels and, ironically enough, in generally undervalued technical or vocational education, this orientation tends to fade as students enter higher grade levels that are oriented to getting them into college. Acquisition of facts and the ability to know enough of them to do well on standardized tests so that better students can get into college is a dominant focus of high-school education. With some exceptions, high schools are very well characterized by the fragmented, knower-oriented, passive-learning model just described.

Even in more progressive schools, there is little time for teacher interaction or staff development. Teachers seldom have time to discuss their teaching methodologies, teaching goals, or student needs, even informally since they are involved with students for the greater part of the day and when school is not in session, teachers are on vacation, hence not involved in their own or their students' development. As an example, at my son's school in a progressive city with a reputation for good schools, the PTA brought together a group of teachers to present a session on the ways in which process writing was used in different grades. At the PTA meeting, which was attended by many of the rest of the teachers, teachers were surprised to find consistencies in their own classroom goals across grade levels. One teacher commented that this was the first time that she had understood how her own work in the classroom was placed in the context of what was going on in the overall elementary curriculum. This is a sad statement for a progressive school system in the 1990s in a town where there are two regular staff development meetings a week. One can only imagine the lack of knowledge in less progressive schools or schools with even less staff development time, which are the majority.

This is not to say that in most schools there is absolutely no staff development. Periodically, in most schools, there is something called in-service that takes place, in which teachers are provided with new materials, new ideas, or new programs. Just as with students, the assumption is that teachers will become knowers about these ideas, absorbing them and presumably magically incorporating them into their teaching plans. In general, however, few of these new ideas make their way into teaching because there is little opportunity for teachers to work collaboratively to solve some of their problems or implement new ideas. Just as teachers themselves provide for little opportunity for their students to learn to work together (indeed, many teachers would call cooperative learning outside of a specific assignment cheating), so too many are unfamiliar with teamwork and cooperation as a means of achieving better overall organizational results. Unlike many businesses, where meetings provide an opportunity for interaction and the development of common goals or approaches to problems, schools are structured with little built-in time for interaction among the professional staff. The result is that teachers continue to work in relative isolation from each other and fail to gain the benefits that might be associated with learning from what others are doing. The sometimes open conflict between teachers and administrators, the us-versus-them attitudes that sometimes exist, do not help to build the bridges that are needed to develop a more cooperative approach to meeting students' educational needs.

Teacher education itself has historically not focused on issues of team building or collaborative learning, or even on the learning process as much as on the knowing process, so teachers and administrators (who come predominantly from the ranks of former teachers) have little experience or knowledge of these processes. In any case, as Sizer points out,[5] educational processes that focus on learning rather than knowing are difficult to fit into fifty-minute periods. The emphasis on knowing and the lack of interaction among both teachers and students in the learning process has rather completely disempowered students.

Empowerment, of course, is a theme that is faddish among school officials today, but the impacts of the disempowerment, which the system as it exists has fostered, are important and need to be dealt with in the long term if real system change is to come about. Far better understanding of the ways in which the system works and the implications on work, on student learning, on teachers and administrators is needed for structural change to make a difference. Otherwise any attempts at change will become "just another program" and, as with reform efforts in the past that went only part of the way toward system change, will fail because they have failed to take into account the system effects of the structure and forces that are operating.

Thus, lack of knowledge about organizing and about the overall system in which they operate on the part of teachers and principals, then, can be considered a major problem in the reform of schools. There are knowledge gaps about the role of organization in enhancing learning, about organizational processes, about collaboration and cooperation (not surprisingly, in light of the whole society's individualistic orientation). There is lack of understanding about the interactive effects of the structure and system that has been created, both with external and internal forces. This gap results in the program orientation, an orientation that implicitly suggests that significant problems can be solved if only another program is added.

COMMUNITY CONDITIONS

Although schools still largely perceive themselves as islands of security, safety, and discipline in a world that is too often harsh or even violent, keeping community problems from penetrating school boundaries has become increasingly difficult, not to say impossible. These social or community problems, as will be discussed below, come into the schools in the form of children who are affected by their own lives outside the school. They are evidenced in outbreaks of violence, selling of drugs, and students carrying weapons to school. And increasingly these problems are not limited to inner-city schools, but are becoming more prevalent in suburban schools as well. So while school officials might find it desirable to pretend that social problems affecting them could be wished away, they must deal with their consequences every day.

The economic and career situations of parents are different than were those of a generation ago; these differences have strong implications for schools. Community and family support networks that may have once existed have been eroded by career shifts, mobility, and economic circumstances. Problems of poverty and broken homes create numerous difficulties for young people and, at the same time, our expectations of those young people are rapidly rising. Without demands coming from the community and parents, teachers and principals have had little real incentive to undertake the difficult and demanding changes for which astute observers of the educational scene are calling.

Pressures affecting schools evidence themselves as a series of problems confronting schools, which have their origin in the social fabric. Among the problems most commonly cited by eighth-grade students in one survey are alcohol use, school vandalism, student conflict, drugs, robbery or theft, and verbal abuse of teachers.[6] Teachers generated a similar list, however, ranking verbal abuse of teachers first, followed by alcohol, conflict, drugs, and vandalism.[7] Not surprisingly, these problems were more significant to both teachers and students in poorer neighborhoods than in more affluent ones, which is one measure of the impact that the local community has on the schools.

The general public takes a slightly different perspective, rating drugs, lack of discipline, and lack of proper financial support as the most significant problems facing schools.[8] It is interesting to note that the problem of drugs invades schools from the community, rather than emanating from the school. Discipline is a problem in part because children are undisciplined when they reach schools, and many of the tools that teachers and principals used to have to make discipline effective have been taken away in recent years. And, while the public may perceive lack of proper financial support to be problematic to schools, there has been little willingness in recent years on the part of the general public to pay more taxes to support the schools.

In a series of interviews conducted over a two-year period at a variety of different schools mainly in large cities, I heard a consistent message from educators and others involved in school improvement initiatives. The external problems that penetrate schools are reflected in both the teachers' and students' perceptions cited above, but, if those people interviewed are to be believed, the actual extent of problems afflicting schools is both broader and deeper than the data above suggest. The severity of problems mentioned consistently across the schools I visited, of course, may have something to do with the significant urban and economic development problems that these cities were facing. Thus, these problems are presumably more characteristic of inner-city schools than they would be of surburban or rural schools, nonetheless there is at least some possibility that they penetrate all schools.

Problems of Community

As business leaders have become more involved in school improvement and partnership efforts, some have begun to realize that the failures of education are in part really the failures of community. Recognition dawns that, as one individual who coordinates a partnership program, indicated, "Business is now close enough to see what we're doing with kids, what we're up against, and that we're not just making excuses. The reality is that sometimes teachers can't teach because of social problems." Poverty, drugs and alcohol abuse, violence, abuse and neglect, hunger, homelessness, teen pregnancy and parenthood, and unemployment are only some of the community-based issues with which schools, particularly those in inner cities, have to contend. No schools are completely immune from these problems. In general, community infrastructures and support systems have been eroded, leaving schools with the problems that communities once picked up.

On the issue of teen pregnancy, for example, one person interviewed commented, "Not all teens who have babies keep their children, but we do have several [in an alternative program for teen mothers] who, because they are still learning, have a parent or grandparent raising their children. The parents take in the teen's baby. . . . We are looking at thirty-four-year-old grandparents and great-grandparents at fifty-four. We have a generation of teen parents." When teenagers have children, they compound the problems that they themselves face, making climbing out of difficult circumstances even harder. Yet some teens may see no alternative or may believe that having a baby is a way to be loved when no one in their own lives seems to care.

Problems of Family

Just how do the problems of family confront the schools on a daily basis? One teacher was eloquent in her portrayal of the situation:

Families are overwhelmed. There are new things they've never dealt with before. Counselors now are seeing things they've never seen before, child abuse, single parent homes, crack babies, and parents with deprivations in their home life. There's a breakdown of the moral structure of society and the family. The do-your-own-thing era is hitting us in the face. But you can't have twenty-five little people in a room doing their own thing. There has to be control and order.

Kids have survival techniques. They're creative and you have to capture that. They'll use it one way or another, mischievously or productively. Too many parents don't know what to do or how to do it. They don't have a handle on parenting. We have to encourage them at home, to talk to their children every day, allowing the kids to exchange with the parent. Children are having children. These are real hard core issues. Then children come to school and this is all they have. These kids are not productive, but they don't want to go home at the end of the day. The school is home for a lot of children. We have to do everything we can to make school productive.

Educators interviewed agree that all children need at least one caring person in their lives, yet for many children, particularly those in broken or poverty-stricken families, for children of children who are not yet themselves mature enough to be responsible for another person, for children without adequate role models in their lives, finding that caring person can prove difficult indeed. Or as the coordinator of a major collaborative effort between business and schools said, "Until we can get parents to fulfill their obligations we will be lacking." Similarly, a principal commented, "I would like to have recognition that there are a number of talented people in our schools. We have to solve more than traditional education issues solved in the prior generation. We need support, input, involvement, both institutional and individual. *Schools can't take the place of families*. We need help and understanding." (Emphasis added.)

This issue of caring is an important one and it combines with the setting of high expectations. Children need someone to care for them and set high expectations while simultaneously assuring that they begin taking responsibility for themselves. In the past, of course, these responsibilities were assumed by family members, often members of the extended family. As community and family structures have weakened, it has become harder for young children, particularly those in poverty but also some in more favorable situations, to find a caring person in their lives. In some schools, mentoring programs have been developed to provide students with a caring adult and a role model, where none otherwise exists.

Although mentoring can hardly be expected to take the place of family support, the rationale behind these programs suggests what is missing for many young people today. One educator commented, "I want kids to be as successful as they want to be. We need to show them there's a reason to exist for many, someone to do this for, someone who listens. We need to teach them about accountability, someone who cares if [the child goes] to school. It can be a path to college or work. It's friendship, helps them borrow someone else's eyes, be special, it's become a status symbol now to have a mentor here. It's a link to success, a foothold. Mentors open doors for kids that might not otherwise be there. It makes the connection why they're in school, that you need skills to be a successful, productive adult.

Some kids don't make the connection that it's not just luck but takes hard work. In the absence of resources of a network, a family, a sense of natural nurturing, it provides a sense of direction."

Another mentoring program coordinator commented, "This program provides a mentor for careers. I don't think the partnership goes deep enough. The mentors have knowledge on the surface, they need to come into the trenches and *see* what goes on [in the schools and children's home lives]. They don't see what these kids bring to school every day, or what teachers have to deal with. Kids may have [an] alcoholic father, mother is gone. They can't focus on their algebra grades."

The lack of caring about youth and children in society was mentioned by many people interviewed. Many stated that as a society we have abandoned our children or that many children today are "hope-less" with good reason, for they have little economic opportunity, little chance at advancement, and few people around to provide the nurturing and support that underpins successful development. As one individual work-ing on an inner-city collaboration commented in an interview, "There's a tremendous lack of structure in our students' lives. Fifty percent are from single-parent families. Parents lack knowledge of how to help their children. Some schools resist parent involvement but parents value education and insist children get it. But they're not sure how to help. Parents want to help children but some schools do not want parents involved and parents sense that."

For far too many children there are few family or community struc-tures available to provide that caring support. As one individual stated, "We have a society that says that children are important but constantly takes away resources. Ideally you want to bring all these people together in a kid-centered approach. It takes so much organized structure to allow someone to grow and be successful. We need to ask, how can we help each other to work with the whole human being? If people really believed that kids were a priority, they would put money, resources, and brain-power into the ghetto. But the generation that supported education is gone.

"People don't care about schools if they don't have kids in schools. The church and community used to have a sense of caretaking and people were committed to a vision of that. But it's not real any more. Society is not willing or able or ready to fill that vision. The priorities have changed in the last thirty years and a lot of institutions are falling apart. We don't know how to make it work anew. Values have shifted, so that there's no inherent set of values today and we've become a more egocentric kind of society and have lost our sense of community."

Problems Related to Equity

There are other issues. Schools in the United States have historically been asked to contend with broad social problems of equity and integration. During the early 1900s, schools were the primary social vehicle for integrating masses of immigrants into the nation and providing for them a semblance of common ground and understanding. From the 1950s into the present, schools have been asked to cope with the still unresolved integration of black and white cultures in the United States and the racial traumas that the process of integration has entailed. More recently, problems of equity and integration have been extended to other ethnic minorities, in particular Hispanics from a variety of backgrounds, but also Asians, who come from a wide range of different cultures.

The integration process, which is aimed at social equity, has created difficult problems of adjustment for schools because of clashes of culture and sometimes outright violence associated with bringing together people of different backgrounds. The violence resulting from the 1970s ruling on busing to achieve racial integration of formerly all-white schools has left a bad taste in many people's mouths with respect to the schools. Yet, if we carefully considered the school's role in this process of integration, it should become clear that neither teachers nor administrators necessarily had the background or preparation to deal with the significant problems of achieving racial harmony. Despite this, when schools' attention was drawn away from education toward matters of achieving integration, we too frequently failed to recognize that the problems associated with achieving racial integration, however noble that integration may be as a goal and however desirable to society at large, had the net effect of distracting schools, teachers, and students from their primary task of education.

Schools have, in effect, proved a touchstone for issues such as racial integration because they provide an opportunity to reach individuals when they are very young and presumably still able to be influenced. Also, nearly all children pass through school doors, making schools one of the few and one of the broadest reaching access points available to public policy makers dealing with such issues. Perhaps schools were also asked to take on these tasks because school officials were less powerful in speaking out in the public arena or in private forums. Business coalitions, however, might have been asked to forcibly integrate the workplace, and civic organizations might have been asked to assume this very civic responsibility they were foisting onto the schools, or churches might have provided the moral leadership needed to effect this type of social change.

Indeed, ultimately, of course, public policies forced many of these other institutions to deal with the same racial and integration issues as schools have had to deal with.

Currently, schools are being asked to integrate children with disabilities and special needs into the so-called mainstream classroom. Laudable as the goal of achieving integration is, it again drains schools of important resources and in too many cases focuses a great deal of attention and resources on a few children to the detriment of those children left in the mainstream. Please don't misunderstand, it is not that integration of any group is a bad thing to attempt to do; indeed, the value of equity is a fundamental tenet of our Constitution, one that we all presumably value. It is a reality, however, that asking schools to assume the primary burden for achieving social equity is a distraction from educational purposes, especially when few or no resources in the way of additional funding or training are provided to help the schools cope with the added demands that such burdens place upon them. For example, the turmoil that an emotionally disturbed child creates within a classroom is disruptive not only to him or herself but also to the rest of the class. The difficult issue is what should be done to deal with problems of equity in circumstances where the goal of integration is important and valued, but the problems of resources, attention, and training have yet to be weighed into the evaluation of why schools are failing.

Economic Conditions

Hopeless is another word that frequently came up in interviews, especially in cities where the economic structure has deteriorated and where few upwardly mobile—or indeed any—jobs are available. Perhaps nowhere is the situation more acute than it is in Detroit, where the population is diminishing, companies have had massive layoffs or moved away, the economy has changed, and the tax base has been eroded. All of these factors affect the schools. For example, Detroit is a city in which there are few economic opportunities left and little chance that many young people will achieve even the limited economic status that their own parents achieved unless fundamental change takes place. One observer commented, "Hope. Children here don't have hope for the future and they're right. They are correct, there's no support and there's no reason for hope."

Consider what has happened to jobs that used to pay a middle-class wage in many locations. Some jobs have become technologically more advanced and require greater skills than are locally available. Many companies have relocated their operations out of the inner city to suburbs that are less congested and more pleasant, leaving few well-paying jobs available in some cities, like Detroit. Still others have moved out of the suburbs to foreign locations where labor is cheap and abundant. Even more companies find themselves restructuring, which typically means downsizing and laying off in order to become more competitive. Each one of these actions eliminates jobs that once paid good wages. What jobs are left? Reich has argued[9] that the bulk of jobs left under these circumstances will be either service jobs or knowledge jobs. Although some service jobs pay well, the majority of them are in personal services, such as hairdressing, child care, or garage attendant, and barely pay a living wage. Knowledge jobs, or what Reich terms "symbolic analyst services,"[10] pay better, but there are still far fewer of them than are needed, and they require far more advanced education than personal services do.

This situation puts conflicting demands upon the schools and indeed upon society. If schools gear up to meet the demands of the knowledge-based economy as arguably they must for our citizens to be competitive with citizens of other industrialized nations, then there may not be enough jobs available in which to place all the knowledge workers. If schools fail to gear up and produce such knowledgeable citizens, choosing instead to educate the masses for the service economy that is widely presumed to exist and to be capable of sustaining the quality of life that Americans have come to expect, then many people, while working, will be in the position of merely scraping by.

CURRICULUM EXTENSION

Although the length of neither the school day nor the school year has expanded, many schools now have added sex education, character or values education, environmental awareness, sensitivity to the handicapped or disabled, drug awareness and resistance education, parenting skills, antismoking campaigns, abuse and violence protection, and computers and information technology, among numerous other topics, to an already fully loaded curriculum. Some of the problems in society that have been taken on by schools have thus been incorporated directly into the curriculum, typically as add-ons to what is already being taught. In a curriculum that is already fragmented into short periods, simply adding in more elements makes for a curriculum soup, largely consisting of separate chunks of material that have not been well integrated with each other and that are delivered piecemeal.

Although each new curricular item may be important and valuable, simply adding it on to what already exists means that essential time is taken away from important academic subjects. Little time is available for teachers or administrators to step back from the demands that are made with respect to the curriculum to set priorities about what should and what should not be taught. Various proposals have been put forth over the years to help schools focus on the curricular choices they are making. A back-to-basics movement during the 1980s focused some schools on the traditional three "Rs" of reading, 'riting, and 'rithmetic, but did little to eliminate or restructure what was being done. In any case, it is not clear that the three "Rs" are a sufficient base for today's world, given the changing political landscape, the technological shifts that are rapidly occurring, and the global integration in the world economy that only seems likely to increase in the near term, as we shall see in the next section.

COMPETITIVENESS AND EDUCATION: REFRAMING THE DEBATE

A number of forces have made clear the interdependencies that exist among companies, schools, families, social agencies, and government. For businesses, this interdependence has manifested itself in a number of ways that are increasingly becoming a necessary way of doing business. Technology is one growing source of linkages among organizations.[11] Phone lines used as data networks, local area networks, satellite linkages, FAXs, computer hookups, and teleconferencing create instant communication. People in different organizations are brought closer so they can work together in ways that were previously not possible. Such speedier and closer relationships among separate entities enhance the ability to communicate among businesses that "do business" with each other and also foster more relationships with other stakeholders with whom business organizations deal.

Alliances with suppliers, customers, government, and even competitors have eroded organizational boundaries and created interlinked networks of organizations that explicitly recognize the ways in which they depend upon each other. Such alliances have become necessary concomitants of organizations attempting to achieve global competitiveness[12] because of the efficiencies they offer. Several observers have noted that the network organization is likely to be the dominant organizational form in the future.[13] Whether permanent, as in many supplier-customer alliances, or temporary, as in catalytic alliances for social problem solving,[14] or opportunistic as in many public-private partnerships, it is clear that such structures foster and use interdependence to strategic advantage. The impact of networks is that boundaries between organizations have become increasingly transparent as "boundary spanning" roles developed to deal with external stakeholders that impact firm activities, for example, governmental agencies, community-based groups, and public interest organizations. Pressures by these entities have forced many businesses to deal explicitly with the web of institutions with whose activities they are inextricably linked.

Network structures bring together competitors in R&D or other consortia, suppliers and buyers, and, in addition, foster collaborative interaction between businesses and government (e.g., economic development), businesses and schools (e.g., adopt-a-school), and businesses and community-based or government organizations (e.g., job-training partnerships). The more than 100,000 education-business partnerships established over the past decade suggest that this process of opening up boundaries has also affected educational institutions. Pressures for more parent involvement coming both from within schools, which need parental support to achieve educational objectives, and from parents who desire to know more about what is going on in schools, has further eroded traditional barriers.

Many of these alliances are closer to so-called communitarian values that are more similar to foreign competitors' values than traditional individualistic American values.[15] In the communitarian value system, relationships for the common good are a way of doing business. American businesses, using ideologies based on individualism and cutthroat competition (aided by public policy measures prohibiting interaction and collusion), have generally been slower to engage in collaborative relations than many global competitors. But in practice, communitarian behaviors have tended to reduce adversarial relations and decrease notions of organizations as collateral systems, while enhancing understanding of interdependencies among them. In Japan[16] and Korea[17] companies operate as linked networks, supported by government actions, and fostering through their own behaviors strong educational systems. In the United States in contrast, businesses may complain about government actions or weak schools, but collaborative action to make changes has traditionally been fairly limited. Acting collaboratively is still quite new to many business executives, not to mention schools and government, since like businesses, schools have been presumed to operate collaterally. It is becoming more and more obvious, however, that the network organization demands a more collaborative and interactive than collateral and independent approach.

Linkages between business needs, society's problems, and education have also been dramatically illuminated by demographic shifts. Most businesspeople were unaware of the links between demography and the health of their organization even ten years ago (and many still do not believe that their firms will suffer). When the workforce was plentiful, businesses did not worry about finding qualified workers. Now that the population of high-school graduates has been growing more slowly for some time, many business leaders have been forced to confront the realities of demographic change and to become aware of the ways in which their businesses are dependent on schools and family structures. The Hudson Institute's influential study Workforce 2000 (Hudson Institute, 1987) was instrumental in fostering this recognition, and real-life difficulties in recruiting employees have reinforced it.

Further, scarce (and becoming scarcer) resources are increasingly forcing schools, social service agencies, and businesses to think more in terms of doing what they can do best and link with other agencies or groups for what they cannot do. This need to strip away surpluses or duplication of efforts and pare down to a core organization is one of the main rationales behind the emergence of the network structure and so many alliances. Paring down to the essentials requires working cooperatively and collaboratively with others who offer the still needed, but outsourced services. Such coordination requires a web of relationships, that is, a network of cooperating organizations, if organizations are to achieve their purposes. Thus, a new paradigm of collaboration and cooperation is developing that recognizes that the health of society, ultimately its competitiveness, depends on the health of its institutions and they in turn depend upon each other in a whole system.

IMPACT ON THE SYSTEM

The abandonment of youth and the frustration for the conditions that too many children face may result in what one novelist has termed a slow-motion riot.[18] The pressures for competitiveness add another dynamic that makes scarce good paying jobs and the need for educational improvement more piquant. As one observer in Detroit commented, "The rebellion is already started, it started a long time ago. You may think not, but it will be a different type of rebellion and where will your business go when it can't function here any more? Drugs are more available than ever before. The reality of the situation is that it's already started. Will we sit idle and wait till it comes to our front door?"

The demands on curriculum and from the social and community environment of students have caused some schools to become de facto social service agencies, attempting to cope with the multiple societal problems they have been handed. Whatever services schools do pick up, it is clear that they must somehow find a way to return to their more basic purpose: providing education for all. Perhaps that purpose requires some rethinking about whether that education is for citizenship, as it has historically been framed, or for work, or perhaps for both. Whatever the ultimate conclusion, schools are there to educate and we, as a society, have not been letting them do their jobs in the past few decades.

One of the national education goals highlights the ways in which the problems facing American schools today have shifted in the past half century: Every school in America will be free of drugs and violence and will offer a disciplined environment conducive to learning. Problems of drugs and violence are symptomatic of the reasons why schools are so widely perceived to be failing. A primary underlying cause of schools' failures, which is not to take responsibility away from schools for changing themselves, has to do with the decay of the social fabric of communities. Added to the decay of the social fabric is the fact that achievement of a globally competitive standard of living and globally competitive industries now requires a far greater skill base than was needed in the past. Achieving this skill base clearly means that schools do need to change, both in method and structure. But the social fabric inherently affects the schools as well.

The educators, businesspeople, and others I interviewed sent a consistent message about the problems of today's child: these children, especially those from dysfunctional, broken, or economically deprived families bring with them to school a multitude of problems. Even suburban children have changed because of changing family and work situations. The ultimate message: as a society, we have largely abandoned our kids.

We bring them into the world, then effectively desert them, sometimes in front of the television which is a less-expensive babysitter than a real one, and a whole lot easier to find. Sometimes (if we are poor or working too much) we leave them out on the street, sometimes home alone as a latch-key kid. Not all of us do this, of course. Many of us try to be responsible for our children and to instill in them a sense of their own responsibility for themselves. But too many of us are forced by the exigencies of a stressful existence into small abandonments that mount up over time.

If we are lucky we can find adequate child care for our children's pre-school years and after-school care during their school years. If we are unlucky, that care is whatever we can scrape together. We are busy, too busy frequently, to spend a lot of time with our children instilling the values that our own parents taught us. Anyway, we seem to believe that the school will teach them everything they need to know. And if it doesn't the principal, the school board, and the local newspaper will hear about it.

In the inner city, where poverty, lack of education, and few economic opportunities prevail, the situation is far worse than in the suburbs. Here a higher proportion of parents may be jobless, on welfare, on drugs, or subjects or agents of violence and abuse. Many such parents are unable to provide an adequate role model for their children, a role model ultimately that says that studying hard and education are important. Affected by the general attitude that education is not really a problem, parents in these circumstances as well as those in more fortunate circumstances, find it difficult to place too much emphasis on education. Stressing education is even more difficult when economic opportunities are few and the rewards of education through job opportunity or advancement to higher levels of education seem distant indeed.

As poverty has persisted and grown worse in certain inner-city and rural areas, as the plague of drugs has grown to mean that some children have parents who are absolutely incapable of assuming parental responsibilities, and as violence has grown throughout our societies, schools have taken the brunt of our failure as a society to quell these problems. Indeed, there is a great deal of consensus about problems in and of the educational system over many years. Among these problems are establishing the relative priorities of content versus process, dealing with equity among students with vastly different abilities, interests, and intelligences, the lack of national goals for education, the relatively passive posture students are expected to assume, and the relatively low status of teaching as a profession in the United States.

There are some signs that the rhetoric is shifting slightly as we approach the year 2000. The word responsibility seems to be slowly re-entering our vocabulary. We may have begun to recognize that with the rights that our Constitution grants and the rights that many of our public policies have granted in the past decades also must come a degree of responsibility. Part of that responsibility, arguably, has to be to take better care of our children.

NOTES

1. Much of this chapter is based on field research and telephone interviews conducted under a grant from the Spencer Foundation and in assessing the National Alliance of Business's Compact Project. In addition to the twelve-city National Alliance of Business Compact Project studies reported in S. A. Waddock (1992b and 1993a), the Spencer Grant permitted in-person visits and interviews in five Compact cities as well as two other cities, and with policymakers in Washington, D.C. I also spoke with officials in Boston.

2. N. Postman (1979), *Teaching as a Conserving Activity* (New York: Delacorte Press), makes this point.

3. "Society," of course, has done no such thing. We who elect public officials, work and pay taxes, and raise children *are* society. As a nation, however, we seem to have chosen to either ignore major social problems or to ask that schools take them on so that we can try to avoid responsibility for them. Unfortunately, as the thesis of this book suggests, schools cannot handle all these problems alone.

4. See, for example, T. Sizer (1992), *Horace's School: Redesigning the American High School* (Boston: Houghton Mifflin Company); or D. Perkins (1992), *Smart Schools: From Training Memories to Educating Minds* (New York: Free Press).

5. T. Sizer (1992), *Horace's School.*

6. In National Center for Education Statistics (1991), *The Condition of Education 1991*, vol. 1. (Washington, D.C.: U.S. Department of Education).

7. National Center for Education Statistics (1991), 8–9.

8. National Center for Education Statistics (1991), 9.

9. R. B. Reich (1991a), *The Work of Nations: Preparing Ourselves for Twenty-first Century Capitalism* (New York: Alfred A. Knopf).

10. Reich (1991a).

11. See, for example, S. M. Davis and W. H. Davidson (1991), *2020 Vision: Transform Your Business Today to Succeed in Tomorrow's Economy* (New York: Simon & Schuster); A. Toffler (1990), *Powershift: Knowledge, Wealth, and Violence at the Edge of the Twenty-first Century* (New York: Bantam Books); and S. Zuboff (1988), *In the Age of the Smart Machine: The Future of Work and Power* (New York: Basic Books).

12. See, for example, C. Handy (1990), *The Age of Unreason* (Boston: Harvard Business School Press); R. M. Kanter (1989), *When Giants Learn to Dance* (New York: Simon & Schuster); Davis and Davidson (1991); and K. Ohmae (1990), *The Borderless World: Power and Strategy in the Interlinked Economy* (New York: Harper Business).

13. For example, R. E. Miles and C. C. Snow (1986b), "Network Organizations: New Concepts for New Forms," *California Management Review* Spring, 28(3): 62–73; Kanter (1989); and S. M. Davis (1987), *Future Perfect* (Reading, MA: Addison-Wesley).

14. See S. A. Waddock and J. E. Post's paper (1991) "Social Entrepreneurs and Catalytic Change," *Public Administration Review* 51(5): 393–401.

15. G. C. Lodge (1990), *Perestroika for America: Restructuring Business-Government Relations for World Competitiveness* (Cambridge, MA: Harvard Business School Press); and G. C. Lodge and E. F. Vogel (1987), *Ideology and National Competitiveness: An Analysis of Nine Countries* (Boston: Harvard Business School Press).

16. See, for example, M. Gerlach (1987), "Business Alliances and the Strategy of the Japanese Firm," *California Management Review* Fall: 126–142; Lodge and Vogel (1987).

17. Lodge and Vogel (1987).

18. Novelist Peter Blauner wrote a book of this title depicting the crack culture in New York.

Chapter 5

Not Alone: Outside in Thinking

Schools need not be alone in accomplishing their educational mission, despite the fact that our traditional linear view places them in that position. Changing our conception of the schools, however, requires a fundamental shift in the paradigm or model through which we view schools and their activities, as well as a shift in the dynamics of the relevant systems. As has been suggested in earlier chapters, this new paradigm involves a wholly different set of assumptions about schools than are traditional.

The first new assumption is that schools are *not alone responsible* for education: education is fundamentally a responsibility that is shared among the important institutions that constitute society. These institutions include the families and communities, businesses and other employers, governmental agencies, educational organizations including governance bodies for schools, institutions of higher education, especially those that educate teachers, human service organizations, health care organizations, and churches and other values-framing institutions.

Conceptually, we can think of schools as the center of the spider's web of influences identified in the previous chapter. The strands together determine how strong and sturdy the web will be in accomplishing its task;

Much of the discussion in this chapter comes from two papers by S. A. Waddock: (1993c), "The Spider's Web: Influences on School Performance," *Business Horizons* September–October: 39–48; and (1992a), "The Business Role in School Reform: From Feeling Good to System Change," *The International Journal of Value-Based Management* 5(2): 105–126.

the number and sturdiness of the strands determine the web's strength and flexibility. We can place schools at the center of the web. The national level is represented by the outside strands, along with three important levels of influence: state, community, and family. The interdependence among the strands suggest that society's overall well-being is determined by the relationship that exists between the number and strength of supporting strands. This analogy to the spider's web illustrates the type of interdependence that exists between schools and the rest of society. Ultimately, such a model may offer a useful perspective on school reform that mitigates the loneliness schools have experienced in educating children.

Thus, the second new assumption is that schools are *inherently interdependent* with these other institutions. Because of this interdependence, schools need to work more collaboratively with other institutions than has been traditionally their wont. A move toward a more collaborative systems approach requires thinking about how new relationships between schools and other social institutions can be structured, about what the current structure is, and about the systems dynamics inherent to that structure. In this and the next two chapters, we will deal with these important structural issues and the ways in which they affect schools.

UNDERSTANDING RESPONSIBILITY FOR EDUCATION

According to our implicit expectations, schools are expected to pick up the most of the responsibility for education, as well as for solving the many social problems that we as a society have chosen not to deal with through other mechanisms. But we have not provided means of empowering them to do so. As the next two chapters will demonstrate, the solutions we have used to deal with problems affecting schools until now have effectively taken responsibility away from other institutions and transferred those responsibilities to schools. By steadily decreasing their resources, expanding their mission and increasing the population they are expected to educate, allowing them to take on new responsibilities with which it is almost impossible to cope, and conveying our lack of trust through the media, the political process, and our lack of respect for educators, we have steadily eroded the ability of schools to educate children. School officials, in their turn, have allowed us to do these things to them. They have largely failed to take action on the problems they face, have been passive (albeit hurt) in the face of criticism, have not clearly delineated their own mission and goals, and have accepted without question the burdens added to the already hefty set of responsibilities that education of the young entails.

Thus, for too long we have expected too much of schools without according them either the resources or the status to reach our expectations. Indeed, some of our expectations of schools may be both unrealistic and impossible for them to achieve because, as must be clear from the previous chapters, schools alone cannot be responsible for the upbringing and education of our children. But simultaneously with expecting so much of schools, we have lowered our expectations of other social institutions especially with regard to education and to our children. The family, the church, the community as a unit, used to be a source of values, of commitment, of stability and strength for children—and not incidentally very real providers of education. Each of these institutions has been seriously eroded in recent times with significant negative effects on education.

Schools have been expected to pick up the slack. Yet schools are simply, by their nature, their goals, and the background of their staffs, not up to the task.[1] One business executive, who is deeply involved with school reform, puts it like this, "Schools can't duck accountability because of the problems of society. But they can't do it alone. The biggest problem in school reform is that for every problem in American education, there is today a successful solution to the problem. Our inability as a society to *adopt* those success models broadly is criminal. It's a mind-set—if problem solving is successful, we need to use it—we need to get rid of that not-invented-here attitude."

Let us consider for a moment where responsibility for education should lie and whether or not there might be leverage points that structurally begin to reshift the burden back toward those more appropriately responsible. Arguably and obviously, responsibility for education needs to be assumed by students, teachers, administrators, and district-level policy makers: by the students for their own learning; by teachers for assuring that learning takes place; by faculty for designing learning systems for children that facilitate learning processes; and by school and district administrators for bringing together the resources of time, money, equipment, energy, and ideas that permit creative ideas about structuring education to begin to flow.

But there are whole other groups that bear some responsibility for education as well, especially when we consider the system that impacts school performance explored in the previous chapters. If healthy families and communities are indeed part and parcel of high-performing schools, responsibility for education needs to be assumed by others, that is, by those we might call external groups: by families and communities, for instance, who need to put priority on education, reinforce its value through attitude and conversations about the worth of working hard in school, and who need to provide the structure and support for children so they come to school prepared to learn; by businesses who employ parents and determine their wages, working conditions, and family-leave policies, who explicitly or implicitly expect employees to work beyond their scheduled hours; by human service and health care organizations who provide services to families and children in need; by the media that sets the tone and expectations for schools, shapes public attitudes through the stories created, and creates a set of values that has the power to value or devalue the work of educators; by governmental agencies, the churches, health care providers, and policy makers; by museums and cultural institutions; and by sports organizations. In short, supporting education is everyone's responsibility. These other institutions make up the strands that have the capacity to strengthen the schools or, if they are broken or distorted, to cause them to stretch and even fail.

THINKING ABOUT THE POSSIBILITIES

Fragmentation of purposes might work in a world in which a whole child or a whole family was not at issue. But in the real world we are dealing with people and families, who have a variety of needs. And we are dealing with schools that cannot be expected to cope with all of society's problems without others taking on their own fair share of the responsibility. Further, the entire effort to institutionalize responsibility for education and for children, whether within the schools or within other formal institutions, has resulted in an erosion of much of the sense of personal responsibility. This erosion affects parents, children, and probably even teachers for failures to learn that characterize our nation.[2] As Charles Sykes puts it, we have become a nation of victims.[3] The very word responsibility pretty much disappeared from our public discourse during the 1980s, replaced by words like rights, entitlements, and victims. All of these terms suggest that instead of accepting responsibility for our actions, we are entitled to certain benefits with few or no countervailing duties. In a sense, along with the disappearance of community, we have experienced a disappearance of caring about each other,[4] a caring for our young that suggests that we recognize the responsibilities that come with bearing and bringing up children.

The executive director of the Cincinnati Youth Collaborative, interviewed during research for this book, stated, "We use two terms, one is that the development of children and youth is a shared responsibility and all youth-serving agencies are responsible and have to take this message in. Second, it's a misnomer to say that we have a business-school steering committee: it's really one-third business, one-third social service deliverers, and one-third others with stakes in the development of children and youth.

"Finally, the development of the child is central, not just education. If a child is born healthy and given prenatal care and medical and health attention before he or she is five, then that child will achieve better results. We need to bring all these things into alignment. We need to work with neighborhood organizations as a go-between, meet with the urban [locally, the Appalachian] council and community schools, to see what kinds of programs are needed. We need to work with the health clinic for grants and proposals, be co-signers to the grants sometimes. We need to work together for the child and the family."

One teacher who had recently come back to teaching after a ten-year absence commented, "I am amazed at what schools now have to deal with—all these major social problems. Schools don't have 'product control,' the way businesses do. Teachers have to accept kids, teach them how to go to the bathroom, brush their teeth, be guidance counselors because we need to socialize the kids. *You can't just teach any more.* Kids don't express their appreciation: these kids are hungry, pregnant, on drugs, on parole. Teachers are being asked to do things they are not trained to do and don't have the aptitude to do, for example, finding a place for a kid to sleep. Teachers don't have the skills or interest to do these things." (Italics added.)

STRANDS OF THE WEB: A NEW PERSPECTIVE ON EDUCATION

Let us consider for a few moments what the spider's web of influences affecting education looks like. The web provides us with a snapshot, essentially a static picture, of the situation of education. This snapshot provides insight into some of the forces that influence the ability of schools to do their work; however, it is less helpful in providing insight into the dynamic qualities that affect the system as a whole. For that we will look to systems dynamics theory in the following two chapters so that we can begin to understand how the process of social change can begin.

First, the strands affecting education consist of a series of nested levels at the center of which is the school. The levels are family, community, state, and national. Children's performance within schools is the central unit of analysis for the macrosystems perspective we are developing, which explores the influences of the spider's web system. Aggregated at the school level, the performance of a school can be said to be the overall level of performance of all of the children in a school or, more broadly, of a school system comprised of multiple schools. We will look first at the levels and then at the strands to determine some of the ways in which school performance is influenced and, by inference, what responsibilities they bear.

Nested Levels of Influence

Moving outward from the school's boundaries, there are four levels of influence that form a network of nested systems in which schools are embedded: the family, the community, the state, and the national level. The inner nest, and the one that most directly and probably most power- fully affects school performance, consists of the family system. As we have seen, there is significant evidence that family structure and stability in the United States has significantly deteriorated within the last thirty years or so. Given that families are the first educators of children and probably the most important long-term educators, the stresses of divorce, dual-career and/or earner families, and single parenthood have put significant down- ward pressures on the ability of parents to provide a safe, secure, and educationally appropriate environment for their children. Learning is difficult when children are distracted by more fundamental issues, such as wondering where the next meal will come from or whether anyone will be there when they get home. No wonder that in interviews I conducted about schools, a number of observers commented that as a nation, "We have abandoned our children."

This abandonment has happened as well at the second level of influence on education, the level of community. Families reside in communities, such as local neighborhoods, small towns, or very large urban areas. But in our communities our sense of common good is also seriously in trouble. Where once neighbor would support neighbor, where when someone was ill or in trouble, the community came together to provide help and concern, today there are many communities, suburban and urban, in which neigh- bors are so busy with fragmented lives that they barely know each other. In fact, because few realize that the old mechanisms have disappeared or are aware of the consequences of that disappearance, there has been precious little discussion of real mechanisms to replace our lost com- munities and even little awareness of the consequences that lost com- munities have for education.

Other elements of the community also greatly affect the status of families within the community, particularly socioeconomic factors. The economic base provides potential resources that can support schools financially, if that base is sound. When it is not, schools almost by definition will be troubled because they will not have sufficient resources to do their jobs. The political base provides for the willingness or unwillingness of the taxpayer to support schools. In too many instances over the past decade a prevailing "get mine first" attitude has caused taxpayer revolts that have forced communities to make serious cutbacks in the services they provide and schools have been greatly affected by those cutbacks.

Because public policies are very important in affecting the conditions under which schools, families, and communities operate, both state and federal policies also must be considered. State policies, laws, and norms form the third level of institutional influences on schools in the United States. The fourth level is the federal level, encompassing national culture, ideology, and attitudes, as well as large businesses and the federal government itself. At the state level, policies are promulgated that affect schools directly and indirectly, economic development activities take place, and agencies exist that provide the much-discussed safety net.

At the federal or national systems level are bodies that provide broad umbrellas of both ideology and action that influence activities at lower levels. For example in the business community, a national-level group like the Business Roundtable (BRT) could establish a set of guidelines of an action plan for its members to deal with issues of education and advocacy in each of the fifty states. BRT has also published numerous reports that attempt to develop policy positions and influence members both nationally and more locally. These activities represent one way in which actions at the national level take place and filter down to other levels.

Influences: The Strands

The strands supporting the web surrounding education include educational policy makers, the economic system, teacher organizations, including unions and colleges and universities, social service organizations, governmental agencies, and value-shapers, which include the media, interest groups, publishers, social and political activists, and churches.

Educational Policy Makers

One of the predominant and most direct influences on education is educational policy. At the national systems level, the Department of

Education sets national policies and, more recently, goals for education. In the United States, however, the federal educational agencies have historically had relatively little direct influence on local schools, which are run by local school boards under the auspices of state education agencies. The federal government role until quite recently has largely been one of assuring civil rights around educational issues, disbursing grants and loans primarily for higher education, and administering the funding for disadvantaged youth.

With the promulgation of the national goals for education, the U.S. Department of Education has attempted to assume a more proactive role in setting a national education agenda. Because the primary responsibility for education belongs to states and local communities, the education department must attempt to achieve its goals by trying to persuade local communities and states to accept and endorse the goals, rather than by direct action. Nonetheless, whatever their limitations, the national goals for the first time set a target for schools to attempt to achieve, against which actual achievement can be measured.

In 1994 Congress passed GOALS 2000: Educate America, which will continue implementation of the six education goals, plus the two added goals of teacher development and parent partnerships. Ultimately such national-level thinking will impact schools at the local level, since communities must voluntarily join the program and develop locally based means of implementation.

State boards or departments of education are primarily responsible for setting state educational policies for all of the local school districts that fall within their domains. They may provide funding support, determine funding policies in general (e.g., use of property vs. other taxes), or choose textbooks for the entire state; teacher contracts may be negotiated at the state level. At the community level, local school boards, more than 16,000 in the United States, hold primary responsibility for the delivery of educational services, for local school policies and procedures, for staffing, and for direct service delivery. These boards exercise the most potent and direct control over school policies, curriculum, teacher and principal assignments, and other staffing issues, as well as local funding decisions, in conjunction with other local authorities. To the extent that school boards work in the interest of children and the schools, they can be effective political and governance advocates for schools. To the extent that they are embroiled in local politics and focus their attention on minutiae (micromanagement), they may actually impede schools' educational missions.

In turn, at the family level parents can become involved to some extent in school policies by working together with teachers and principals in parent-teacher associations or organizations (PTA/PTO). In recent years, many schools have responded to pressures for improvements by establishing policies of site-based or decentralized management, frequently engaging interested parents in advisory and even governing boards that directly influence individual school policies, programs, and procedures. These types of mechanisms and other similar mechanisms permit parent voice in the affairs of schools. Until quite recently in some schools and still on-going in most schools, this voice has been limited, at least as far as curricular or school policy matters go. PTA/PTOs have generally done more fund raising than policy setting and many advisory or governing boards including parents have had difficulties in establishing real power over school policies.

In general, although schools claim to want parental involvement, many schools have actually erected barriers of professionalism, short open hours, and difficult access that have kept parents from having much voice in their own children's educational processes. Some of this is changing now through the work of Comer[5] and others who have demonstrated the importance of parent involvement in achieving effective education.

Teacher Organizations

Teacher organizations include unions, which exist at national, state, and local levels, the universities and colleges that prepare individuals for positions in teaching, and to some extent teacher participation at the local level in school governance groups, including advisory boards, PTA/PTOs, and school committees. On one hand, unions have attempted to help assure teachers of their professional status; improve working conditions, pay, and status; and provide a mechanism for communicating with teachers throughout the nation. On the other hand, unions have also diminished teachers' status as professionals by imposing the types of work rules, standards for performance, and inflexible systems that have kept blue collar workers from more creatively working in alliance with managements, and have sometimes fostered adversarial teacher-management relationships, set up barriers to entry into the profession, and taken teachers out on debilitating strikes. Union structures exist at the national, state, local, and building levels and, depending on the attitudes and stances taken by members, can greatly affect the ways in which teachers do their jobs, interact with administrators and students, and organize themselves.

While unions may resist changes that many observers perceive to be necessary to improved education, representatives of both the American Federation of Teachers and the National Education Association, in interviews with the author, recognized the need for significant changes in the teaching profession. One indication of movement is that certain key union leaders have been speaking out in favor of radical change. For example, as we have seen, Rochester's Adam Urbanski is an outspoken national figure advocating for structural changes in the relationships between schools and teachers and in performance standards for teachers.

Another subject of much criticism has been the colleges of education that train future teachers. Often criticized for irrelevance and lack of rigor, education schools are beginning to respond to increasingly demanding challenges, some posed by changing statutes that require more liberal arts or subject-matter education for future teachers. The relatively low regard in which teaching as a profession is held by U.S. society, combined with the opening up of other professional opportunities for women over the past twenty-five years, has further eroded the profession's ability to attract the most qualified individuals. Currently, however, there are many efforts under way to improve the curricula of education schools and attract more qualified students into the teaching profession. Some state regulations are shifting to require more rigorous academic preparation of education majors, which should have the effect of having teachers better prepared over the long term.

Human Service Organizations

Human service organizations include all of those organizations whose stated mission is to better the lives of individuals, families, or communities. The relative strength of these organizations provides the much-discussed safety net for families struggling with various types of social problems, such as lack of adequate housing, unemployment, illness, or other problems. With some exceptions, services offered by human service organizations in the United States tend to be fragmented into specific problem areas (e.g., hunger, homelessness, employment, training) with little emphasis on meeting the needs of the whole individual or family. Although this is changing in some places,[6] on the whole social services are still offered in largely fragmentary fashion.

This fragmentation of services which occurs nationally, statewide, and locally, makes it difficult for schools, which have to deal with whole students and the panoply of problems that they may bring to school with them (of course, too many schools are not student oriented). Complicating the schools' situations is the fact that many of the social problems that used to be handled in other forums, particularly by communities, families, churches, and community organizations, are now handed to schools for resolution. Schools have been asked in recent years to deal with problems of day care, latch-key children, child abuse and neglect, and broken homes. Schools have also been asked to teach children basic values, teach AIDS and sex education, and deal with disciplinary problems that used to be dealt with in the home. In many communities, the social service organizations do provide some helpful services, but only in a few are these services linked closely at all to the work that schools are trying to do. Because services are so fragmented, schools must often pick up pieces that others have dropped and incorporate them into an already crammed school day, whose daily or yearly length has not changed in many years.

Government

Government agencies operate in what have been called policy sectors.[7] Each policy sector tends to deal with different types of problems, such as housing, welfare, employment, defense, environment, and, of course, education. Through the years many government initiatives have developed into highly rigid bureaucracies, each of which develops its own sets of rules and regulations to guide decision making.[8] The educational policy sector, as noted above, is separately discussed because its influence on schools is fairly direct and more obvious than that of other policy sectors. Nonetheless, the interaction—or lack of interaction—of government agencies in other key policy sectors whose policies affect family welfare, economic conditions, and community status can also be cited as one of the institutional influences on school performance. Like the community services noted above, the services delivered by government agencies have tended to be highly fragmented, seldom dealing with whole individuals, families, or systems, but rather tackling each problem in piecemeal fashion.

Only recently has there been any move to get dominant government agencies to collaborate on educational issues. For example, with the issuance of the Secretary's Commission on Achieving Necessary Skills (SCANS) report noted earlier, the Department of Labor at the national and state levels began to work with the national and state level Department of Education representatives on attempting to get the national education goals implemented in communities and to incorporate SCANS considerations into that implementation. Of course, the human services piece of the puzzle was notably missing in this interaction; however, it did represent a step toward a more-systemic approach to education. The lack of such an approach in the past has meant that most of the problems of schools have, like many human problems, been dealt with institutionally and programmatically through narrowly defined programs or policies.

Value-Framing Institutions

The attitudes and values that a society holds are shaped in a variety of ways, in families, including their cultures and community values, in the ideology that dominates the culture, in the religious and moral training that churches and other religious institutions provide, and, at least in the modern world, in the values shaped and promulgated by the media and the political and public policy processes.

Arguably the most important value-framing institutions are the family and community systems within which children are directly embedded. In the United States, as was noted above, these institutions are not in good shape. The strength and security that these once provided is now much weaker than it has been in the recent past. Because parents are so busy and extended families tend to be scattered, children are less likely now than in the past to find support at home or in the community for the hard work that learning necessarily entails. Further, as the workplace drifted farther and farther from the home through the process of industrialization, the connections between learning and work have become weaker. Nowadays too many children find it difficult to make the connection at all. Additionally, too many parents are under so much stress that it is hard for them to find the time to help motivate their children to learn, instill a set of values, or focus on the importance of community building.

Coupled with a weakening family and community structure is a highly individualistic national ideology.[9] This individualism gave rise to the materialism, self-interest, and market orientation that dominated the national culture during the 1980s and early 1990s and played a significant role in the public's unwillingness to pay taxes to support schools or provide the necessary social and human services infrastructure to support families in need. Combined with public policy systems, such as welfare, that foster dependency and a victim status for far too many people, the individualism has resulted in the sense of wilding that Derber[10] discusses, an unwillingness, even an incapacity, to work together for the common good. Schools receive the brunt of this individualism, since many young children now have little sense of overarching values or doing for others. The result is that discipline and commitment to learning are hard to come by in many places.

Churches, social, and civic organizations might have been expected to fill in some of the missing value structure and provide a rationale and infrastructure for community building. But many churches are themselves struggling to maintain membership. Church leaders who have been outspoken advocates of community building or support for education have been altogether too rare, presumably because they do not view this as their role. Nor have many churches developed mechanisms that might help struggling families maintain their own sense of community or belonging. Churches might, for example, provide support for the particular struggles of modern-day life, such as pre-school child care, before- and after-school care, or other ways of supporting the family, which would by their very nature support schools. They might bring together elders, who have time on their hands, with children, who need role models, so that the adults might provide not only role models but values with which families who belong to the churches could identify.

Political organizations at the national, state, and local levels also help shape attitudes and values related to participation in a representative democracy and capitalistic economy. Political organizations and the political process shape the general ideology of a nation, which in the United States has generally been an individualistic (and in recent years, dominantly "me" oriented ideology in the United States) one at both the individual and organizational level. The bully pulpit of the presidency and other elected officials has not been well used in recent years to foster a sense of togetherness, wholeness, or belonging. Instead, values of individualism and materialism have taken precedence in too many instances, again leaving schools to deal with the product of a "me" culture.

The media is also an important shaper of values and by and large those values have been dominated by materialism, instant gratification, and, again, individualism, especially in the mass media to which many young children are most exposed. Many young children watch many hours of television each day, according to surveys. While the impact of television can certainly be positive in some cases, much programming exposes children to very short segments, a good deal of violence, and set of values that suggests that getting as much as you can as soon as you can is the overriding value in life. Teachers are now coping with children who bring short attention spans, combined with a desire for the glitz, glamor, and immediacy that television conveys. In contrast, the process of learning by its very nature is much slower, more difficult, and requires much more effort than simply passively viewing a television or video show.

Economic System

The final sector is the economic system, in which businesses play the most prominent role. Historically in the United States, there have been few direct linkages between businesses and schools, other than the fact that businesses have hired young people upon their graduation from high school or as part-time workers while they are completing high school.

Since the publication of *A Nation at Risk* in 1983, however, the linkages that exist between the preparation young people receive in school and their preparedness to take their places in the world of work have been more explicitly identified. This linkage became explicit at the national level with the U.S. Department of Labor's SCANS reports,[11] which defined the skills needed in the workplace that should be acquired in schools for graduates to be effective in the so-called high-skills workplace.[12] There is a conundrum surrounding the rhetoric on high-skills workplaces, of course, that affects both schools and employers. Few employers, as was noted earlier, have actually made the transition to high-skills workplaces. At the same time few schools are producing graduates equipped for that type of workplace. Which comes first or how schools and businesses pressure each other interactively to move forward simultaneously is a difficult, though important, issue.

There has been a shift away from the general indifference of business toward education that characterized the business environment during the heyday of the baby boom era when entry-level workers were in bountiful supply. Today many businesses evidence much more concern with the quality of the workforce and, by extension, the schools because of the debate about global competition that has taken place. Some of this concern has translated into advocacy on the part of business groups or individual businesses attempting to influence educational policy. Other aspects of business's influence on education have more to do with the economic conditions generated by business decisions. Businesses play several influential roles with respect to education.

Business as Business: Increasing Demands for Links

Businesses, other employers, colleges, and the military are the traditional recipients of high-school graduates in the form of entry-level employees. Of course, society at large is the recipient of the twenty-five percent or so who do not make it through the educational system, for whom there is a shrinking supply of low-skilled positions. Society has to bear the burden of lives that may not be economically productive, of individuals who may even drain the system through their dependence on welfare or because they are involved in the criminal justice system. That is, of course, purely an economic perspective. A broader perspective would suggest that society must bear the cost of individuals who are incapable of performing their duties related to informed and active citizenship, who cannot or do not engage in the broader community, and who take more from society than they are able to give back.

Employers absorb the products, the graduates, of the U.S. educational system. Until quite recently, business's stance has largely been to take a hands-off posture with respect to schools. Businesses and other employers simply absorbed whatever product met quality standards and rejected the rest, exerting very little overt influence on schools. While schools themselves may not have been subject to the whims of the market, in general their successes or failures *are* subject to those forces.

Businesses and Schools in the United States

Unlike businesses in some European and Asian nations, most U.S. businesses have followed the relatively individualistic ideology described in an earlier chapter. In doing so, they have maintained a hands-off stance with respect to the schools (as well as to government, at least rhetorically. I leave to others the assessment of the reality of the hands-off stance). In the case of schools, however, until the partnership movement began in the early and mid-1980s, businesses were in actuality largely separate from schools in the United States.

In fact, despite the many, many partnerships that exist, most do little to bring schools and businesses (or other employers) into better alignment because they are programmatically, not systemically, oriented. What this means is a program will be overlaid on top of existing programs and curriculum, for the schools, but few or no changes in day-to-day practices will be made. As a result of this implicit distancing, employers, the military, and even colleges have had relatively little say about curriculum, standards, or expectations of school students. Such matters have been left in the hands of school professionals, few of whom have ever worked outside the school environment or have direct knowledge of the norms, expectations, or demands of those workplaces.

Indeed, few employers explicitly make the linkages for graduates or students between performing well in school and making the transition to work, say, by asking for transcripts, diplomas, or school recommendations. Even colleges in their desire for continued growth have tended to devalue real academic achievement in school and admit many applicants to fill their classrooms, without real regard for their academic achievement in high school. The military has exerted even less influence until fairly recently when increasing technological demands have forced various branches of the service to raise their entrance requirements.

Today many businesses evidence much more concern, fueled by the need for entry-level workers and changing demographics, with the so-called quality of the workforce and, by extension, the performance of schools. Some of this concern has translated into advocacy on the part of business groups or individual businesses attempting to influence educational policy, with educators and other social activists criticizing the relatively narrow focus on work-related skills that some business leaders are perceived to have.

Another aspect of business's influence on education has more to do with the economic conditions generated by business decisions. Many businesses have been forced over the past fifteen years to restructure themselves to maintain their competitive posture vis-à-vis global contenders. As a result, many strategic decisions have fostered outsourcing or location of facilities either outside the firm, frequently outside the nation. As a result of the loss of jobs involved in such displacements, some communities have fewer available jobs for high-school graduates. Students attempting to determine whether working hard in school makes sense may in some cases justifiably conclude that it does not: there are few opportunities for them even should they obtain a decent education and, as Albert Schenker points out, if they decide to go to college, to the extent that relatively low-skilled jobs are available, graduates will very likely be accepted somewhere no matter what their high-school performance.

By the early 1990s, school-business linkages were being framed as an issue of high skills versus low wages.[13] If employment opportunities are to encourage students to perform better in school, it is argued, then business enterprises need to create high-skilled jobs that tap the talents and energies of graduates. Since many of the lower-skilled jobs that traditionally absorbed less well educated school-leavers or graduates are being outsourced to low-wage countries and since those that are still available domestically do not produce enough income to support a family, the low-skills, low-wage choice is not promising for either the future of education or of the nation. In (relatively recent) recognition of the relationship that exists between school performance and jobs, many business leaders have assumed new, far more active, roles in their attempts to influence school performance.

Employers' Family Policies and Work Loads

Critically important to the health and well-being of families whose members are employed in businesses or other types of organizations are family policies that shape the amount of time and energy family members will have for each other. There is increasing evidence that in the United States over the past fifty years, working hours have actually increased rather than decreased.[14] With the entry of women into the labor force, this increase in working hours suggests that there is less time for dealing with issues such as paying attention to children, ensuring that homework is completed, or dealing with children's problems that arise at school or in the home. Suzanne Gordon has documented that the pressures created by so much work have resulted in a substantial lessening of both concern for community and for caring.[15] Workplaces in general are not amenable to concerns about children or caring.

Family policies of different types of employers reflect a similar bias against caring and ultimately against children and education. With few exceptions, most companies do not allow employees time off for dealing with their children's births, sicknesses or other problems, and even where there are family friendly policies in place, cultural norms about how much work needs to be done often prohibit employees from exercising their right to use these policies.

The very existence of these many types of influence on school performance suggests in an interdependent system each of these institutions also bears responsibilities for the entire system that influences education. In the next chapters we will explore in detail the systems dynamics that affect schools and the ways in which leverage points within those dynamics might be found to begin a long-term process of social change.

NOTES

1. See N. Postman (1979), *Teaching as a Conserving Activity* (New York: Delacorte Press).

2. N. Postman (1979), deals with this topic. See also C. Sykes (1992), *A Nation of Victims: The Decay of the American Character* (New York: St. Martin's Press). For a discussion of victimization in the black community see S. Steele (1990), *The Content of Our Character* (New York: St. Martin's Press).

3. See Sykes (1992).

4. See S. Gordon's remarkable book (1991), *Prisoners of Men's Dreams: Striking Out for a New Feminine Future* (Boston: Little, Brown and Company), for a lengthy discussion of what she terms the caring agenda, particularly Chapter 5 and the Conclusion; and also C. Derber (1992), *Money, Murder, and the American Dream: Wilding from Wall Street to Main Street* (Boston: Faber and Faber).

5. See J. P. Comer's four articles: (1984), "Home-School Relations as They Affect the Academic Success of Children," *Education and Urban Society* 16(3): 294–337; (1987), "Our National Dilemma: Building Quality Relationships," *EDRS* November: 40; (1988), "Educating Poor Minority Children," *Scientific American* 259(5): 42–48; and (1989), "Child Development and Education," *Journal of Negro Education* 58(2): 125–139.

6. See, e.g., D. W. Osborne and T. Gaebler (1992), *Reinventing Government: How the Entrepreneurial Spirit is Transforming the Public Sector* (Reading, MA: Addison-Wesley).

7. J. K. Benson (1982), "A Framework for Policy Analysis," in D. L. Rogel, D. A. Whetten, and associates (eds.), *Interorganizational Coordination: Theory, Research, and Implementation* (Ames, Iowa: Iowa University Press).

8. See Osborne and Gaebler (1992), for examples.

9. The work of G. C. Lodge (1990), *Perestroika for America: Restructuring Business-Government Relations for World Competitiveness* (Cambridge, MA: Harvard Business School Press), is most insightful on this topic.

10. C. Derber (1992).

11. Secretary's Commission on Achieving Necessary Skills (1992), *Learning a Living: A Blueprint for High Performance, A SCANS Report for America 2000*. Issued by the U.S. Department of Labor, April.

12. SCANS report (1992); and also National Center on Education and the Economy's Commission on the Skills of the American Workforce (1990), *America's Choice: High Skill or Low Wages!* (Rochester, NY: National Center on Education and the Economy).

13. National Center for Education and the Economy (1990).

14. See, e.g., J. Schor (1991), *The Overworked American: The Unexpected Decline of Leisure* (New York: Basic Books); and S. Gordon (1991).

15. See Gordon (1991).

Chapter 6

System Dynamics of School Failure

In the last chapter, we explored some of the external pressures that schools are facing, some of which have caused significant problems for the educational process. In this chapter, we will explore the most significant obstacles to change as we look at the structure of schools as a systems dynamics problem. In education, the problems of poverty, class, race, economic opportunity, equality and equity, community, and workforce quality interact powerfully with the educational process, affecting deeply children and their performance in school. At the same time the external and internal pressures constitute a set of systems that schools are embedded within and create a dynamic process that results in their continuing actual or perceived failures. Senge has pointed out that problems like those that afflict education are insidious in their character, creeping up on society rather than making themselves known more immediately through a crisis.[1] This insidious character is difficult for human beings to contend with, according to Senge. People are more capable of dealing with catastrophes than with slow change or what in a previous chapter was termed the "slow-motion riot" that is affecting our schools today.

Senge proposes that the solution to insidious problems like the failing education system or those social problems that interact with the schools is necessarily a systems approach. In a systems approach, the interaction of structure and policies of the system can be understood so that the dynamic of failure can potentially be shifted to a dynamic of success. This chapter explores the system dynamics that have resulted in school failure (or perceived failure), so that potential trigger points for change can be identified.

The previous chapters have made clear that issues related to students, society, and structure all contribute to the problematic performance outcomes of schools, but as yet have not explored the ways in which these problems and issues interact with each other to form a system. From a systems perspective, we might classify problems related to schools into three categories: student problems, societal problems, and structural problems within schools. Each of these sets of problems creates a dynamic that affects the ultimate performance of schools, as Figure 6.1 suggests. The dynamics of these three categories of problems are, however, far from simple: each constitutes its own system dynamic and combines with the others to create the tremendous complexity facing educators and policy makers desiring to improve the performance of schools. This chapter will focus on understanding the systems dynamics of school-based problems that are evidenced structurally, student problems that are evidenced in their own behaviors and performance, and social problems as they affect students and the curriculum of schools.

Using the work of Senge as the basis of this analysis we will develop a series of systems diagrams that will help us to think holistically rather than in fragmented fashion about the problems of schools.[2] Systems thinking, according to Senge, means being able to see *interrelationships*, not just

Figure 6.1
Overall Dynamics of Education

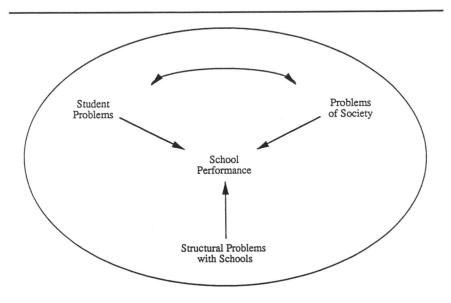

linear cause-effect links, and to see the processes of change or the dynamics of these interrelationships rather than viewing the situation as a static situation. Many, if not most, of the ideas that have been put in place in efforts to improve the schools have been overly simplistic—or based on linear thinking—rather than understanding the dynamics of the problems that schools face. Below we will adapt the systems dynamics model to the situation of schools in attempting to better understand the problems from this systems perspective and gain insight into what Senge terms the "leverage points," or those places where significant improvements can be made.[3]

STUDENT PROBLEMS

Take as the symptom problematic student performance, which is modeled in a simple systems diagram in Figure 6.2. The student lives primarily in a family and community context outside of the school (only about 9 percent of a child's life is actually spent in school). To the extent that the student is experiencing problems in that life outside of the school she or he carries into the school the attitudinal, behavioral, and academic consequences of those problems. For example, if a student is in poor physical health, is hungry or malnourished, or is subject to abuse, neglect

Figure 6.2
School as Problem-Solver

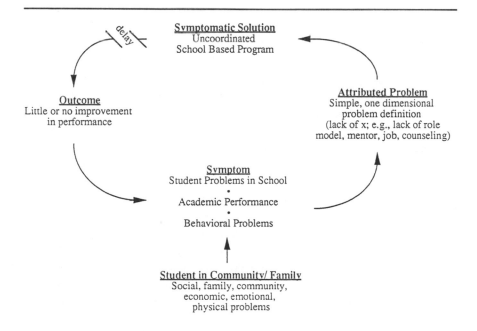

or violence at home, all of which are sometimes consequences of poverty situations, learning may be difficult or behavior problems may develop. Because it is hard to pay attention when physical or emotional conditions get in the way, the student may misbehave in order to get the teacher's attention or simply underperform on tests or in other assigned work. Homework may not be done, the student may be disruptive in class or have a limited attention span.

If teachers recognize that students are actually underperforming because of problems that are externally caused, then action may need to be taken to deal with the symptoms manifested by the students. Students and families must somehow be made aware of the need to take responsibility for themselves so that school work is not adversely affected. Despite the fact that the causal conditions exist outside the school, school personnel typically feel responsible for putting in place a program to deal with some of the consequences of the students' family and community problems, partly because if they don't put such a program in place, the situation is likely to remain unchanged and the problems will continue unabated.

Thus, if students come to school hungry, for example, a breakfast program may be put in place to feed them. If there is violence or drug sales in the neighborhood, security guards and metal detectors may be at the school's entrance to provide a sense of security and safety. If children are being left outside the school early because parents have to get to work or are going home to empty houses, early morning and latch-key programs might be developed, stretching the school's already limited resources and deflecting energy and attention away from education toward these behavioral and attitudinal problems.

At the junior high or high-school level, a youngster considering dropping out of school because he or she does not see the worth of completing his education may be put into an "at risk" program, assigned a mentor, or put into a school-to-work transition program. A pregnant teen may be put into a parenting or drop-out prevention program. Courses will be offered on parenting skills to youngsters who have become parents. Drug abuse counseling may be offered through the school. Teens who are sexually active may be offered human sexuality programs and condoms may be distributed through the school. Teachers may be asked to cope with problems arising in the home or community. To deal with lack of knowledge about the world of work, a school-to-work transition program may be developed. Part-time jobs may be offered to some students through school-business partnership programs. Guest speakers may arrive at the school. The largely unintended end result is a proliferation of programs, each of which attempts to deal with one aspect of the problems that students are manifesting. Generally speaking, these programs will be uncoordinated and will be developed rather linearly, as if the problem on which they were focused could be resolved simplistically through the program and were unrelated to the social context in which the student and the school were embedded.

The actual problems of students' lives, as must be clear by now, are very complex. Dealing with them requires a sophisticated and holistic approach rather than program overlays on top of existing structures. The family and community situation creates the context in which the student learns and the school functions, a context that however much the school might want to isolate itself from, it cannot. The causes of much of the misbehavior, attitude problems, social and emotional issues, and lack of attention to school work are rooted in the students' home and community life. The result of symptomatic treatment is a proliferation of relatively simple programs aimed at dealing symptomatically with the students' problems. But most of these programs ultimately fail because they do not address root causes or involve family and community organizations in taking responsibility for resolving the fundamental issues that caused the problems in the first place. Instead, the school through its programs assumes the burden of responsibility.

Additionally, because the panoply of programs that is created is seldom considered holistically or coordinated so that the whole student and his or her problems are being dealt with, the fundamental problems are rarely solved. The outcome, as the figure suggests, is that there is little or no improvement in the students' situations, performance, or behavior. The result is a systems dynamic that Senge calls "shifting the burden" or, alternatively sometimes, a dynamic of "fixes that fail."[4] Such activities drain resources from education and take time away from the tasks of planning, coordinating, and implementing significant educational reform. A few students exhibiting specific symptoms may be helped by these program interventions. For the vast majority whose problems lie outside the ability of a fairly simplistically designed program to solve, there are few real changes in their lives that would help them better cope with the demands of school.

The pioneering Boston Compact, which was briefly discussed in the first chapter, is an excellent example of such a programmatic and ultimately overly simplistic approach to what is actually a systems problem. The student problem on which Compact planners focused was the high dropout rate among adolescents. The symptom with which they chose to deal was the lack of access to jobs, which was believed to be a key reason why so many students dropped out. So with all the best intentions, the Boston

Compact was developed as a jobs program, a program that would hold the carrot of a job out to students who finished their education and improved their school performance, including grades and attendance.

The fact that many of the youth at risk of dropping out had little understanding of the world of work, few role models who actually worked or could share with them the rewards of a good career and make the linkages between working hard in school and succeeding on the job, or had the support and incentives from home to work harder in school was not understood or taken into consideration. Further, the fact that many of the academic and behavioral problems evidenced by students in the schools were rooted in years of failures, in socially and economically deprived backgrounds, and in families that were barely holding together and who provide little support for education was also not well understood.

Not surprisingly, although the business community had lived well up to its own commitment to provide access to entry level jobs, the schools' overall performance in terms of attendance, drop-out rates, and test scores did not improve measurably during the program's first five years. The programmatic approach developed dealt only with those symptoms most readily observable and failed to deal with the systemic causes of the students' school failures. A similar analysis could be applied to many of the programmatic solutions that schools develop to contend with student problems. Sometimes all these programs result in a vast array within a given school. Because of the delay associated with the feedback processes, however, frequently there is not a lot of improvement in students' performance or much abatement of their problems.

The impact of the programmatic approach to dealing with student problems within schools is ultimately to take responsibility away from the family and the community for helping students to build stable, emotionally supported, and productive lives *outside* of schools, so that they can perform better *in* school. Since schools develop programs to deal with each symptom, they implicitly accept the responsibility for whatever problems students bring into the school with them. This acceptance permits those outside the school system, parents and other relatives, human service organizations, churches, government agencies, health providers, police, and neighbors, for example, to walk away. These others can readily believe that the problem is being resolved without their input and without their having to accept much, if any, responsibility for children because the health, safety, security, counseling, and general caretaking needs of the children will be dealt with by the schools.

The dynamics of this systems problem create a vicious circle in that each time a symptom is addressed through development of a program, people expect that the problem will be solved. After a significant delay it becomes clear that the problem is not being solved, so more programs are added and the program proliferation becomes worse without solving the problem. The continued development of programs takes more and more responsibility away from those outside the school system who might otherwise be expected to assume it, for example, for families providing a supportive and caring environment that encourages education, for human service agencies to coordinate their initiatives with respect to families so that whole families' needs are considered rather than just pieces. Until thinking about the fundamental causes of the students' lack of performance in school is changed, arguably little will change in schools. Until those responsible for ensuring that proper attitudes, nourishment, behaviors, discipline, and support and caring are provided to children, along with high expectations for their performance, are asked to take on these respon- sibilities, the vicious circle will continue unabated. In the next chapter, we will explore the leverage points that may exist for dispersing some of this responsibility to more appropriate sources.

SOCIETAL PROBLEMS

The second systems dynamic has to do with incorporating social prob- lems into the domain of schools. Name your social problem: reducing smoking, disabilities, environmental degradation, sexuality, AIDS, drug abuse, race, social equity, conflict and violence, parenting skills, child abuse, even bicycle safety. Go into almost any school and you will find curriculum dealing with many, if not most, of these problems, all of it added with good rationale to the existing curriculum. Falling test scores? Add a component on test-taking skills and drill for the test for weeks prior to its administration, forcing students to memorize facts likely to be contained in the test. Whatever the problem, one popular solution seems to be to add a curriculum component. Attitudes toward the environment need changing? Create an environmental curriculum and add it to history, social studies, math, science, reading, and the other basic subjects. Stu- dents engaging in sexual activity? Distribute condoms in the schools and develop a human sexuality curriculum. Drug abuse, conflict among stu- dents, dealing with differences, all of these and many other social problems have been the focus of additional curriculum components in recent years.

Another typical response of schools to the emergence of these social problems and curriculum demands is the programmatic one: to overlay program after program on top of what already exists. This dynamic has already been illustrated in the systems diagrams related to student performance and social problems. The result of this program orientation is that in one school, which is viewed as highly progressive, the principal and teachers can barely keep track of the programs that are under way. Teachers tend to view innovations as "just another program." Even though this school has a strong set of core values reflected in a relatively straight-forward mission statement, it is not clear to either the principal or teachers just how all of the programs relate to the mission. And the irony is that even though the principal is aware of the need for strategic planning to deal with the fragmentation that the array of programs has produced, there is no time built into the teachers' contracts for such activities. Invariably, serious planning activities are put aside in the interests of fire fighting the maelstrom of problems that students bring to the school each day and in carrying out business as usual. Under such circumstances, little thought can be or is given to the fundamental restructuring, the working smarter not harder, the need to have the school itself become a learning organiza-tion, the student orientation, and the focusing of the programs that are offered on specific and systemic needs that are arguably necessary.

What's wrong with this picture? What's wrong is that because in too many schools there are no fundamental structuring principles or goals that underpin the general curriculum, there are few useful guidelines for decision making about what goes into the curriculum and what stays out. While many parents, for example, believe that human sexuality is some-thing that ought to be taught in the home, the AIDS crisis combined with a freeing of sexual mores has resulted in many schools adopting sex education curricula and some high schools now distributing condoms. In my own hometown, the nature of this education has caused considerable controversy. Some parents take the fundamentalist position that sexuality should be taught in the home, be based on religious or moral principles, and be based on so-called traditional values. Others, including many on the school committee, take the position that students should be taught tolerance for different life-styles and the facts of life. All of this recently raised considerable controversy, distracting the school committee, the educators, and many parents' attention away from other curriculum issues that potentially deserved more attention because they provide the basis for informed and responsible citizenship.

Controversies such as this one do have the beneficial impact of raising some serious questions about the core content that is being taught in the schools. Other curricular additions may just take place without anyone asking the basic question: should we be teaching this at all? What do we expect of our students and what should we expect? What are the basic skills? What are the areas of academic competence and knowledge that all children should have? Fundamentally, what is the purpose of education and what fits into that purpose? But answering this question is difficult because there are few arenas in which the basic questions are raised and the solutions generated, in typical linear fashion, tend to be focused in the development of new curriculum initiatives to deal with whatever the problem of the moment is.

Thus, in addition to dealing with the behavioral, attitudinal, and academic problems of students, schools have been expected to take on many of the social burdens that have been documented in previous chapters. Similar to the vicious circle dynamic that occurs with student problems, solutions to social problems also generate their own vicious circle (see Figure 6.3) that ends up in an ever-elaborating curriculum. Some social problems are dealt within the programmatic responses to student attitudes, behaviors, and problems discussed just above. Others, however, are broader societal problems that get addressed either through social programs like the busing program of the 1970s, which attempted to achieve racial integration in schools. More popularly, curriculum additions are made, adding new materials to an already overloaded school day.

In the case of busing or other means of forcibly integrating the schools, the schools were used as a means of achieving, in the long term, greater racial integration. It was hoped that more harmony and equity between the

Figure 6.3
Dynamics of Shifting Education's Goals

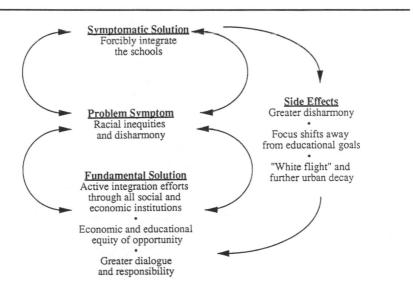

Symptomatic Solution
Forcibly integrate
the schools

Problem Symptom
• Racial inequities
and disharmony

Fundamental Solution
Active integration efforts
through all social and
economic institutions
•
Economic and educational
equity of opportunity
•
Greater dialogue
and responsibility

Side Effects
Greater disharmony
•
Focus shifts away
from educational goals
•
"White flight" and
further urban decay

races would emerge as a result of the racial integration, closer contact, and greater knowledge that was achieved through school integration. In many instances, of course, a very different systems dynamic was established in a typical pattern of shifting the burden.[5]

The fundamental problem was one of racial inequities and disharmony. The symptomatic solution attempted was to forcibly integrate the schools through busing in some instances or police presence in others. Unfortunately, the unintended consequences or side effects were greater racial disharmony in the short term, less ability on the part of schools to actually deal with educational matters, and a long-term problem of what has been called white flight, that is, whites moving out of areas that were to be racially integrated, leaving schools more segregated in some instances than they had been originally. Additionally, as schools deteriorated, safety and drug problems (among others) exacerbated, and businesses tended to leave some areas, resulting in further economic decay in some important population centers, in a typical vicious circle dynamic.

A more fundamental solution to the problems of racial inequity and disharmony would surely involve the schools, since they are a basic part of American life, but would recognize that schools are only part of the solution. But obviously their central role in society makes schools an easy target for dealing with big social problems like equity and racial harmony, like the environment, like AIDS, like drug abuse, and so on. In part, this is the case because the schools are there to educate: by necessity, they must assume responsibility for providing information and creating awareness of these problems as well as for potentially generating individuals capable of creating solutions to these problems in the very long run.

But the net result is that schools take on all of these problems and the "solutions" are long term indeed unless supported by other measures, such as changed laws or public policies. And unfortunately in too many instances schools' own educational goals are unfocused and fragmented, and their fundamental purposes are allowed to remain undefined. The U.S. system has left defining school goals in local hands, but locally few have the time or inclination (perhaps the knowledge or understanding) to ask the important questions, that is the bigger questions such as what is the *mission* of the school, and how should that mission best be accomplished. Developing a mission, a set of core values around that mission, and a structure to achieve it represents a kind of *strategic* thinking with which few school administrators are familiar. Even fewer teachers have had any experience in developing an organizational strategy. Businesses, on the other hand, are constantly forced to think about their strategies because of the competition they face. This lack of so-called market forces has fueled the school choice debate, but as we shall see in the next chapter, choice is far from a panacea for the schools.

Thus, here we see the vicious circle of shifting the burden once again. The symptomatic problem is that social problems like environment, smoking, AIDS, sexual activity among youth, violence, drug abuse, or equity exist. Compounding the situation is the lack of goals consensus about education's fundamental mission and a lack of acceptance of responsibility for dealing with these issues elsewhere (or simultaneously) in society. The diagnosis generated is that schools should adapt their curricula and take on the task of educating children about whatever the particular social problem at hand is. This curricular adaptation provides a symptomatic solution to the problem, with recognition that any action to result will be long in coming as children grow up and presumably change their behavior as a result of their new knowledge. The unintended consequence, however, is that the curriculum becomes even less focused and more fragmented than ever. It becomes difficult for students to distinguish the important from the unimportant. Because the amount of time available for instruction remains unchanged and because the teaching methods also remain largely unchanged, more and more content is squeezed into the same amount of resource, time.

Because the system we have structured is based on local autonomy, fundamental questions about the purpose of education have traditionally not been addressed at the national or even the state level. Rather, it is left to each individual community to develop its own response to these questions. The impact of this particular systems dynamic, as Figure 6.4 indicates, is that social problems are diagnosed with an assessment that schools should adapt their curricula and take on the burdens of society by providing a better understanding of these issues to students (who presumably will be better equipped to deal with these problems when they graduate). Other implications are that social problems addressed primarily through educational mechanisms will be a long time coming in their resolution. Of course, there is no guarantee that knowledge alone will solve, for example, the problems of AIDS, of race or equity, or of the environment. Thus, the educational solution alone is too narrow.

A narrowly focused curriculum solution, like the programmatic solution described above, permits other social institutions, those that ought to be developing public policies, media campaigns, organizational policies, or public debates to deal with these matters, to sidestep the issues. Of course, this is far too simplistic a description; it overdraws what is actually a complex, interactive and iterative process in which public policy is presumably being made and in which at least some other organizations are

Figure 6.4
Dynamics of Curriculum Additions

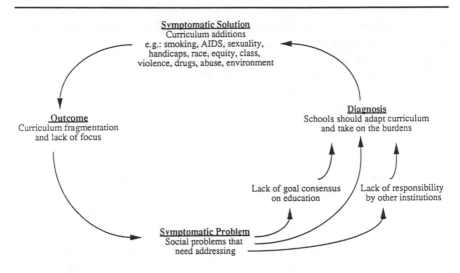

dealing with some of these problems. The very complexity and interactive nature of problems like AIDS or the environment, as we shall see in later chapters, means that *multiple* organizations must become engaged in their resolution.

SYSTEMS DYNAMICS OF CHANGING SCHOOLS

Earlier, this book raised the question of why haven't schools changed in the face of the intense criticism they have received, the competitive problems of the nation, and the obvious problems that children are facing. In the two previous sections, we have looked at some of the systems dynamics surrounding student problems, which are symptomatically addressed through a variety of programmatic interventions overlaid on regular school activities, and at social problems, which when foisted onto the schools are manifested through the development of an increasing array of curriculum items. Another systems dynamic is at work in the relative stability that schools have enjoyed over the years and may help to explain why it is so difficult to begin to move schools toward radical reform. This dynamic is even more complex than those discussed above because many more factors feed the dynamic that creates a force for stability or change in the schools.

Compounded by the same type of linear thinking that implies that programmatic or curricular solutions will resolve complex problems, the social forces that were described in earlier chapters create a dynamic that results in lack of change or inertia for schools. Even when the rhetoric surrounding schools suggests that radical reform ought to be attempted, schools have remained virtually unchanged because the existing dynamic is one that fosters stability rather than reform, since there is far less pressure for change than there is for stability in the system. As Figure 6.5 indicates, there are a number of gaps that create the dynamic of stability that we see with schools. These gaps include lack of goal consensus, lack of will (compounded by the prevailing sense of complacency), lack of knowledge and vision about the organizational processes involved in change and about what restructured schools might be, lack of time and resources to implement change strategies, and natural resistance to change. As with the other systems we have studied, this structural system creates a vicious circle in which forces for stability override the impetus for change of which the rhetoric speaks. Each of the elements of the system will be discussed below.

Lack of Goal Consensus about Education's Real Mission

Gary Watts of the National Education Association (NEA) pointed out in an interview that schools today are designed on a factory model. The system is premised on an assumption that children learn by "having things

Figure 6.5
Dynamics of the Attitude Problems about Education

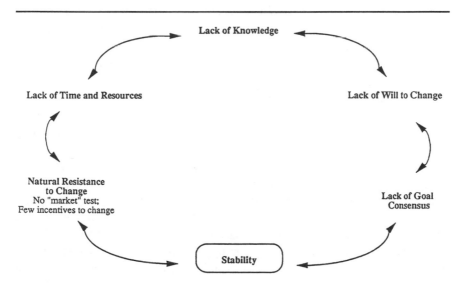

poured into their heads." Uniformity and efficiency are the goals. This system is formulated on Frederick Taylor's model.[6] The premise of the current system, the old paradigm, is this: you take off the top of kids' heads, and you pour things in, different things depending on the class. Some heads fall off, but it's OK for one third to be failures. We've set up the school system this way. That worked fine when people were being trained to go to work in factories where creativity was not necessary. The school system was emulating what business was doing. Business wanted these 'products' as well."

The problem is that the world has changed, according to Watts. "The world, students, families, the content base have all changed, but we still are saddled with the old system." The problem with most change efforts, according to Watts, is that we keep looking for the "silver bullet," the one program or tactic that will by itself save the schools and transform the system. "We tried the idea of open classrooms. It was a failed conception because we made only one change. You have to deal with balance. Any single idea today will equally fail in and of itself. The problem of education is not solvable by a silver bullet. The problem is also not motivation—you take more of the same and screw it together." The problem, that is, is a problem of the system, and when one element of the system changes, the rest of the elements need to change with it: curriculum content, pedagogical approach (or teaching methodology), organizational structure, and the reward system all need to change simultaneously.

One union representative commented, "If you have a common agenda, core curriculum, standards, and shared frameworks about education, there's the basis for a real rich dialogue between parents and schools about what's happening to individual children. These can be combined with assessments and then you have the basis to engage the parents—and they should be engaged, and held responsible for the nonschool part of the agenda that relates to education. If that means not watching TV, then it's clear what's expected. And then you know which parents are doing it and which are not." But the problem is that this shared agenda does not exist for most of our schools. Consensus on the goals of education is notably lacking.

Others suggest that part of the problem is that there's little common understanding of what teachers are supposed to do in the classroom. Common practice is to leave teachers largely to themselves, assuming they know how and what to teach, based on curriculum guidelines provided by the state or district. Lack of time for interaction and isolation in classrooms with the children means that teachers infrequently talk to each other about teaching. Anyway, for many teachers, talking even (or maybe especially) to other teachers about what to do in the classroom would imply that they do not know how to do their jobs. Because there are no standards or goals that are accepted even within school districts, teachers and school administrators frequently find themselves reinventing the wheel to solve problems that have already been dealt with elsewhere. From a strategic perspective, the lack of interaction means that few common goals emerge even *within* a school. Because classroom activity is left to individual discretion (admittedly with sometimes overly restrictive guidance from districts that limits creativity), there is no good way of checking to determine the ways in which long-term goals are being met on a daily basis.

Among other problems with the current system is the emphasis on passive learning by students, too frequently with the sole active member of the classroom being the teacher. This situation contrasts to learning by everyone in the school, as well as the school as a system. Systems thinking is aimed at developing learning organizations,[7] but ironically, despite their emphasis on education, the schools as currently structured focus more on stability than on the constant change and improvement implied by the term learning organization. Teachers are understandably reluctant to change their roles from promulgators of knowledge to facilitators of learning, since they have neither the training nor skills to assume this very different classroom role. Simultaneous with emphasis on passive learning is a focus on students as knowers—knowers of information, facts, dates—rather than as learners. As the NEA's Watts points out, knowledge is measured on standardized tests. Learning is much more difficult and accordingly much more costly to measure.

Understandably, the lack of goal consensus about education creates one of the foundation problems for system reform. It is difficult to reform a system unless you know what you want it to accomplish and where you want it to go. Until there is a national, state, or at least local agreement about whether education's primary purpose is one of socialization, of educating citizens for a democratic society, of creating the workforce of the future, of helping the country become more competitive, or of some other goal or combination of goals, it will be difficult to set a direction for reform. The national goals, adopted by the U.S. Department of Education during the Bush Administration and continued under the Clinton Administration have provided at least one part of that direction, though arguably they are incomplete and focused as much on social problems as they are on what education itself ought to be about. Still, they represent progress and, as we shall see in the next chapter, a potential leverage point for changing the system. But these problems of lack of goal consensus are compounded by the next problem, which is a very real lack of will to change the current system.

Lack of Will: Attitudinal, Ideological, and Political Impediments

The second major factor that feeds into the structural change dynamic is the lack of will to change. Fed by the complacency that suggests that my school is OK, even if all the others are not, U.S. society faces a serious lack of will to change the educational system. There has been very little real public pressure for real reform, few teachers or principals willing to admit that they have something to learn about the transformation of their schools, and not many people willing to undertake the strenuous set of activities involved in transforming the system. The attitude problems highlighted earlier have thus kept real school reform largely off the public agenda. The result is that there is little real public will to change the schools. Rhetoric about crisis in the schools has fueled a certain amount of consternation and focused attention on business involvement in education, but significant change has yet to occur.

A more pervasive and certainly more difficult aspect of the attitude problem has to do with the fact that the nation has never educated all of its citizens to the high-school graduation level. Expectations about the role of school have changed, as one individual from Pittsburgh who was interviewed for this project indicated, "The United States was never set up to educate every citizen, woman, or minority. It was set up to make sure that certain groups of kids got a special education and everyone got a certain baseline. Kids are basically selected to education, so we have selective education. Equal education is education for everyone, and we need every man, woman, and minority. The baseline has to be increased. Kids need to learn to write, read, think, analyze, do teamwork. Everyone needs these skills."

But this statement implies a very different set of expectations and requires a different system to achieve than the current system, which essentially skims off the intellectual cream and allows the rest of the milk to be used for purposes that are less productive. The changing global economy has, as has been noted earlier, fostered recognition that this strategy is less than productive for society in the long run; however, changing both attitudes that create the strategy as well as the system that supports it has proved more intractable than was imagined in 1983 when *A Nation at Risk* first highlighted the connections between competitiveness and education.

Even today, after all the rhetoric, the nation seems to have a mind-set that devalues education, encourages little support for education within many families or from the broadcast media, and is satisfied with relatively low-achievement levels. This attitude is fostered by an anti-intellectual bias in the media, particularly on television, and through social norms that consider "eggheads" or "achievers" to be "dweebs" or worse. None of this seemed to matter during the baby boomer years following World War II when low-skilled mass production jobs that paid well tended to proliferate and when there was plenty of labor to go around. It is just those low-skilled but high-paying jobs that have disappeared, but the public mind-set has not yet caught on to the shift.

Nor, in reality, have most workplaces made the shift. While other nations have recognized the need to educate people for high value-added jobs, the United States continues to follow a mass production mind-set in education that implies that there will be jobs for those of low-skills levels. Other nations, such as Korea and Japan have strong family structures and social norms that place great emphasis on educational achievement and establish high expectations that *all* children will learn to a reasonable level, even if it takes some children longer than others to get there. Some, like Germany, have developed strong apprenticeship and school-to-work transition programs that ensure that even those individuals not proceeding to higher education receive adequate schooling.

Certainly there is far more homogeneity among the populations in many of these other nations than in the United States, which is already characterized by demographic diversity and which is projected to grow still more diverse in the near and intermediate term. In any real effort to educate all of the nation's children, significant resources will have to be devoted to children who are substantially different in appearance and cultural values from the dominant white majority. The fact that in some places the white majority is being replaced by an Hispanic or black majority has not made much difference yet, since it is these populations that have historically received the worst educations. There are serious power implications in truly educating all—and those implications frequently go unstated while simultaneously posing tremendous obstacles to real reform.[8]

The plurality that characterizes the political system in the United States means that different perspectives are brought to bear upon the schools. Plurality means, in part, that everyone who has been through the educational system—that is, virtually everyone—thinks that he or she knows what needs to be done to improve education. When very many different perspectives are brought to bear on a complex problem like education, it is difficult to come to consensus about what should be done at all.

Lack of Knowledge and Vision

School structure also reflects lack of knowledge: few school administrators and even fewer teachers are aware of the different organizational structures that might be available to them, which might change educational process, establish links to share responsibility, or create a solid strategic vision for a school. Nor is there much understanding of organizational change processes necessary to get to a radically different type of school that accomplishes its purposes better, such as the school described by Sizer in *Horace's School*.[9] Nor even is there a clear understanding of what restructured schools would or should look like, particularly since there is a strong local component to the ways in which U.S. schools are structured and operated.

Dealing with day-to-day crisis and duties, few teachers or administrators have had an opportunity to think much beyond "what is," to begin thinking about "what might be," especially as schools are structured to deal with external constituencies. Because there is so little time for interaction, it is difficult for teachers to find time to think beyond teaching methods, content, or approaches that have either been supplied by their districts, by textbook publishers, or by professors when they were themselves in college. Teachers and administrators alike have suffered with the consequences of the social problems, curriculum demands, and resource constraints that have been imposed upon them. Many teachers will acknowledge that the problems they face go well beyond the school's corridors, but, for the most part, they have had neither the knowledge nor the time for thinking, let alone planning, about how to change.

Reform or restructuring in the current management parlance, requires thinking beyond the boundaries that currently exist, breaking those boundaries if necessary. Yet breaking existing boundaries is very difficult: it requires that we see what might be rather than what is. When people, such as teachers or school administrators, are mired in the day-to-day crises and demands of real-life students, they not surprisingly have little time or inclination to go beyond what is. Legislatures and local school boards have provided few resources or models that they might emulate—and where such models exist, following them is extraordinarily difficult. Change such as is imagined here is not, nor can it be easy. The process of change requires considerable expertise to negotiate, and there is little of that expertise available within schools. Some schools, for example, are attempting restructurings based to some degree on total quality management (TQM) methods first introduced in businesses.[10] One of the first things that researchers note when they attempt transformation is that the entire system is involved; the second thing they note is that the transformation process is extraordinarily difficult to achieve and requires considerable attention to maintain.[11]

There is, of course, as the TQM experiments illustrate, considerable research and experimentation going on in some schools. Some of these efforts provide role models for the type of organizational change efforts that will be needed to shift from the stability of what is to the dynamic processes of constant improvement, attention to learning by everyone within schools, and greater participation by all in the learning that would appear to be needed in our schools. Although the models reported by the Conference Board as one set of examples are very different from each other, they share the characteristic that they are undertaking a comprehensive review of the entire *system* and *structure* of the schools, and that they require extensive planning, implementation, and thinking time around issues of what the school should look like and how its goals should be achieved.[12]

Lack of Resources: Time, Trust, and Money

Real reform requires resources of both money and time, as the figure also suggests, and the lack of adequate resources inhibits the system change process. To date, the American public has been unwilling to expend more resources on a system that rhetoric suggests is failing because there is little trust that the same educators who are now said to be failing could make the necessary moves to turn the system around. Of the resources perhaps the most critical is time and training for staff development, on the organizational change process, on the emerging goals for education, and on how to restructure to assure that appropriate responsibilities are assumed by those outside the school.

Time is a key to successful change because the current structure of schools isolates teachers in classrooms essentially all day long with little time to collaborate, talk about teaching or student needs, or ways of really changing what is done within the school. Teacher contracts typically further limit what is expected of teachers and how much preparation time they will be allotted.

In one Boston school, attempting to develop a strategic plan for the school year to meet systemwide objectives, simply finding time for teachers to meet required going around the limits imposed contractually. Some teachers are unwilling to meet this "extra" demand for participation. Days are limited and the school year is limited, and there seems to be little public willingness to fund the extra time that would be necessary not only to bring the number of hours that U.S. students spend in school to international standards but also to provide a little "slack" time for teacher development, management-teacher interaction, and collaboration. Finding this slack time may ultimately require extending both the school day and the school year, which ultimately requires more spending on schools. As the tax revolts of the 1980s made clear, there is little public desire for more taxes, particularly when the system is already in trouble.

Further, there is a significant attitudinal barrier because many teachers view participating in developing programmatic approaches to teaching, restructuring the school, collaborating, and participating in decision making as management tasks and, therefore, outside of their domains and responsibility. Unions have helped to foster this "us-versus-them" attitude of teachers toward administrators, and it takes considerable energy, attention, and willpower to begin breaking down some of the barriers thus created.

Natural Resistance to Change: Institutional Impediments

The existing structure of schools is essentially symptomatic of the lack of a deep sense that schools in fact *need* to change as well as itself imposing significant obstacles to change and the stability that is created by this structure provides natural resistance to change from within the schools themselves. The stable, highly bureaucratic, and isolating structure of schools creates its own set of dilemmas for school staff, who are both buffered from and buffeted by many of the changes going on outside the school. Also, union contracts for teachers and custodians place serious constraints on change initiatives. As resources have been squeezed over the past decade, the general response of school administrators has been to cut back programs that are viewed as nonessential (while adding those to help certain groups of students, as noted above), eliminate or reduce elements of the curriculum (such as art, music, or gym), or lay off staff and increase class size rather than to change the ways schools operate. Except in unusual cases, the notion of restructuring both the processes and content of education, what businesspeople might call not working harder but working smarter, is seldom attempted.[13]

As the proponents of school choice have been saying for more than a decade, schools do not change because they do not have to change. Unlike businesses, which can go under when they are not effective in achieving their goals or remaining profitable, public schools, at least until very recently, have had no "market" pressures on them. Proponents of choice suggest that market forces, that is, allowing parents to choose which school their children will attend, will serve as a mechanism for fostering significant improvements in schools. Such choice advocates look at higher performance levels in private and parochial schools as resulting from the fact that parents can and will take their children elsewhere if the school fails to perform up to snuff.[14]

Arguably, however, the causal arrow goes in the opposite direction, or at least the arrow may be bidirectional: private or parochial schools may perform better simply because parents do *choose* to invest in their children's education. That investment is more than money, however; it is very likely attitudinal, involving high expectations, stress on the importance of education, and a set of values that emphasizes hard work as well as ability. Parents who send their children to private or parochial schools, that is, would seem to be more likely to understand the importance of education, stress that importance to their children, and maintain a consistently high set of expectations and values around the educational process that children absorb. This is not to say, of course, that many parents whose children use public schools lack these same values or high expectations, but simply that there is probably a biased distribution of parents who are truly concerned about education whose children are in private and parochial schools as compared to those in public schools. In the public schools, prevailing attitudes that accord education low status, that are satisfied with whatever the expected performance level is, and that reward ability rather than hard work are more likely. Despite a public advocacy of school choice by some policy makers, few communities have moved to systems in which real choice is offered. As a result, the conditions that are posed by lack of competition among schools, except in wealthier communities where parents can and often do choose to send their children to private or parochial schools (or, simply, where the choice involves living in a community with notably better schools in the first place), remain. Schools are still seldom allowed to go out of business.[15]

Battles about turf represent another obstacle of considerable importance to school reform. Earlier it has been argued that the problems of today's children can be addressed only by creating a system that ensures that all of their needs are met—by families and, where necessary, by an alliance of businesses, social service agencies, community organizations, and schools. The fragmentation of services that currently exists, with each agency or organization carefully maintaining its rights to its own turf, combines with the individualistic ideology prevalent throughout the nation to make collaboration difficult. Although many, many so-called partnerships have been established in recent years, few of them really grapple with systemic issues that cut to the heart of their organizational enterprises.

Finally, it is well known that any large-scale organizational change meets resistance. It is much easier to stay with the status quo, much less risky, and much simpler since no new patterns have to be established and little new will have to be learned. Change is hard and it is readily understandable that when there is no gripping sense of crisis, no serious pressures for reform, the forces of inertia would cause the system to remain relatively stable.

The pragmatic things, changing people, are perhaps the most difficult aspects of school restructuring. As Gary Watts of NEA points out, "When NEA went through its merger of black and white affiliates twenty-five years ago, it was a painful struggle. After you got through the philosophical issues, pragmatic things held up the merger. The human things were the toughest to crack. That's true with school restructuring too. Even if you can get the key people on retreat and they can conceptualize the change, then to go back and undo all these threads one by one is very difficult. You have state regulations, interpersonal issues. It's a three-to-five-year effort. You need to start, work it, have setbacks, rebuild relationships. There's no magic answer."

THINKING TOWARD SYSTEM CHANGE

Because my perspective is one of the outsider looking in, the changes I propose will focus on the internal and external linkages that schools can make, and the ways in which leverage points might be found for each of the systems dynamics we have discussed above. Rather than focusing directly on pedagogy, curriculum, or school goals per se, on which I have little direct knowledge, using organizational theory about change processes, I will suggest that both internal and external structural changes will be necessary to develop necessary links between schools and the other institutions on whom they depend and to begin the process of changing in a positive direction the systems dynamics we have been exploring.

Others, more knowledgeable about curriculum and internal school processes have better dealt with curriculum reform, for example Theodore Sizer in his *Horace's School* and David Perkins in *Smart Schools*. These changes involve active participation in and responsibility for their own education by students, with teachers assuming more of a facilitative role. More long-term, cooperative projects and emphasis on learning rather than knowing underpin the philosophies behind these school restructuring proposals. Such proposals would thoroughly reconstruct the educational process and deal with significant content issues as well, since they would force an evaluation of what gets taught along with how it is taught.

Many proposals for restructuring curriculum and pedagogy focus on what happens inside the school, assuming that the pressures that come from outside can be safely ignored. There is, of course, some evidence from the work of Comer and Sizer that good schools can be created even under the most difficult circumstances.[16] But without significant support and change in the operating policies and ways in which schools relate to external constituencies, success requires heroes of the sort represented by Jaime Escalante of *Stand and Deliver* fame. Since most people are not heroes, it would arguably be more prudent to create a system and a structure for schools that can work effectively whatever the external circumstances. This approach would mean that every school's structure would look different but could potentially be adapted to the needs of the local community. When external forces are understood, the possibilities for structuring will become more apparent since it is likely that principles for their reorganizing can be found.

NOTES

1. P. M. Senge (1991), *The Fifth Discipline: The Art and Practice of the Learning Organization* (New York: Doubleday).

2. See Senge (1991), Chapter 5 and Appendices 1 and 2, in particular.

3. See Senge (1991), Chapter 7, in particular.

4. See Senge (1991), Appendix 2.

5. See Senge (1991), Appendix 2.

6. Frederick Taylor is considered the father of principles of scientific management.

7. See Senge (1991). The subtitle of the book is, of course, *The Art and Practice of the Learning Organization*.

8. J. Kozol does, of course, make this very point in his (1991) *Savage Inequalities* (New York: Crown), but he is among the few mainstream writers to do so.

9. See T. R. Sizer (1992), *Horace's School: Redesigning the American High School* (Boston: Houghton Mifflin Company).

10. See, e.g., S. B. Wolff and G. C. Leader (1993), *Business and the Public Schools: The Potential for a Partnership Based on Total Quality Management* (Boston: Human Resources Policy Institute, Boston University).

11. Sandra Byrne of the National Alliance of Business, Washington, D.C. has conducted an extensive study of schools implementing TQM systems. Personal communication.

12. S. A. Waddock (forthcoming), *Collaboration for Systemic Reform in Education: The Fourth Wave* (New York: The Conference Board).

13. T. R. Sizer (1992) documents the process of change and what an excellent restructured school might look like from a curriculum and internal structure perspective, as well as the difficulties in achieving such changes, in his wonderful book. D. Perkins

presents similar ideas in a more theoretical framework in his book (1992), *Smart Schools: From Training Memories to Educating Minds* (New York: Macmillan).

14. Perhaps the most outspoken school choice advocates are J. E. Chubb and T. M. Moe. See, for example, their (1988) "No School is an Island: Politics, Markets, and Education," in W. L. Boyd and C. T. Kerchner (eds.), *The Politics of Excellence and Choice in Education* (New York: The Falmer Press), 131–142; and their book (1990), *Politics, Markets, and America's Schools* (Washington, D.C.: The Brookings Institution).

15. This is not a statement to advocate choice as a panacea as some observers would do, because I believe that choice has serious limitations for students whose parents are not deeply involved in their children's education and has the potential to leave those children in circumstances even worse off than they were before choice was implemented.

16. See T. Sizer (1992), cited above, and also J. Comer's three articles: (1984), "Home-School Relations as They Affect the Academic Success of Children," *Education and Urban Society* 16(3): 294–337; (1988), "Educating Poor Minority Children," *Scientific American* 259(5): 42–48; (1989), "Child Development and Education," *Journal of Negro Education* 58(2): 125–139.

Chapter 7

Structure as Possibility

The discussion of economic, social, and family changes that have occurred since World War II suggests that our society is undergoing a massive transformation. The technological innovation of computers alone has permitted massive organizational restructuring of a kind not possible in earlier times. Organizations everywhere are struggling with the need to integrate economic and social goals, with pressures from numerous external stakeholders or constituencies, and with the need to work more cost effectively. Many organizations, both public and private, have faced serious necessity of redesigning or transforming themselves if they were to remain at all competitive. Businesses, some governmental agencies, nonprofits, and health care institutions, like the family, are straining for survival under the many constraints that their external environment places upon them. Schools are no exception to these trends.

Interdependence among institutions has been highlighted by technological changes, the emergence of the global village, and a heightened awareness of connections through partnership programs, which bring different institutions into increasingly close contact with each other electronically and organizationally. These linkages ultimately will force the development of new institutional infrastructures. This infrastructure is the linkage that connects all types of institutions in much the same way that our roads link cities and towns or telephones link individuals and businesses. These linkages are literally reshaping the way organizations are structured and how they operate.[1] The rapid emergence of computer technology has, in effect, forced us to recognize and deal with the interdependencies within which we exist. Globally, markets are merging; far-flung divisions of companies are in constant communication via electronic networks. We have seen that what happens in Japan or Germany does indeed affect what happens in America, economically and in quality of life. More locally, we are linked by instantaneous access to news and information around the globe via television and computers.

Many businesses are installing computer equipment in other organizations to increase direct access to those organizations and, not a by-product, sales. Electronic networks are an important reality of many modern organizations. These networks connect people daily in ways never before conceived. These technological linkages symbolize the interdependence that has always existed but has gone largely unrecognized when we have shaped our institutions and communities. Till now, as the systems dynamics models in the past chapter suggest, we have allowed each institution to work on fragmented pieces of problems, installed program after program to deal with one aspect of a problem, or fought about whose turf this piece of information was on rather than worrying about what the problem we were trying to solve was. Recognition of the inherent interdependence among us, particularly with respect to the performance of schools, makes this type of thinking no longer workable.

Thus, in the past, it was possible for schools as well as businesses to attempt to exist as if they were largely independent of other institutions. But the same forces of interdependence that are technologically connecting the rest of the world are also connecting schools to the world. In past chapters, we have explored the impacts that social problems and forces have had on schools and the issues that lack of attention to these connections have raised. Recognition of interconnectedness of problems, families, and institutions relative to schools and their current relative isolation in society has slowly been growing in the past twenty years. Slowly our understanding of the systems dynamics at work is beginning to come to the forefront. This dawning recognition, which comes about in part because of increased attempts at collaboration, demands for restructuring and reform, and cries of failure and crisis in schools, means that educators, policy makers, business leaders, and governmental officials are all seeking new ways to think about structuring of schools.

The Carnegie Foundation for the Advancement of Teaching recently studied the issue of school choice extensively. The study concluded:

The evidence is overwhelming that the crises in education relate not just to school governance but to pathologies that surround the schools. The harsh truth is that, in many communities, the family is a far more imperiled institution than the school, and teachers are being asked to do what parents have not been able to accomplish. . . . And if they fail anywhere along the line we condemn them for not meeting our high-minded expectations.[2]

Taking a similar perspective to the one that this book has been developing, the report continues, "educational excellence relates not just to schools but to communities as well."[3] The implication of this thinking, according to the Carnegie report, which ultimately suggests that school choice is not at all the panacea that some would like to claim it to be, is that "If we are truly serious about better education, the time has come to launch a national effort on behalf of children. It's time to acknowledge the interrelatedness of the home, health clinics, preschools, the workplace—all of the institutions and social forces that influence children's lives."[4]

The forces identified in previous chapters have thus eroded the notion that organizations in society can operate independently of each other or in what is termed a collateral systems manner.[5] These forces have also enhanced awareness of and heightened actual interdependencies that have always existed between, for example, home and school, community and school, businesses and school. Slowly, but perhaps inexorably, the recognition is dawning among those who wish to improve schools that a new way of viewing relationships among organizations both within and between economic sectors is needed. We need a new organizational infrastructure, a new way of viewing the communities within which schools are embedded as they influence the schools. In a few places, such as Louisville, Kentucky, and Pittsburgh, Pennsylvania, this new way of viewing relationships among organizations may actually be beginning to take hold. Based on a concept of interdependence among organizations and a mutuality of interests for at least parts of separate organizations' goals, this way of viewing the relationships among major social institutions can be called collaborative systems perspective.[6]

Earlier scholars developed a similar notion term: the interpenetrating systems conception of social institutions. Interpenetrating systems mean that "Neither are the two systems completely separate and independent nor does either control the other."[7] In this view, society is presumed to exist as a macrosystem and institutions and other units within society as microsystems. School systems, governmental units, social service agencies, and business enterprises constitute the dominant macrosystems attempting to improve schools. None of them, not even the schools, because they are interdependent with other institutions, can achieve the goal of school improvement alone, since actions in one sphere affect operations, behavior, and outcomes in others, as the systems diagrams suggest.

While they certainly need to change, schools cannot by themselves achieve the desired outcomes of good educational performance of their graduates without inputs and assistance from other key stakeholders. On-going collaboration is necessary because schools, for example, are dependent on families to produce children who are willing and able to learn, on the support of governmental institutions for funding and policies, on businesses to hire graduates, and on the ability of social service agencies to perform their jobs adequately. Family members, in turn, are partially dependent upon their employers to enact policies that enable them to adequately parent their children so that they are, in fact, ready for education. We will call the perspective that suggests that interpenetration among institutions needs to be formally recognized a "collaborative systems view."

Taking a collaborative systems view means that individuals and organizations accept a *shared* responsibility for the education and development of children. They then need to begin working together toward common goals. In the economic arena, a similar view of competitiveness among business organizations tightly links customers, suppliers, and even competitors in a network of interdependencies. A collaborative systems operating mode explicitly recognizes this inherent interdependence; institutions and organizations do not attempt to act as if they were completely independent of each other. Rather, they form coalitions and alliances; they work hard to define a common agenda or common set of goals: they think about the common good, instead of the purely individual good. They acknowledge the importance of community and of both individual and institutional responsibility for behaviors and for outcomes.

Those who take a collaborative systems view of schools and other institutions explicitly recognize the multiple responsibilities that exist for educating children successfully. In practice this might mean, to use some simple examples, that teachers and administrators meet periodically with local businesses to discuss the types of skills that are required in local jobs and that some attention is then paid in the curriculum to assuring that students gain those skills. It might mean that school staff and parents work together to assure that homework assignments are completed and that children come to school prepared to learn: well fed, with adequate sleep, and with an appropriate attitude toward school and learning. It may mean that community infrastructures, for example, day-care support systems, safety and security, neighborhood watch and neighborhood improvement programs be begun. It might mean that local employers work closely with schools to develop family-friendly corporate policies, so that employees can participate actively in school activities, such as teacher conferences, school plays, assemblies, and provision of in-class parent help.

Further, schools might acknowledge their dependence on parents to provide safety, shelter, and support for children, factors that will be continued when children are in school. Having acknowledged this inter-dependence, teachers and principals can then expect, demand if necessary, parental involvement in assuring that homework is done and in encourag-ing disciplined attitudes toward school and studies. In turn, parents can reasonably expect or even demand that schools will provide adequate foundations of knowledge in key areas such as reading or mathematics. Businesses could recognize that because they depend on schools for a quality workforce, they need to work with schools to assure that the standards they demand are being met. Further, they might need to change their own policies to assure that children can, in fact, receive adequate parenting. Recognition that reinforcement of these knowledge areas is necessary in the home if students are to successfully absorb them bridges some of the gap between home and school.

These types of things already happen in piecemeal fashion in many schools. The many adopt-a-school and program-oriented partnerships established during the 1980s have helped to reinforce the need for a collaborative approach to education. The difference between the collateral and collaborative systems views is that in the former little consideration is given to the rationale behind any activity beyond its immediate value to the individuals or groups involved. In the former, there is little, if any, discussion of the common good. Programs are fragmented and not viewed as part of a long-range plan. In the collaborative systems view, the relationships of home and business activities to the educational develop-ment of the child and to the school's achievement of its goals is explicit, planned, and part of a systemic approach to educational development. Common good and win-win strategies are explicitly developed and defined for all involved parties in the collaboration. The activities developed thus form part of an entire system designed to enhance the role and performance of the school and support educational institutions and their goals.

With this background, it is now time to consider what restructuring schools demands of teachers, principals, parents, human service organiza-tions, and government to name only a few of the most important actors, and the ways in which the systems dynamics can potentially be altered. As school officials begin to recognize what is needed, they can begin to reassert their own responsibility for what they must by rights do: educate children. Then they can articulate what others must by their own rights do:

take care of the relevant aspects of children's and their families' lives. This chapter will focus on the demands of restructuring schools so that the possibilities that exist can be tapped by exploring the ways in which leverage can be found to change the systems dynamics affecting schools to improve performance.

LEVERAGE AND SYSTEM CHANGE

If the systems dynamics of the current situation of schools are problematic, then the potential for improvement lies not necessarily in new programs, not in new curriculum additions, and not in a maintenance of the status quo structurally. The potential lies in finding the leverage[8] points in the *system* so that the dynamic processes of the system as a whole can be shifted in a more positive direction. In other words, the problems of education are such that linear thinking that overlays program or curricular initiatives will not work. The entire system dynamic must be shifted so that the forces at work push in new, more positive directions than those of the past.

Good performing schools require the interactive effects of healthy students coming from strong families living in strong communities, surrounded by a healthy society, and coming into internally and externally restructured schools (Figure 7.1). This is the macrosystem in which school performance emerges: it has to do with internal curriculum and structure, expectations and demands upon students, and teacher quality and performance, that is, the usual suspects. But it also has to do with the external considerations of community and students themselves and the ways in which these factors influence what happens in schools. The relationship between communities, students, and schools, then, is complex and *interactive*, not simply one sided.

As complex and difficult a task as finding them has proved to be, there must be leverage points within the dynamics of students' lives, social problems, and the structuring of schools that foster significant changes in the overall system. Just as a lever provides the mechanical advantage that permits a small force to move a much greater weight, so the leverage points in a system can establish powerful new patterns of behavior and interaction that result in a changed dynamic and ultimately a changed outcome. Thus, while the changes that are needed to effect school reform may seem massive, by seeking out key points of leverage, we may be able to use the existing resources to much greater effect than we have in the past.

In thinking about initiating change efforts that might work for schools, the discussion of the three systems dynamics that affect schools in the last

Figure 7.1
A Healthier Dynamic for School Reform

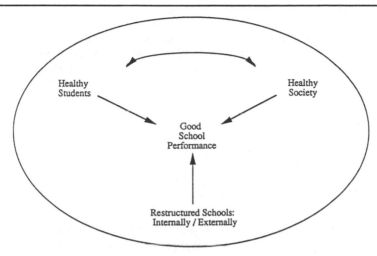

chapter indicates that the dynamics of at least those three different but related systems must be shifted in order to achieve effectively performing schools. Figure 7.1 indicates that desired outcomes include "healthy" students, that is, students who are supported by strong families and are able to participate actively in the demands of schools; healthy communities; and internally and externally restructured schools. We cannot hope to achieve long-term improvements in school performance unless our communities, schools, and students all improve. The key question is, where should the restructuring begin?

Changing only one element of the tripart system shown in Figure 7.1 would probably not impact the entire system or achieve the desired outcomes noted in the figure. For example, schools might restructure internally along the lines that Sizer describes, so that they are project oriented, involve active learning strategies, and encourage participation and responsibility by students and teachers for their own learning. Some schools are trying to do this. But if only schools change and students continue to come to school from communities and families that are disintegrating and provide little support, it is highly unlikely that the school changes alone can successfully transform these students into successful and productive citizens.

Given the impact of external forces on schools, the depth of problems that students face, and the need for having multiple constituencies assume responsibility for educational outcomes, it is unlikely that schools alone provide enough of a leverage point for change. Although clearly there are exceptional schools, even in highly troubled communities, the Carnegie Foundation's recent assessment of school choice makes clear that simply changing the school is insufficient:

Consider . . . District 4. In this poverty-ridden section of New York City, more than half the children come from homes headed by single parents. Almost 80 percent are eligible for the free lunch program. Years ago, school choice brought a new sense of energy and creativity to this district. Yet, even today, far too many students are academically deficient, and District 4 schools still struggle against almost overwhelming odds. Even with the positive influence of school choice, is it realistic to expect an island of academic excellence in a sea of social crises?[9]

Clearly, the answer to the question raised by the Carnegie Foundation is to deal systematically with the more fundamental problems, while *simultaneously* attempting to change what happens in schools. Changes in *all* of the systems are necessary since healthy students come from healthy communities and enter schools that are both structured to deal with those issues they do bring with them and that encourage the type of learning and problem-solving skills necessary in the modern competitive environment.

So how do systems change? Organizational theorists have developed ways of thinking about restructuring that provide insight into what is needed to effect the type of major shifts in systems dynamics that are needed to improve schools. Many companies have undergone dramatic restructuring processes in recent years, including Ford and Xerox. These companies and others transformed themselves from essentially uncompetitive, inward-looking, bureaucratically bound-up entities that failed to focus much on quality or on customers to much more customer-oriented, quality-focused, and less bureaucratic entities. Researchers David Nadler and Michael Tushman[10] have gained insight into what it takes to effect such transformation. By taking some of these researchers' ideas and applying them to schools, we can, perhaps, gain insight into some of the potential leverage points for improvement in schools.

There are two types of change, as Nadler and Tushman see them: incremental changes, in which organizations simply change slowly to adapt to changes in their external environments, and strategic changes, which address the whole organization and "change the frame, either reshaping it, bending it, or, in extreme cases, breaking it."[11] The addition of programs and curriculum innovations that we have seen is characteristic of schools representing the incremental type of change. But, as we have also seen, such changes have done little or nothing to change the systems dynamics of schools. The result has been that schools have remained largely static despite the apparent public outcry and evident need for reform.

Based on the analysis in previous chapters, schools require strategic change, because to improve their performance they must change the dynamics and outcomes in the entire system, internally and externally. Indeed, major social change, a dramatic rethinking of the way we view schools, their roles in society, and the ways we relate to them is necessary. Arguing for such change actually takes us to a broader perspective, above the level of schools themselves to thinking about the interactive effects of the social system in which schools exist. This is strategic change at the community level for sure and probably at the state and national levels as well. This new perspective begins seriously assessing what schools can and cannot legitimately accomplish, what their fundamental purposes are, and the ways in which we, as a society, hope to have schools achieve those purposes.

Think about the levels of change that are required: schools need to change internally and alter their external relations; communities need to be reconfigured so that they once again provide supportive environments for children and families. At the state and national levels, rules, regulations, and policies that affect teacher education, the profession of teaching (including union regulations), curriculum, funding, and operations must all systemically be shifted in support of new responsibilities for everyone involved in education, less bureaucratic restrictions, and more openness to continued learning and improvement.

Further, it must be recognized that the old ways do not work any longer because the world has changed, so new ways of building community and supporting families must be found if schools are to succeed. Schools, like other organizations, need to incorporate concepts that enable them to not only have their students learn constantly but they themselves need to become learning organizations.[12] Concepts like total quality and continuous improvement or learning must be built into the systems of schools, not as overlays on top of what already exists, but as a basic aspect of the way that schools operate on a day-to-day basis. Alliances internal and external to the schools, cooperative and collaborative strategies, and new approaches to learning by students, teachers, and administrators inside the school, and by those who "partner" the school from the outside, that is, parents, businesses, and other organized institutions become a central and new way of educating. These are goals that make sense for schools as they face the difficulties of the twenty-first century.

Fundamentally, the argument is that everyone is responsible for education. The details of these responsibilities will be explored in the concluding chapters of this book as we examine the ways in which alliances and collaborations can be developed between school and home, school and business, and school and other institutions so that responsibility for education can be shared. The remainder of this chapter will explore systems change and schools, and the systems dynamics of the three areas that most directly impact school performance: schools themselves, students, and communities. Organizational theory will help us better understand the process of large-scale system change demanded in the restructuring of schools and the responsibilities for education.

SYSTEMS CHANGE AND SYSTEMS DYNAMICS: ORGANIZATIONAL CHANGE

Nadler and Tushman[13] propose that there are three clusters of activities for the kind of significant change that they term "frame bending," which is what schools need to do. These clusters are initiating change, content of change, leading of change, and achieving or implementing change.

Initiating Change

Initiating change begins with three principles. First is solid diagnostic thinking that identifies the major problems, strengths and weaknesses, and critical success factors for the organization. Obviously, the specifics of these principles will differ for each school. The type of systems diagrams that were developed in the previous chapter provide a reasonable starting point for diagnosing some of the systemic problems facing schools, which are both internal to schools and external to students and community. Basically, the diagnosis that we have come to at this point is that the problems of school performance are threefold: they are community, student, and school problems. We also conclude that the student problems, community problems, and school problems are interlinked in a systems dynamic that needs major reorientation if school and student performance is to change. That is, improvement in school performance demands improvement in family and community strength as well.

Next, to achieve a successful reorientation, leadership needs to develop a vision that is rational, encompasses key stakeholders, incorporates core or end values, defines performance objectives, and identifies the ways in which organizational structure and processes need to change. The public debates about school reform to date have focused largely on school choice and on the notion of "restructuring" schools, but without necessarily defining any clear sense of what these restructured schools would look like or what they would accomplish that is much different than what they accomplish today. The assumption seems to be that changing a few things or putting "market" pressures on schools will dramatically alter the system. This assumption is probably unrealistic, as the quotation from the Carnegie Foundation cited above suggests, and it provides little or no unifying vision or direction for school reform.

Indeed, simply changing the schools, as we have discovered, while necessary is not sufficient to improve long-term performance. Nor do many of the public debates propose ways in which relationships between schools and the many constituencies that affect them should be changed to achieve the desired results. And however much good the market may do to improve the competitiveness of businesses, the public nature, historical development, and realities of location make the use of simple market forces alone an unrealistic tool for school reform.[14]

Thus, the type of vision suggested above: that each school become a learning organization, incorporate concepts of continuous improvement, and devote itself to active participation on the part of both students and teachers in their own learning processes might serve as a unifying vision. But it is a special sort of vision: one that permits each school to find its own way in achieving these ends, to meet the demands of local conditions, and to bring individuals into its own system in a way that engages them in the process of change and on-going improvement.

Finally, Nadler and Tushman indicate that there needs to be a great deal of energy behind the transformation. Leaders need to generate a sense of urgency before change can be accomplished, because organizations are inherently stable. Strategic change creates pain because people are forced to rethink what they do daily, because the old familiar patterns no longer work, and because new learning must take place. However much schools might like to view themselves as learning organizations,[15] the constant development and change involved in the continuous learning, continuous improvement dynamic established in a learning organization requires considerable energy and momentum to maintain its trajectory. Certainly more energy is required to sustain continued learning and improvement than is necessary in a stable bureaucratic organization that does not respond flexibly to changing internal or external conditions.

The difficulties of maintaining a stance of continuous improvement are obvious in schools that have attempted to implement total quality management systems, according to a study undertaken by the National Alliance of Business, but so are the apparent benefits to students of such approaches.[16] Bureaucratic structures, isolation of teachers in classrooms, and lack of imagination and information create significant impediments to development of this type of energy that have to be overcome before continuous learning can be achieved. But the outcomes for students, which may or may not show up in improved test results, suggest that students in such systems are highly involved in their work, are active participants in learning, and are excited about their education, a far cry from the boredom and drudgery of worksheets and lectures in the traditionally structured school.

Content of Change

The actual content of change involves another set of principles: centrality and the "three themes" principle.[17] Centrality implies that change must be linked closely to the entire organization's core purpose, thus, defining the goals of education, a key component of the structural problems that schools face, becomes critical. The "three themes" principle means that change agents need to carefully focus their efforts on what Senge terms the leverage points, that is, a few key themes, in order for the change to be effective. While the goal is to change the entire system, the development of themes for change can help those involved articulate both what needs to be done and how it is to be done. As an example, my son's school attempted to develop a set of what we termed "core values." When effectively implemented, core values provide a framework against which any activity, program, or curriculum change can be thrown to determine whether it fits with the overall "theme" or mission of the school. Whether these themes are called goals, mission, core values, or by some other name, it is critical that there be some central focus that helps orient the change effort and determine what fits and what does not.

Other aspects of the content of change involve issues of leadership. In the successful changes that Nadler and Tushman studied, there was an individual leader they termed a "magic leader."[18] These are leaders who can envision the desired change, energize people to move forward, and enable or help them through the change process by creating appropriate processes, rewards, structures, and resources to effect the change. In schools bound up by union rules, administrators with little or no management training, and severe resource constraints, developing such leadership has been problematic. Below we will explore some of the potential leverage points for developing the needed magic leaders in schools.

But, according to Nadler and Tushman, magic leadership is not enough by itself. A critical mass of people must be built within the organization in order for change to take place, including finding champions for key initiatives. Thus, in a school, the magic principal might identify teachers to lead the structural reform, others to develop goals, and still others to focus on curriculum changes. In Sizer's description of *Horace's School* a team of teachers from a variety of disciplines was assembled to plan and initiate the needed changes and to "sell" those changes to the broader community. Such broad-based support is essential to effective change strategies, whether within the wall of the school or externally in the community. Indeed, even changes occurring within the schools, if they are to incorporate the systems dynamics thinking we have been discussing, will need to include the broader constituency of parents, businesses, human service agencies, health providers, and policy makers who need to support education reform if they hope to be effective. Additionally, many studies confirm that school improvement demands at minimum significantly more parental involvement than is traditional in many schools.

Achieving Change

The next cluster of the change process involves implementation of the changes or what the researchers term achieving change. Nadler and Tushman identify three key principles for this stage: planning and opportunism; many bullets; and investment-and-returns. Intensive planning is necessary to achieve frame-bending organizational change and change the dynamics of a system. Such planning is time and resource intensive in that it must involve a significant number of people, as Sizer illustrates in *Horace's School*.[19] Most attempts at school reform have failed to recognize the type of investment in planning that is necessary to successful change. The mentality has been that change can be achieved through overlays on top of what already exists or with little effort to really understand the dynamics of what has been happening in the school. That is why the notion of systems dynamics is so powerful: it permits a very different way of assessing the problems of schools, one that does not lay blame upon students or faculty or administrators, but rather looks at the system and attempts to shift responsibility. Once this recognition takes place, then planning processes can be set in motion that focus on the necessary changes in the system.

The many bullets principle is necessary because of the natural resistance to change that exists in all organizations, which is particularly notable in highly bureaucratic and unionized organizations, such as schools. The experience of the past decade of efforts to improve schools without changing internal processes or external relations confirms the "forces that work for stability" of which Nadler and Tushman speak. To overcome these forces for stability, it is necessary to change multiple aspects of organizational life simultaneously. This is what Gary Watts of NEA is recommending when he says that the classroom structure cannot be changed to open classrooms and result in immediate and dramatic improvements. Simultaneously, the reward system for teachers, the availability and demands of planning time, the curriculum, the structure, and the goal orientation for students, among many other factors, all need to change. This is what Nadler and Tushman mean by many bullets: changing a number of things that provide leverage to shift the system dynamics in the desired direction. Then, if one of these shifts is not working, it is possible that others will work. The authors indicate that what needs to be addressed, at minimum, using many bullets are standards and performance measurement, rewards and incentives, planning processes, budgeting, resource allocation, and information systems.

The final principle for change is one that is frequently overlooked in school reform efforts: the investment-and-returns principle. Changing any organization is expensive. The need for extensive planning highlights the resource intensity of system change. Without a willingness to invest major amounts of time, money, and energy and commitment by staff and concerned constituencies, little real change is likely. Again, the effort described by Sizer in *Horace's School* is suggestive of the resource needs to achieve major improvements.

IDENTIFYING THE LEVERAGE POINTS FOR CHANGE

The diagnosis given above suggests that all three of the systems dynamics discussed in the previous chapter need to be shifted in more positive directions in order for schools to improve. The organizational analysis suggests some possible leverage points for change within the school as organization and may also be helpful in identifying leverage points in the macrosystem of schools.

Student Problems

Student problems in school are at their core not just individual problems but problems of family and community translated into the individual. Some problems, of course, *are* directly attributable to individual behaviors, decisions, attitudes, and abilities; students must assume much of the responsibility for resolving these problems. Others, however, are a product of the circumstances in which the students find themselves. Too frequently, of course, we allow students' life circumstances to become an excuse for abrogating responsibility for their actions.

But as the evidence presented earlier suggests, some problems do arise because of the circumstances that students are in, which deeply affect their lives and have secondary effects that require that others assume part of the responsibility as well as the students. As long as the attitude is "I'm not responsible," whether it is students, families, community agencies, or school authorities, making the implicit or explicit statement, whatever problems exist will go unresolved because there is no one willing to tackle them head on. If the dialogue around problem resolution is shifted from attempting to transfer the problem and the responsibility for resolving it to different shoulders, toward a language of everyone assuming part of the responsibility then the situation changes.

As an example, in one high school visited, the principal interacted with a black male student who was sent to her for causing a problem in the high school by telling him, in effect, "It's too bad that you're poor, it's too bad that you're black, but unless you want to end up on the street or dead like a lot of the other young black males will, you had better straighten up and get working." First she acknowledged that he had real problems, thereby affirming him as a person. But then she shifted the burden of responsibility for his behavior and his performance back to him, where it belongs. This principal knew that to allow the student to use his poverty or his race as an excuse for his behavior problems would be to commit him to failure for life. Similar stances can be taken toward other types of responsibilities.

Dealing with student problems using this more collaborative approach, in which responsibility for action and impact is shared, means that both community and family need strengthening, responsibilities need clarification, and individuals need adequate support so that they can assume responsibility for their own lives. What is needed, however, is support rather than sustenance or assistance. The assumption needs to be that appropriate responsibilities, actions, and behaviors can and will be assumed by individuals, families, and institutions, rather than that some outsider will "do" for them. This type of stance creates a difficult tension to manage, since both individuals and the institutions that represent them need to assume significant responsibilities and since support needs to be there without causing dependency. Thus, neither the supported nor the supporter can shed responsibility, lest we truly become, in the words of Charles Sykes, "a nation of victims."[20]

To deal with the problems that students bring to schools, for example, both family and community structures will need to be strengthened (see Figure 7.2). The Persistent Poverty Program in Boston is one example of an effort that includes the long-range goal of school improvement, while

Figure 7.2
A Collaborative Approach to Societal Problems Affecting Education

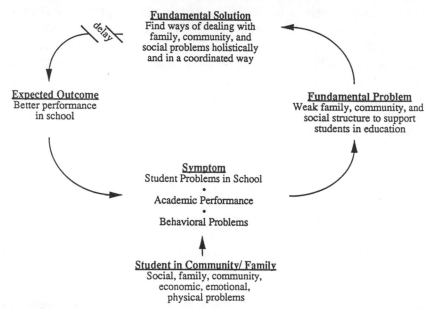

recognizing that at base, the critical factor in producing what were above termed "healthy" students is a healthy surrounding community with strong families supporting their children emotionally, physically, and financially.

Healthy communities are those in which there are enough jobs and other types of economic opportunities to provide living wages to families, where the transportation and communications infrastructure is adequate to support neighborhoods, indeed, where there are neighborhoods that permit residents to have a sense of community. Healthy communities provide support services where they are needed, have adequate affordable housing for the income levels of residents, and include citizen activism and sufficient police protection that safety is not a major concern. In healthy communities, children can grow up without fear of being shot at if they are outside, where they are not accosted by drug pushers on the way to school, where gangs do not play the major role in providing social supports.[21]

The Persistent Poverty Program in Boston, which is sponsored by the Boston Foundation and funded by a grant from the Rockefeller Foundation, attempts to use the development of community infrastructure as a leverage point for fundamental change. The program's aim is to eliminate chronic, intergenerational poverty in Boston. To accomplish this task, the Persistent Poverty Program takes a new tack: it brings together a broad-based, cross-sectoral, multicultural alliance to develop new ways of dealing with community problems and issues. How this is being attempted will be discussed more fully in the next chapter. The important thing to note here is that the leverage is found in the dialogue that is emerging among representatives of different sectors, ethnic groups, and socioeconomic groups. The potential for action, Charlotte Kahn, director of the program believes, lies in linking these individuals and the organizations or groups they represent in entirely new ways and with a new set of assumptions about both what can be accomplished and how it can be accomplished.

A similar effort underpins the community-oriented implementation plan of the GOALS 2000 program, through which the education goals are to be achieved. These activities involve the bringing together of key actors within local communities to brainstorm about how the education goals might be implemented in their community and about what needs to be done to bring all of the key actors within the community into the education picture. Thus, teachers and school officials, business leaders, representatives of the media, health providers, local elected officials, university representatives where available, nonprofit and human service organization representatives, church and opinion leaders, and representatives of key local government agencies are among those invited to participate in discussions about the original America 2000 program of the Bush era and its implementation.

Continuing with much the same collaborative spirit, a spirit that recognizes the need to involve the entire community in improving education, the Clinton Administration's GOALS 2000: Educate America attempts to ensure that all segments of the community participate in education reform at the local level. Together these initiatives represent a marked break from the old way of thinking that schools alone could be responsible for education. The legislation builds into public policy initiatives the shared responsibility for education that this book has been arguing is necessary for the long term. There is, of course, the need to recognize that this more collaborative and holistic approach will not necessarily achieve immediate results, and just working to talk about change will not effect change. But, on the whole, this perspective may have a better chance of changing the systems dynamics of school performance than any one effort or new program might, because it explicitly recognizes the important role of many constituencies in education, especially once such coalitions move to action steps.

Social Problems and Curriculum

Another systems dynamic that needs addressing is the overlaying of new curriculum on top of what already exists. Finding the leverage point for dealing with this problem probably involves clarifying and identifying the goals of schools at the local level more explicitly. The six national goals for education, while helpful in clarifying what the atmosphere, expectations, and attitudes surrounding schools should be, do little in the way of focusing the curriculum or pointing in directions that suggest what should and what should not be left out of the curriculum. The notion of learning organizations, continuous improvement, and active involvement in and responsibility for education by all parties provides a starting point for change. But further goals about *what* should get taught are necessary through the same type of collaborative process through which responsibility sharing comes about.

Because both federal and state levels, as well as elected officials, can potentially provide a bully pulpit at least for beginning the process of elaboration of educational and curricular goals, it is critical that a dialogue about what should and what should not be in curricula begin at these levels (see Figure 7.3). But schools in the United States are controlled and directed at the local level and this independence is likely to be maintained, so the best that the federal government can do is to provide a framework that suggests the direction in which schools might head. As with GOALS 2000: Educate America and its predecessor slogan, America 2000, individual communities will have to "sign on" voluntarily to any articulated

Figure 7.3
Impact of Changing Attitudes on Schools

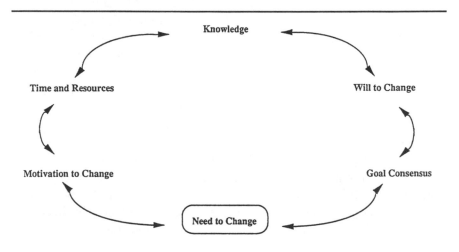

goals. But a goal such as "first in math," is not enough. What math? How should it be taught? What should be accomplished and what should students be able to do in math if we are to know that this goal has been met? Indeed, the math curriculum development process sets an example for how such goals can be targeted in a pluralistic nation such as ours, where independence of schools is maintained at the local level.

Since the goals define what ultimately is taught and even the way in which it is taught, an extensive public dialogue about the goals of education and some definition of those goals as they relate to curriculum would be an important first step in helping schools at the local level determine what and how they are to teach. In the process of creating this dialogue, which might be lead by creative teachers' unions, by the Departments of Education nationally or at the state level, or even at the community level through the coalition building process inherent in the GOALS 2000: Educate America concept, other institutions could be encouraged to review their own responsibilities for education and begin changing some of their own practices, policies, and behaviors.

While clarification and discussion of the goals of education in America will not solve all the problems of curriculum, they will help schools at the local level to become more aware of the problems associated with simply adding on curriculum with little thought to its integration into what else is being taught. In the sense of strategic change, such goals would provide an important and guiding vision for schools, one that each school could attempt to achieve in its own way using local rule, but that provides an overall coherence to education that is now lacking in the United States. Thus, it would seem that the critical leverage point for reforming curriculum problems in schools has to be to start with the goals.

Structuring Within and Without the Schools

If there is one point within the overall system that impacts school performance that is shown in Figure 7.1, it is probably the way in which schools themselves are structured. Typically, when school structure and school reform are discussed, attention is paid to what happens in the school itself. Indeed, what happens in schools and the ways in which they structure themselves internally are vitally important to achieving any set of education goals, to the attitudes and well-being of teachers and students alike, and to what is learned and how it is learned, as Sizer's work has aptly indicated.[22]

Internally, using Sizer's *Horace's School* as a model, we can suggest that schools need to structure themselves to be much more open and flexible. They need to be more oriented toward active learning with teachers serving more as facilitators of students working on projects focused around some core curriculum areas than as fountains of knowledge. They need to foster problem-solving and communication skills, student initiative, and a love of learning that lasts throughout a student's life by focusing on active learning methodologies. Sizer does an excellent job of illustrating one model for achieving these types of goals and there are many others that might also be pointed out.

But what is too often overlooked in the discussions of school reform are the ways in which the school structure might be modified to deal with the important external constituencies that have been discussed in earlier chapters (see Figure 7.4). In the next chapter I will more fully explore these relationships and the ways in which schools can restructure so that they are linked to these constituencies using a form of alliance building that reshapes the school from an inflexible, highly centralized, heavily bounded bureaucracy into an open, flexible, and adaptable learning organization intimately connected with those important groups and organizations in its environment. Many business organizations have adopted this form of organization, which is called a network organization and found that it has enabled them to far better cope with the external conditions they face. This is not an easy organizational configuration to adopt, because responsibility and power for achieving results are shared among allies, those with whom an organization is linked. But the very

Figure 7.4
A Solution Taking the Social Burden Off Schools

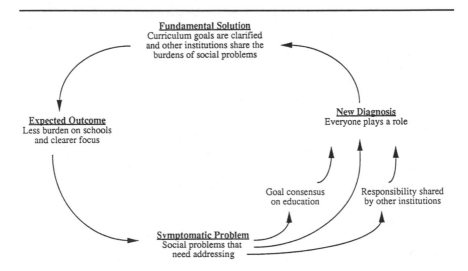

sharing of responsibility for education is what this book has been arguing is absolutely necessary for the long term.

THE PROCESS OF RESTRUCTURING

Problems of education are what are termed metaproblems or messes, that is, they are problems without clear boundaries or ready solutions. They are problems for which simple programs will not work and that single institutions cannot handle alone. As a nation we can no longer afford to have each of our institutions act as if it could accomplish its purposes single-handedly (if indeed, we ever could) or to have individuals or institutions abrogating the bulk of their responsibility for forming and maintaining communities.

Ultimately, metaproblems require that multiple actors become involved in a lengthy, sometimes contentious, and often difficult, process of collaboration if they are to be resolved. For example, problems of environment, social decay, poverty, and poor education cannot be handled by one institution, whether it is the family, the school, or the government. Such problems by their very nature cannot be solved by *single* institutions, yet as Bellah and colleagues have recently pointed out, "we live through institutions" and, as they further point out, "we have begun to lose trust in our institutions."[23] Since single-handed solutions are unlikely to work, collaborative or coalitional solutions then become necessary. It is this perspective that enables us to make progress in the reform process.

Organizational transformation of the sort that is represented by systemic restructuring into a collaborative model is difficult, time consuming, and costly. If one believes that the real problems lie elsewhere then undertaking that transformation becomes unlikely. Still, there are some signs that the problems with which schools are being hit have begun to erode slightly the sense of complacency that exists in the public. Among many educators, perhaps particularly those in the inner-city schools, which are facing the most serious social problems, there is growing recognition that something needs to change. Finding the vision, the will, and the wherewithal to actually make changes, however, is not easy.

Arguably, this process can be begun through an enlivened process of public dialogue about the roles, responsibilities, and expectations for schools and the constituencies surrounding them. Dialogue, of course, is not enough, however, since attitudes and perceptions are critical to establishing a sense of urgency that schools do in fact need to change, raising a serious and nonideological conversation[24] about schools.

NOTES

1. See J. B. Quinn (1992), "The Intelligent Enterprise: A New Paradigm," *Academy of Management Executive* 6(4): 48–63.

2. Carnegie Foundation for the Advancement of Teaching (1992), *School Choice* (Princeton: Carnegie Foundation for the Advancement of Teaching), 76.

3. Carnegie Foundation (1992), 76.

4. Carnegie Foundation (1992), 77.

5. L. E. Preston and J. E. Post use this term along with the term to be discussed below, "interpenetrating systems" in their seminal book, (1975) *Private Management and Public Policy: The Principle of Public Responsibility* (Englewood Cliffs, NJ: Prentice-Hall).

6. See, for example, three papers by S. A. Waddock: (1992b), "The National Alliance of Business Compact Project: Business Involvement in Public Education," *Research in Corporate Social Performance and Policy*, 13; (1993a), "Lessons from the National Alliance of Business Compact Project: Business and Public Education Reform," *Human Relations* 46(7): 849–879; and (1992a), "The Business Role in School Reform: From Feeling Good to System Change," *International Journal of Value-Based Management* 5(2): 105–126.

7. Preston and Post (1975), 27–28.

8. P. M. Senge in (1991) *The Fifth Discipline: The Art and Practice of the Learning Organization* (New York: Doubleday), suggests this concept of leverage.

9. Carnegie Foundation (1992), 76.

10. See, e.g., D. A. Nadler and M. L. Tushman (1989), "Organizational Frame Bending: Principles for Managing Reorientation," *The Academy of Management Executive* 3(3): 194–204. Much of the following discussion will use the ideas of Nadler and Tushman to frame organizational changes that might make systems changes within schools feasible.

11. Nadler and Tushman (1989), 196.

12. See Senge (1991). Senge's concept of the learning organization forms the core concept for continuous improvement, innovation, and reform that is central to the restructured internal and external relationships that will be proposed in the ensuing chapters.

13. Nadler and Tushman (1989), 197–199. The ensuing discussion follows their model for large-scale organizational change efforts.

14. See the Carnegie Foundation report on School Choice (1992), for an in-depth discussion.

15. Senge (1991), develops this concept in detail.

16. Personal communication, Sandra Byrne, Project Director, National Alliance of Business.

17. Nadler and Tushman (1989).

18. Nadler and Tushman (1989), 200.

19. See T. R. Sizer (1992), *Horace's School: Redesigning the American High School* (Boston: Houghton Mifflin Company).

20. See C. Sykes (1992), *A Nation of Victims: The Decay of the American Character* (New York: St. Martin's Press).

21. See, e.g., A. Kotlowitz (1991), *There Are No Children Here: The Story of Two Boys Growing Up in the Other America* (New York: Doubleday) for a compelling

description of the lives of inner-city children facing the "sea of social problems" that the Carnegie Foundation identifies.

22. See Sizer (1992).

23. R. N. Bellah, R. Madsen, W. M. Sullivan, A. Swidler, and S. M. Tipton do a remarkable job of defining some serious problems in society as well as the need for reforming some of our institutions in their book (1991), *The Good Society* (New York: Alfred A. Knopf), 3.

24. E. Freeman and J. Liedtka discuss the importance of good conversations in (1991), "Corporate Social Responsibility: A Critical Approach," *Business Horizons*, July–August: 92–98.

Chapter 8

Structure as Solution

Over the past forty years, there has seemingly been a steady but persistent decrease in the amount of attention that schools are able to pay to content and curriculum of education as the goals of education have become less clear, curriculum has expanded, and social problems have been dumped into schools for resolution. Concurrently, then, there seems to have been a steady increase in the social content with which schools have to contend. This dynamic is illustrated in Figure 8.1, and is highlighted in reports of what students and teachers pay attention to. In the 1940s and 1950s, major concerns were disciplinary, but related to issues of chewing gum, tardiness, or talking in class. By the 1980s, the issues had shifted to drug abuse, violence, and safety, among others.

This same problem can be viewed another way by suggesting that the amount of education that is actually delivered in the schools may vary systematically by socioeconomic category. Higher socioeconomic families can still "purchase" a good deal of educational content for their children, either by moving to expensive suburbs where schools are still considered to be working reasonably well or by sending their children to private schools. Children of middle-income families receive a good deal of educational content, but also experience more social programs geared at dealing with problems in their communities and the mix of families in attendance. For low-income families, especially those in poverty-ridden inner cities and rural areas, the "social" content of schools tends to dominate education concerns as these schools serve more as

Figure 8.1
General Shift of Education's Focus over Time

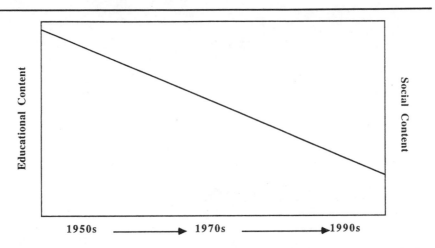

custodial or social service institutions, struggling to maintain discipline
(see Figure 8.2, for a sense of what this dynamic looks like).[1]

Arguably, until we as a society make a serious commitment to deliver
the same educational content to all of our children as the children of the
higher socioeconomic categories receive, we will be miserably failing our
children. But to deliver equal education, we need to deal with the systems
dynamics that have been discussed in recent chapters, to make different
assumptions about teachers and administrators, and to share responsibilities

Figure 8.2
General Focus of Education by Socioeconomic Level

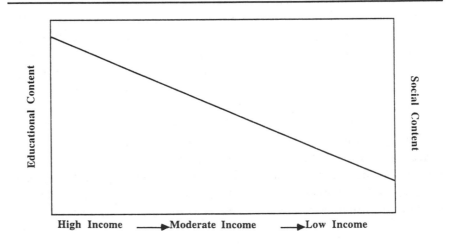

for education with those other institutions in society that rightly bear those responsibilities. In this and in the next chapter, we will see an organizational and systems dynamic strategy for dealing with these issues systemically, while shaping each school to its own local situation. Obviously such a strategy involves the direct and indirect participation of many "actors" other than school officials.

As we have seen, business and government leaders became intensely involved in education reform issues during the 1980s and into the 1990s, along with many reform-minded educators. Too many initiatives, however, took place only at the margins or, in the case of many well-publicized conferences and studies, apart from the world of education. Most efforts did not distinguish the systems dynamics that represented the underlying problems or attempt to deal with those dynamics systematically. Too few recognized the essential interdependence of schools with other institutions and the ways in which their actions influence each other. In the end, too many of these initiatives had the appearance of imposing change from without, rather than fostering change from within. The result was that there was little substantive change within schools through the 1980s or into the 1990s.

By the early 1990s, however, there were signs that things were beginning to change, albeit slowly. The partnership movement had progressed and knowledge about the complexity of education's problems had spread. More studies and policy reports were produced showing the complexity of education's problems and its linkages to other social problems. As these initiatives spread, greater recognition that *all* relevant parties, including educators, parents, and community organizations, needed to work together began to grow. By way of example, by 1993, the Committee for Economic Development, which had a long-standing interest in education reform, produced a report entitled *Why Child Care Matters*,[2] the subtitle of which was "Preparing Young Children for a More Productive America." This report explicitly links child care, parenting, education, and workforce productivity in a way suggestive of systems thinking. Thus, it seems that some of the problems of systems dynamics and external influences affecting schools were beginning to be understood more broadly than in the past. In addition, some schools and school systems began addressing some of the underlying issues more systemically through radically restructuring their internal and external operations.[3]

It has also become increasingly clear that school reform must come from within and cannot be imposed from without. Whatever some reformers might desire, it is unlikely that existing personnel and school systems will be eliminated to begin again in a sort of zero-based reform approach.

Therefore, current school officials themselves must eventually become able to think creatively and strategically about the reform, regeneration, and, ultimately, radical restructuring of schools, just as many businesses and even public agencies have had to do over the past decade (and, indeed, are still doing). School leaders themselves now need to understand and then make the case for sharing responsibility for education among a range of institutions. In sharing this responsibility, they will be forced to find ways of restructuring their own operations and activities so that the responsibilities actually are shared and that they empower others, as they themselves wish to be empowered. And, unfortunately, they will need to accomplish these tasks in an environment without the bottom-line pressures that market forces place upon businesses and probably without a lot of new resources.

All of this suggests that school restructuring will present difficult, seemingly intractable, and sometimes overwhelming challenges, especially given the difficulties of organizational change already discussed. But I believe that with creativity, insight, and strategic thinking about the structuring of schools these changes can and should be undertaken. We will use the analogy of a school official as a spider weaving a web of the interdependencies that surround schools and sharing responsibilities along the strands of that web, to describe an organizational alternative to the current highly bureaucratic structuring of schools. The alternative is a network structure externally and a rethinking of the internal processes of education that represents a fundamental "reengineering" of the schools.[4]

This chapter, then, will focus on the ways in which schools can restructure themselves to take advantage of the systems dynamics that affect them rather than letting those dynamics affect them negatively as we have seen is now happening. I will argue that by turning themselves "inside out" and forming appropriate linkages, schools can become network organizations that deliberately and strategically work to share responsibility for education with key constituents or stakeholders in their environments. In the next chapter, we will explore in some detail the strands of the web and the ways in which the network structure might be developed, depending upon local circumstances, to develop a holistic approach to education.

NETWORK ORGANIZATIONS AND THE SCHOOLS

Organizational structure and strategy have always been tightly linked in practice as well as in theory.[5] In recent years, many business organizations have shifted their organizational form from the traditional pyramid toward more of a network structure by building in alliances, joint ventures, on-going linkages with suppliers and customers, and social partnerships. Many modern strategies demand flexibility, immediate decision making, and adaptiveness to customer needs through technological and service innovations. The network form of organizing, a form that responds well to the many types of influence highlighted in the spider's web of influences on schools, is proving to be best suited to these demands. Networks permit organizations to respond flexibly to many demands simultaneously, but without committing the whole organization to any one initiative.

The many alliances both internal and external that constitute the network organization push decision-making authority out to the boundaries of the enterprise, where the alliances and linkages take place. Because decisions can take place on the spot, network organizations can provide adaptive, immediate, and flexible responses more readily than can bureaucracies, which tend to rely on the command and control of policies, procedures, and rules. And network organizations have fractal qualities, in that they tend to reflect the whole in their parts; each unit at the boundaries is, in a metaphorical sense, a holistic version of the entire entity, reflecting both the operating values and organizational style of the whole.[6]

Alliances by their nature break down the barriers that exist among organizations; they blur the boundaries between allies and force the allies to create systems that literally and figuratively interpenetrate. They create a set of relationships that help contend with multiple aspects of problems simultaneously by relying on the skills and talents of individuals with significantly different perspectives. By bringing together the forces of more than one type of organization or institution, alliances enhance the ability of an organization to deal with difficult strategic issues, problems, markets, or technologies. They are particularly useful in situations where no one institution can resolve the problem or issue alone, a situation exemplified by education, as the spider's web suggests.

Alliances implicitly recognize the inherent interdependence of the allies. Common to many organizations today, which have entered into what are termed strategic alliances, supplier-customer networks, and public-private partnerships, among other types of arrangements, the network structure is a recent innovation in organizational design. Like the spider's web of external influences on schools that was described in Chapter 5, the network also has the potential to provide strength, dynamism, and flexibility to a school at its center as the school taps those influential institutions and shares responsibility with them.[7] Network structures have the advantage of permitting each school and district to individualize linkages and relationships to the specific needs of the local community and students, while still maintaining their organizational autonomy, specific goals, and operating modes. They represent an adaptive structurally based set of responses to a complex and multidimensional problem.

Network structures have certain disadvantages, too, because they are inherently both complex and fragile. They depend to a great extent for their success on the effectiveness of the *relationships* that are established, relationships that link the nodal points in the network. To the extent that networks depend upon the building of relationships among allies, they also depend on the *processes* on which those relationships are built. These processes include negotiation, mutual interaction and adjustment, interdependence, trust building, and communication. Networks provide the advantage of more heads combined around difficult problem areas, shared responsibility, and shared resources. At the same time, they require greater interpersonal management skills and attention to negotiation, communication, power sharing, and trust building. In the network, the processes of relationship building become as important as the content of the collaborative effort.

Following this line of thinking, I will make the case that schools can use their structures to strategic advantage in achieving their educational objectives by forming alliances, that is, building a network, with key institutions externally and by recreating themselves internally into a loosely structured, but active network that focuses on education and its processes. Schools can, that is, find help to achieve their educational goals if they make appropriate *linkages* to key stakeholders and stakeholder groups, while simultaneously assuming their own appropriate duties and responsibilities. In making this transformation, school officials—teachers and administrators alike—will need to act like the industrious spider, spinning the web anew with each day that passes or each tear that occurs.

Schools will also need to transform their structures away from the traditional, bureaucratic pyramid in which command and control management dominates. As they become networks, schools will have to turn themselves literally and figuratively inside out, tapping the advantages of the network form and minimizing the disadvantages, forging alliances with parents, businesses, local civic and community groups, government and human service agencies, and the media, to name only a few potential allies, on an as-needed basis. This transformation will help schools tap into critical external resources, share responsibility for education, and build support in their external communities, while drawing others into greater understanding of and commitment to education for children.

Schools have traditionally been viewed as what are termed loosely coupled systems.[8] This perspective, however, has typically focused on the internal organization of schools, while the present analysis focuses primarily on the implications of boundary relations. The difficulties of improving performance in schools exist precisely because schools are loosely coupled systems both internally and externally. Loose coupling means that activities within an entity are only loosely coordinated, that individuals may have considerable autonomy (even when they are bound by rules and regulations, as most schools are), and that building consensus and common goals is a difficult process because there are few means in place to bring the groups and individuals within the entity together.

Certainly loose coupling does describe schools, with teachers and administrators often at odds, with each classroom operating essentially independently, and with the many barriers already described inhibiting any "outside" interference with school operations. Loose couplings make school reform all the more difficult to accomplish because so many different groups and individuals must be influenced to change and because they are not tightly bound together. Changing one does not necessarily change them all, though, as systems dynamics theory indicates, the right levers can make a considerable difference. Paradoxically, however, these same loose couplings perhaps also offer the best solution to the problems that schools face providing they can be creatively used.

The invisible barriers that have been erected by many schools create an aura of "professionalism" that prevents many parents from becoming involved in their children's education or other outsiders from influencing—or in school lexicon, interfering—with school policies. Businesses, until quite recently, have been excluded from influencing school curricula or suggesting appropriate outcomes because of decidedly antibusiness sentiments on the part of many teachers and administrators (of course, the feeling has also been decidedly mutual, evidence the saying, "If you can't do it, teach it."). Community organizations and government agencies are kept at bay, offering their services through entirely different policy sectors, which are themselves infrequently linked into a coherent system to provide services in a holistic way.

The loosely coupled system has the characteristic of buffering its technical core from harsh external influences, much as schools have done in isolating teachers in separate classrooms. It is now clear, however, that developing more linkages within schools among teachers to focus on what is being taught, how it is being taught, and why it is being taught is critical to improving schools, as Sizer has poignantly pointed out.[9] Internal networks can and should be adopted that assist teachers and administrators in developing their ideas and in *sharing what they already know and making radical changes in the process and content of education to meet the demands of the twenty-first century*. It is also becoming clear that linkages to external stakeholders will be a critical aspect of sharing responsibility for education and one that educators are only beginning to address.

Here a key assumption needs to be made to effect significant school reform: teachers and administrators *do* have the skills and talent, the ideas and imagination, the energy and the drive necessary to make the changes required for schools to improve their performance and meet the demands of the twenty-first century. *But they need to be given the proper resources with which to accomplish these tasks*, as Sizer so eloquently points out: time (in particular), facilitation by individuals knowledgeable about organizational change, support from the top, help with communication, and money to reward people for their efforts above and beyond the call of duty. Most particularly, they need time and support to establish the dialogues that lead to change.

Trust, in any network of relationships, internal or external, is essential and one of the most problematic things to achieve. If those of us outside of schools do not trust that teachers and administrators have the skills and talents needed to undertake the necessary transformation of the schools, we will never (through taxes and public policies) give them the resources to do so. If, as a society, we assume that teachers and administrators are incapable of the kind of changes that are necessary to improve schools, then we have created a self-fulfilling prophecy. Based on that assumption, we will never develop enough trust in their abilities to provide them with the resources they need to do their job of reform, nor with adequate incentives to deal with the hard work, conflict, and political pressures that systems change necessarily involves, which were described earlier. Time is perhaps the key resource, both in terms of finding time for "good conversations" among teachers and administrators so they can determine what they are about, but also for them to have more time during the school day and year to fit in the many new demands they must ultimately meet in establishing similar dialogues with external stakeholders. Also needed are training, facilitation of the process of change, money for resources and supplies, and support.

Since Sizer has done such a good job of illustrating how internal relations in schools might be restructured to focus on the process of education as well as its content and outcomes, and since this is not my expertise, this area will not be dealt with extensively here. Rather, I will focus on the *external linkages* that schools need to make so that they assure that responsibility is shared among relevant community members.

To develop a network structure that responds to the spider's web of external influences on school performance, it is important that school officials recognize that they need to be open or permeable to external influences.[10] Perhaps even more difficult than the internal changes that must be made, which school officials can be assumed to have significant knowledge of and expertise in, is the mind-set change that must occur so that school personnel themselves can begin rethinking their roles with respect to those groups and institutions they now view as part of the external world. Conversely, these same school officials will need to find the imagination and spark that kindles a rethinking of the school-outside constituency relationship in those constituencies' minds as well.

External influences affect schools through their boundary relationships with other institutions, such as government and social agencies, businesses, and teacher preparation institutions. Arguably then, improving schools dramatically requires substantially altering these boundary relationships and influencing what goes on in these other institutions as well as making substantial changes within schools themselves. In the discussion of the spider's web in Chapter 5, we have already focused at some length on what these external influences are and how they affect school performance, and we then explored the systems dynamics affecting schools because of these influences. Since schools face an extraordinary set of influences deriving from the spider's web described in Chapter 5, perhaps it is time for school officials to begin to view themselves as spiders industriously taking charge of weaving a web that can support the weight of responsibilities that all stakeholder institutions must bear in educating children.

WEAVING THE WEB

Consider the spider. Resourceful: able to build a web based on whatever structures are available in the particular location in which the web is to be built. Industrious and hard working: spinning the web relentlessly, daily if necessary, and repairing it whenever there is a break. Creative, commanding, and ingenious: making the web fit the situation at hand, building linkages where none exist, trapping what it needs for survival and success in life. Aesthetic: beautiful structures emerge from the strands that weave the web. Effective: the web is strong enough to capture the spider's prey. The web does the job and does it well.

Educators need to become spiders in the positive senses noted above, working hard to forge links with their many constituencies, weaving the strands of relationships that currently do not exist. Transforming school structures into webs, networks of allies who can bear some of the burdens of education, repairing the linkages, and building new links where none have previously existed. Making the whole network strong enough to support the needs of students without overburdening any one element. And beautiful and effective: creating a new vision of education that communities can help to weave and that is strong enough to capture everyone's interest and attention. Such vision comes only through the involvement of those people with a stake in the outcome.

What, then, are the leverage points to achieve this transformation? The systems dynamics suggest that the levers may be more clearly articulated goals and a fundamental restructuring of the linkages and responsibilities among schools and other institutions. Clear goals would allow educators to determine what they are and, importantly, what they are not, responsible for. Restructuring through establishing linkages to other institutions enhances the potential for sharing those responsibilities that are rightly spread throughout the network. Internal restructuring along the lines proposed by Sizer also promotes a reconsideration of educational goals, pedagogy, and structure. Rebuilding the community infrastructure so that it supports rather than hinders schools may also be necessary, and could be a part of what occurs through an on-going dialogue about schools and their needs.

The *key* to beginning this process is in establishing an on-going, creative dialogue among those constituents with a stake in education: parents, civic officials, social service agencies, health care organizations, church leaders, media representatives, and local business and labor leaders, among others. In short, anyone with an interest in better education should be an active participant in the dialogue about education. Schools, as the focal point for education, need to be the primary initiators of the dialogue, although, as with the Department of Education's GOALS 2000 program, others can also begin the process.

The focus of the dialogue should be on what the real problems of education in a given community are, what roles various institutions and groups play in education, and how to go about making changes. Once the dialogue is established, it needs to become more than empty conversation. Actual changes need to be made in the way that stakeholders relate to schools, barriers that now exist need to be broken down, and on-going communication lines opened. Schools, in short, need to be "networked" to their "suppliers," that is, the families from whom students come and the educational institutions from which their teachers come; to their "customers," that is, the businesses and other organizations that will employ graduates; and to their "supporters," that is, those other institutions that provide support functions to the schools: publishers, human service agencies, local YMCAs, churches, newspapers, local radio and television stations, and so on.

Ultimately, this strategy of reorganizing as a network retains *primary* responsibility on the shoulders of educators, where that responsibility belongs. It makes educators responsible for establishing key relationships between schools and other important constituencies. The strategy may also make the job of education more complex than it currently is, because of the demands of establishing and maintaining many alliances. But this strategy also places *secondary* responsibility for *dealing with* the influences on education on the shoulders of those with whom the school establishes linkages, thereby spreading out responsibility to the entire web of institutions that impact education. The structural transformation, as with the transformation that is taking place in the business community, needs to be driven by a new vision of what it means to be a school, by fundamental rethinking of the goals of education, and by massive structural redefinition. The definition of goals arguably constitutes a key leverage point for redefining schools and their external relationships. It can determine what is feasible and important for schools to do themselves with respect to education and what others ought to be doing.

The beauty of the network structure is that it can allow each school to define and then establish relationships to *meet its own needs and its community's own circumstances*. Although the approach to school reform proposed here has common elements across all schools in that the network is suggested as a way to structure, the very concept of network permits individualization to the unique needs of any given community.

Under this transformation, educators are specifically responsible for defining curriculum content, goals, and processes, which we have already seen are key leverage points. School officials also need to accept the fact that, while the ills of society that have been dumped on them in recent years do, in fact, need to be taken care of, other agencies or institutions may bear some or even primary responsibility for dealing with those ills. Schools in this model become a *facilitator* for students and their families receiving services they need because they are linked to other organizations that can provide these services. In this way school officials can team up with civic leaders and others concerned about the rebuilding of community infrastructure, without themselves assuming all of the burdens of that infrastructure.

This type of thinking enables schools to both accept responsibilities that they will likely find it difficult to avoid, and to share them appropriately with other institutions, who bear responsibility for certain aspects of problems affecting schools. Depending on local circumstances, schools might find themselves allying with a variety of organizations: social service agencies, churches, day-care centers, businesses, institutions of higher education, governmental and political bodies, to name a few. This model places considerable burden on the schools because both principals and teachers will have to spend significant energy on establishing and maintaining appropriate connections externally. But, if well done, it will also relieve the schools of the de facto social service agency stance they have assumed by default as well as of their "parental" responsibilities.

NOT SCHOOLS ALONE: ALL MUST CHANGE

School officials have to give up something in this new conception and in making the transformations proposed. What they have to give up is the notion that education occurs only in the context of formal schooling.[11] Families are the first and probably primary educators of children and need to be brought much more closely into partnership with schools, breaking down the barriers that have kept them on the outside. Museums, libraries, television, magazines and newspapers, churches, civic, and political organizations and the events they sponsor serve as educational vehicles. Businesses play an important educative role not only with respect to their employment opportunities and economic roles, but also with respect to their family policies, their cultures and values, which are transmitted to employees, and their economic policies. Governmental and human service agencies provide the so-called safety net that supports families in need. Health care organizations are key in providing basic health-related services. Religious institutions and the media generally shape the values and attitudes that prevail in society in important ways.

The important thing to recognize in this transformation is that it is not one sided. While it is true that schools have to dramatically alter their structures and operating modes to achieve better results, the linkages that they make will also demand that other institutions change as well. The process of forming alliances and collaborations is inherently an *interactive* process, demanding change on both sides. Hence, for example, businesses may find themselves altering hiring policies, employment policies, plant location decisions, and family policies, as will be discussed in more detail in the next chapter. Church and civic leaders, for example, may need to take a more active stance in voicing concern about children and in establishing arrangements that substitute for failing community infrastructures.

The media needs to recognize its own powerful role in shaping attitudes and values, as well as its own educative role. The profiteering attitude that has shaped recent history may need to become subject to public discourse and children need to be exposed to attitudes that value rather than demean education. And, as the process of attempting to "reinvent" government continues, it will be important for policy makers and bureaucrats alike to think about the ways in which governmental policies can be brought together into a coherent set of policies that helps people deal with the now divisive issues of race and class that keep us in separate enclaves[12] rather than bringing us together to help our children and their families. Some of the ways in which links might be established so that these interactions can be used to help schools will be explored in more detail in the next chapter.

BOUND BY COMMON VALUES

What is to hold together this loosely coupled network of students, teachers, and administrators with the many allies that they are expected to form? First is that they need to share a common goal about the value of learning and education, about what it is important to learn, and about how one goes about obtaining requisite knowledge and competencies. Education, that is, needs to become a real, and not just an espoused, priority for educators, families, public policy makers, and employers. Putting this "real" priority into action requires real and specific changes in day-to-day behaviors and the attitudes that we convey to our children about the worth of what they are doing.

Next is probably a focus on the worth of children, not just the children of the better off and not just children who look like "me," whatever I look like, but all children. In the currency of modern talk about education, one fundamental tenet seems to be that "all children can learn." This is not common to today's educational institution, but it does characterize the more successful Japanese and German schools. Without such an assumption, schools are probably fated to restrict their best efforts to only those children who look like the teachers and come from the same, more education-oriented class that the teachers and administrators themselves come from. Such a shift may be one of the fundamental levers in the systems dynamics of school reform, one that is too infrequently recognized. This shift also implies recognizing the worth of the work of education and the work of those who "do" education: teachers and administrators.

A third value is the recognition that all parties to the education process have something valuable to place on the table and that the way to determine that value is through an on-going process of dialogue and actions that result from that dialogue. Collaboration necessarily requires dialogue and frequent interaction among collaborators. Raising up the dialogue about education to ask questions of what is to be done and how, by whom, and whose responsibility it is, shifts away from blaming schools or parents for their failures. A dialogue about common goals shifts the discussion toward *solutions* and makes the implicit assumption that, since we are all in this together, we can solve the problem together, that we all have talents that can be tapped to find appropriate solutions for this particular community and its specific circumstances.

A fourth value is to recognize that there is a whole child who lives within a *system* of interactive institutions. Rather than thinking in fragments or pieces of problems, school officials and those they work with need to recognize that actions in one arena affect what happens in other arenas and, with this recognition, to put in place mutually responsive programs.

A final and perhaps critical value important to the restructuring process itself is that nothing is sacred. Like the process of reengineering, focusing on the systems dynamics of school reform requires asking questions that assume that the ways things are done now or the way they have always been done is not necessarily the way that they should be done. Just because, for example, parents have been largely kept out of curriculum decisions in the past, does not mean that they should not influence curriculum now and in the future. Just because teachers have always lectured, does not mean that that is the most appropriate or best method of instruction. Just because classes have traditionally been broken into age groupings does not mean that this practice is pedagogically sound. Just because businesspeople, church leaders, civic officials, and health providers, to name a few, have been kept out of the schools except as occasional guest speakers, does not mean that their future roles need be so limited. And just because instruction has taken place mainly in the classroom does not mean that classrooms are the only places where learning occurs.

WORKING THE INTERSTICES

What would a school that is networked look like? The day might be structured quite differently than it currently is. Many of the old rules and regulations, so sacred to unions and bureaucrats alike, might have to be abandoned, as teachers, for example, start their days with team meetings to determine a particular curriculum for a group of children, or as teachers and parents meet over coffee to discuss discipline and curriculum innovations, while the children play in the gym under the supervision of the gym teacher. Some classes might meet at settings outside of the school, the local hospital or a local business, for example, on a periodic or regular basis, as a way of linking their curriculum with issues they will face in the "real" world (e.g., a curriculum on AIDS and health might be taught by a local epidemiologist and, for students hoping to work with computers, a local business might offer weekly seminars on business computing).

Key to the success of this strategy will be the ability of those individuals who sit at the boundaries of schools and make the linkages to other institutions to envision how the linkages will operate in the interests of the child and of the educational process. The nature of education shifts, according to this definition, with increasing demands placed upon teachers and administrators not only to reshape the way they do their work (or "re-engineer" it to use current business slang), by asking the question, "If we were to start over today, how would we envision education?"[13] In a sense, asking and answering this question is what Sizer has done in *Horace's School*, in which a committee charged with school reform basically reinvents the ways in which education takes place. In the next two chapters, we will explore some of the ways in which such linkages are already being made and make some suggestions about what other types of arrangements might be possible.

NOTES

1. Thanks to James E. Post formerly of Boston University's Management Policy Department and now of The Conference Board for a conversation in which these ideas were clarified and articulated.

2. Committee for Economic Development (1993), *Why Child Care Matters: Preparing Young Children for a More Productive America* (New York: Committee for Economic Development).

3. Examples of cities where such changes were beginning include Louisville, Kentucky; Cincinnati, Ohio; and Portland, Oregon, where at least some of the key actors were looking at the interrelationships that exist among social problems, education, and business success.

4. M. Hammer and J. Champy (1993), *Reengineering the Corporation: A Manifesto for Business Revolution* (New York: Harper Business).

5. The classic book making this point, of course, is by A. D. Chandler, Jr. (1962), *Strategy and Structure: Chapters in the History of the American Industrial Enterprise* (Cambridge, MA: MIT Press).

6. S. A. Waddock (1993d), "The Fractal Organization or Alliances, Networks, and Fragments: How Organizations Adapt to Chaos," presented at the 1993 Academy of Management Annual Meeting, Atlanta, GA, deals with these fractal qualities in some detail.

7. Both the concept of spider's web and the network, by the way, can be applied with any type of institution or social problem at the center. For example, in Boston, the Persistent Poverty Program sponsored by the Boston Foundation and the Rockefeller Foundation places the issue of poverty at the hub of a similar set of relationships.

8. K. E. Weick (1976), "Educational Organizations as Loosely Coupled Systems." *Administrative Science Quarterly* 21(1): 1–11, 19.

9. T. R. Sizer (1992), *Horace's School: Redesigning the American High School* (Boston: Houghton Mifflin Company).

10. See, e.g., J. D. Orton, and K. E. Weick's (1990) article, "Loosely Coupled Systems: A Reconceptualization," *The Academy of Management Review* 15(2): 203–223.

11. L. A. Cremin deals with these arenas extensively in (1988), *American Education: The Metropolitan Experience, 1876–1980* (New York: Harper & Row); and (1990), *Popular Education and Its Discontents* (New York: Harper & Row).

12. See R. B. Reich's (1991a) *The Work of Nations: Preparing Ourselves for Twenty-first Century Capitalism* (New York: Alfred A. Knopf), for a telling analysis of the separation of the upper from the growing under class.

13. This is the fundamental question that Hammer and Champy ask in *Reengineering the Corporation: A Manifesto for Business Revolution* (1993).

Chapter 9 _____
Networks and Schools

Looking at the spider's web, we can generalize about the possible linkages that schools might make and how other institutions may need to change so that they can accept their share of the responsibility for education. We can also look at some instances in which such linkages are already happening, albeit typically in piecemeal fashion. A holistic approach would be based on a complete diagnosis of a community's specific needs, an on-going series of conversations with key constituents or stakeholders (including school officials), in the schools and a plan for making necessary external linkages in conjunction with a restructuring, indeed a re-engineering, internal to the schools. In short, schools themselves must shape the spider's web within which they will reside.

This chapter, then, will explore the potential leverage points in the *linkages* that different stakeholders in the educational process have on the systems dynamics of educational performance. In exploring these linkages, we will try to look not only at what currently exists, but also at some examples of what might exist in holistically designed linkages between schools and their constituencies, a set of relationships that can move the systems dynamics from their current negative spiral downward into a more positive upward spiral. These links if established as needed within communities would, it is posited, spread responsibility for children and for education among a wider range of constituencies than currently accepts that responsibility. These links could also help each stakeholder develop a sense of accountability for the results of the educational process, especially if the focus is on improved outcomes and if standards for achieving those outcomes are explicitly defined through the goal-setting process that, it was argued in the last chapter, is the key point of leverage for changing overall systems dynamics.

FIRST LINK: THE FAMILY

The family level of activity surrounds the school. When parents fail to assume responsibility for providing guidance, educational opportunities, and appropriate attitudes toward education for their children, the schools are left in fairly dire straits, as we have seen. And the reality is that far too many schools are in those straits today as a result of the stresses of poverty, single or two-earner parenthood, divorce, stepfamilies, and other constraints that have placed enormous pressures on parents and made it more difficult than ever to spend the time necessary to raise children successfully. And as we have also seen, schools have been remarkably loath to break down the barriers of professionalism and isolation that have effectively distanced them from parents, except for the efforts of some PTAs to raise money from bake sales and the like for marginal improvements in the school.

The situation described above is not the way that relations between schools and parents are likely to be most effective. There is a wide range of things that teachers and schools can do to 1) establish better and more open communications with the home; 2) break down some of the barriers that exist between home and school; and 3) help parents with their task of parenting, thereby relieving schools of some of that responsibility, so that schools can perform their job of educating. The first two goals can be accomplished largely structurally, through development of systems of communication and better ways of systemically opening up the schools to parents. The third goal probably needs to be tackled programmatically, through developing programs that enhance parents' skills as well as through important dialogues that occur between teachers and parents.

The web of relationships into which parents need to be drawn must realistically assess what the parents can offer and make the kinds of demands that directly involve them in the school in important, meaningful, and significant ways, rather than in the superficial, mostly fund-raising ways that many schools use to keep parents "involved," but at arm's length. Even parents with limited education are typically concerned about their children's own education and their prospects; they can be engaged if their participation is meaningful and if efforts are made to draw them in, keep them informed, communicate the mutual responsibilities that schools *and*

parents bear, and constantly provide feedback on how well those responsibilities are being met.

Although teachers tend to think about the one-to-one relationship
between themselves and their students, a shift toward systemic thinking
that informs parents about what is going on in the classroom, develops
appropriate attitudes and expectations about school performance for students, and illuminates the joint roles and responsibilities of school personnel and parents is critical. Schools need to accomplish these objectives
without being patronizing, since parents are a critical link in the transition
toward a school that is using networks to spread responsibility. In developing the parent-school linkages, the teachers and administrators must first
diagnose the situation they face: What types of families live in the
community? What are their own structural or personal problems with
respect to school (dual-earner families, single parents, unemployed
parents)? How well educated are parents, in general, and what is their
attitude toward education? Are parents likely to be intimidated by the
school? What are the barriers for those families in joining in partnership
with the schools (language, culture, family structure, working patterns)?

Once the diagnosis has been made through an understanding of local
demography and discussions with a representative group of involved
parents, then the process of developing systems within the school that
enhance interaction can begin. There are many possibilities, only some of
which will be relevant to any given school, but some ideas will be proposed
in this chapter (and can be elaborated by the talents of teachers, administrators, and parents in specific schools). The important point to
remember is that a *system* of communicating and establishing on-going
linkages needs to be created to deal with the goals above or those that have
been developed for a specific school.[1]

Traditionally, schools have held yearly open-houses as a ritualized way
of meeting parents. These have been supplemented by parent-teacher
associations or organizations (PTA or PTO) which in general have focused
on issues related to raising marginal funds for school activities, rather than
school policy or curricular issues. Too often run by a few dedicated parents
rather than a broadly representative group, parent organizations, such as
PTAs or the advisory bodies now being created in states like Massachusetts
as part of the governance of schools, have the potential to become deeply
involved in important school issues if only teachers and principals are open
to that possibility. Parent groups can and should be brought into discussions about school goals and core values, curriculum, about school governance, about standards and expectations for students and teachers, and
about policies and procedures affecting students (e.g., homework policies,

discipline). Comer[2] has demonstrated the value of parent involvement in schools, even in the poorest of districts, provided that involvement is real and not superficial. Open-houses in which teachers talk "at" parents may be less effective than engaging parents in a dialogue about expectations for their children, how the curriculum will meet those expectations, and what parents' roles are in helping children.

One traditional vehicle for communicating between school and home is the school newsletter. In these days when families come in a wide variety of structures, including traditional nuclear families, stepfamilies, parents in their late thirties and forties with young children, teen mothers, mothers on public assistance, two-earner couples, single parents of both genders, gay couples with children, grandparents raising children, and across a range of socioeconomic categories, but with some 20 percent of children living in poverty, the traditional newsletter is both imperative and in need of significant change. The weekly newsletter from the school, sometimes put together by teachers, sometimes by parents, sometimes by administrators, is a crucial tool in one-way communication from the school to the home. It provides a forum for a school with a clear set of goals for its students, created through an extensive public dialogue that includes parents, teachers, administrators, and other community-based stakeholders, the newsletter is essential for communicating the core values and key events happening in the school.

But schoolwide newsletters are, in general, one way and tell only fairly general things about what is going on in the school. Though they are more important than ever in conveying attitudes and values about education, as well as what is going on, they do not tell parents enough about what is happening to their own children. Other mechanisms need to be opened up that involve more specific information about a particular child's class and that provide the opportunity for two-way communication and for input by parents into the child's education. One possibility is for each teacher to develop a weekly or biweekly classroom-based newsletter that informs parents in general about what's happening and that invites them to become involved in their child's education regularly. Homework assignments and expectations about how and when that homework will be done, as well as the role that the parent can and should play with respect to the homework, can be articulated in such a classroom note. It can even be both educationally productive and informative to have children contribute to a weekly newsletter, as the first-grade teacher in my son's school discovered. Parents tend to read what their children have written about the elementary classroom; children get practice in writing and are "published"; and parents are better informed about what is happening in the classroom. A newsletter, then, is an important first step in communicating with the home, but only a first step, especially since it is one-way communication. Thinking about the community diagnosis, suppose, for example, that language is a barrier for some parents. Why not ask children, as part of their homework to translate the classroom newsletter for their parents and have parents sign a form attached that they send back, signifying that their children have done this assignment. If overstressed, two-career parents dominate the families, then these notes become even more critical since they can quickly inform parents about what is going on without putting more stress on them, but at the same time, they can accept the importance of parents paying attention to their children's school performance, homework, and out-of-school time.

Many teachers will claim that they can't write or don't have time, or that writing newsletters is not in their contracts, but many of them will be brought on board to such ideas once they realize that many problems they face daily would be solved with better communication between school and home. In some schools, communication efforts have been enhanced by putting phones in the classroom so that teachers can call home, leave a message if necessary, when Johnny or Suzie does a particularly good job (as well as when there is a problem). Even when this is not possible (and cost will probably rule it out for most schools), some systems now expect that teachers will make regular efforts to either phone parents on a regular basis or visit students in their homes. Indeed, one of the underpinnings of school reform in Rochester, New York, was just such an expectation of home visits for the teachers. Although these visits are difficult to schedule and require extra work by teachers, they can be very valuable in developing a working relationship between home and school.

There are other systemic and fairly simple tasks that can draw parents in, that is, that provide possible leverage points for change. For example, how are parents greeted when they come into the school? Do they, like children coming in late, have to report to the principal's office? What is the attitude of the staff to visiting parents? What do signs on the door say to parents about how welcome they are at school? For new parents in particular, are there systems in place for welcoming them and bringing them into the school community, making them feel part of the educational process? One school developed a host family program in which each new family was hosted by a family that knew the school, could explain how things were done, and could welcome the new parents personally.

Schools and parents can create forums or at least a form that can provide information to schools. These methods can be used to elicit parental expectations for their children, their concerns, children's areas of strength and problems, and parental goals for their children for the academic year. In turn, teachers can share similar sets of expectations and concerns with parents in a nonevaluative manner so that parents are better informed about the progress their children are making.

As Linda Braun, director of Families First in Boston, points out,

The first way that schools tend to deal with the changing family structure is to apply band-aids. It's like a therapeutic approach, first you get a social worker, but it soon becomes apparent that many kids need that kind of help. Wider systems are needed to deal with the problems. . . . The next step is to look at this situation as normal. This *is* what families are today and these are the things they need. We *know* that we need to work collaboratively with families; we know that it's better to involve parents and families; but we believe in specialization and professionalization, what we know about schools, we know about education, we know what's good for kids in school, and [sometimes teachers do not] believe that parents *should* be involved in their children's education. Another thing that's operating is that many people who have tried to reach out to parents have gotten burned. It's easier to keep families at arm's length, but it doesn't work.

But for education to work, schools and families *must* collaborate, not necessarily on curriculum, but we can talk to and teach each other. We're all on the same wavelength, we can call on each other, we know we need each other to succeed. We need ways for parents to communicate with schools. We need to look at *systems*, keeping parents informed about policies, curriculum, activities going on, transitions. We need ways for parents and schools to be involved with each other. . . . If you develop appropriate structures, then they'll work for 95 percent of the parents and you'll have fewer disgruntled parents. Most parents are disgruntled because they don't know what they want to know, but if you simply put out a handbook or organize a host-parent program, then you help. These things don't necessarily cost money, but they do require creative thinking, and that's where there are the breakdowns and blocks.

Basic building blocks to attain a more systems-oriented approach to linking with and collaborating with students and their families are fairly simple. Teachers need to be better trained in thinking across the range of students, in diagnosing the needs of the community, in talking with and (importantly) listening to the needs of parents and children, and in sharing what they are attempting to do. Simple things, such as regular times when parents can drop by before school opens (recognizing that many parents work and can't be there at 2:30 or 3:00 P.M.), or providing a teacher's home phone number with one hour a week set aside for calls from concerned parents, or teachers making regular calls to parents, can make a tremendous difference in the attitudes of parents and their children toward school. And, as we have seen in earlier chapters, it is the attitude about school that, broadly speaking, may be a key leverage point in long-term school improvement.

All of these ideas, of course, demand time and attention on the part of teachers and, to some extent, from administrators as well. But if they are well implemented based on the needs of the particular school and its community, they can greatly relieve some of the burdens now faced by teachers when children come to school unprepared to learn, with work undone, or with attitude and behavioral problems.

Two-Way Responsibility

Of course, it isn't just the schools that have to change their behaviors, attitudes, and relationships with the schools and, in some cases, with their own children. Parents and other parental figures have to become more willing to be involved with their children and their children's schools and schoolwork, even when this means setting time aside to go to the classroom, meet with the teachers and administrators, and foster change through exerting pressures. By developing a dialogue about the importance of attitudes toward schools, about the goals and curriculum, and about expectations, parents and teachers working collaboratively can begin to change some of the fundamental, underlying problems that have been discussed at length earlier in this book. Parents complaining about the schools; teachers complaining about parents' lack of involvement: neither of these strategies pushes the necessary levers. Instead, by communicating in open forums, by teachers visiting parents in their homes if necessary, not all parents if some are unwilling to be involved, but the 95 percent that Linda Braun notes do care and are willing to participate, then arguably dramatic changes in the performance of children in school can be achieved. There is nothing like common understanding of clear goals, goals that are at least to some real extent mutually developed, to build a relationship over time that is fulfilling and engaging for parents, teachers, and children.

In terms of family change, parents may need to become more aware of what their children are actually doing (or, in some cases, not doing) in school, make sure that there are sanctions for schoolwork not being done, and foster positive attitudes toward school and schoolwork. Parents, then, also need to be aware of homework assignments on a regular basis (e.g., an assignment book they can check) so that they can determine whether homework is done. They need to be knowledgeable of their role(s) with respect to homework at different ages (e.g., how much help should they give, what is the school policy with respect to homework) and the school policies that affect help with homework. Parents also need to know the school-based consequences of not doing homework or of discipline problems, and to form a mutual agreement about what the home consequences will be—and stick to those consequences when there is a problem (e.g., no television, being grounded).

Teachers and parents together need to agree on what things parents will do at home to support appropriate attitudes toward school, appropriate discipline in school, and the high expectations that both parents and teachers have of children. Only by joining together in lengthy and sometimes difficult discussions and creating joint policies that are revised and renewed annually based on the children's, families', community's, and teachers' perspectives, can significant changes be begun. These changes are systemic, not "quick fixes," and will not happen unilaterally or quickly. But if they are promulgated from the schools, and supported in the home with the very real "buy in" that comes from intensive involvement and real participation in their development that dialogue and policy formation brings, they can be a significant leverage point for positive change because they begin to deal with not just the symptomatic problems but the underlying problems affecting schools.

OTHER NODES IN THE SPIDER'S WEB

Families are but one of many influences, as we have seen, on school performance, albeit they represent the part of the web that directly surrounds the school at every node. But the strands that constitute the spider's web also involve the policy arenas that affect family, including human service, health, and governmental agencies and the programs they foster, businesses or economic institutions that employ parents and graduates of schools, educational policy makers, such as colleges of education and teachers' unions, and value-shaping entities, such as the media, churches, civic and political organizations. And one important set of linkages involves businesses and other employers, both in terms of the types of policies they have for families and in their employment practices. This latter topic will be discussed at length in the next chapter, while other links in the web will be detailed below.

The reason that families are so important is that they operate in virtually all domains: providing a healthy, safe, and supportive home environment, providing economic opportunities from work outside the home, assisting schools with policy through parent organizations, and shaping children's values through constant interaction (or not) along a wide variety of dimensions. The influence of external groups may be somewhat less direct than the family's on children's school performance. Nonetheless some of these institutions function as part of the safety net surrounding families.

Some, such as the media, policy makers, and churches have strong influences because they shape the values and behaviors of individuals and organizations in the broader society.

LINKS FOR HUMAN SERVICE, SOCIAL SERVICE, HEALTH CARE, AND GOVERNMENT AGENCIES

There is a sense in which a wholly new view of the way that human, social, health care, and governmental services are delivered needs to be developed. As a society we can no longer afford the turf battles and programmatic approach that have limited our thinking with respect to families and their needs, and prevented holistic or systemic conceptions of service delivery. Some of this thinking has been recognized in the whole "reinventing government" movement, which if well done would ask governmental agencies to take a more customer-driven, holistic, and systemic approach to their tasks by focusing on services delivered to meet customer or client needs.[3] The whole approach to human services delivery needs to be reconstructed so that families or, at minimum, individuals, and in the case of schools, children, are taken into account. Only then can the current fragmented system be broken down and rebuilt with a holistic set of needs in mind. Agencies, if they are to operate separately, also need to reconfigure themselves into network structures, building alliances with each other and, more importantly for our purposes, with the schools.

Building these alliances and working collaboratively is a major task, of course, and ultimately requires dismantling major bureaucracies in favor of the needs of the public. It also requires new ways of thinking that move away from strict individualism toward instilling a sense of community, of "we are all in this together" into the purposes of organizations that are interacting. Although the prospect may seem unlikely in the short term, the collaborative systems perspective offered here is not a short-term perspective. Collaboration requires long-term, strategic thinking about the ways in which different groups and institutions can come together in the interests of what public policy makers would term the common good. Establishing this common good requires extensive public dialogue of a sort that has been largely missing in recent years, but which has recently begun, slowly and somewhat tentatively to reemerge. Difficult transitions, rethinking the purposes and roles of institutions, and efforts to collaborate where independence was formerly the *modus operandi* require a much more communitarian than individualistic[4] approach than U.S. society is used to. Such an approach requires thinking about a combination of public interest or common good with efforts to maintain the integrity of institutions and economic units like businesses, with their profit orientation.

There is some evidence that some businesses are rethinking their relationship to society through articulation of what they term the "dual bottom line," which focuses both on profitability and common good (e.g., Ben & Jerry's, Patagonia, The Body Shop). This stance is far from the most prevalent theme in business and has yet to characterize public services. Still, certain shifts toward more market-based mechanisms in the public sector also suggest that the reinventing government movement may be making some small inroads into reframing the public dialogue about responsibility. People involved in this movement are essentially rethinking the ways in which agencies oriented toward the provision of human services (broadly defined) might begin to operate in relation to *each other* and to their *clients*.

Using some of the same systems dynamics thinking that this book has been using, combined with a total quality and continuous improvement focus, some public policy makers are thinking exactly along these lines. What is required is combining current programs in a collaborative approach to problem solving that views the school as a central resource for family but that taps into the services provided by different agencies. Thus, health care agencies serving community needs might offer outpatient services to families through an after-hours school-based facility, a day-care center might be willing to locate within the school if the facility were made available after school ended for the day, a church might send in volunteers to read to children or mentor them, and a local agency involved with housing or employment training might use school facilities after hours to bring unemployed parents in for training sessions. Teachers might be used to help develop relevant job skills and supply basic literacy for those needing it, if funds and talent were available. Such techniques would take some of the burden off of the schools, bringing parents into closer contact with the schools, exposing other groups to what is happening in schools, and establishing the basis for an on-going dialogue and further collaborative developments.

Further, a new perspective in which the recipients of services are assumed to be capable human beings interested in helping themselves, may help foster this collaboration and transition. If individuals needing services are seen not as helpless victims, but as people who need some *support* or *education* to succeed, this attitude would provide a powerful leverage point for changing the way that human, health, and governmental services are offered, the assumptions that are made, and the ways and places in which services are delivered.

This perspective is similar to the one that is being used in the Boston Foundation's Persistent Poverty Program, which was described in an earlier chapter. It represents a shift away from making people victims and makes a very different assumption: that they are responsible for their own lives and, importantly, that they themselves are capable of making the necessary decisions and taking action, even when they may need help in improving their lives. Thus, the assumption represents a compromise from a purely market-driven assumption ("Every boat on its own bottom," or "Let the strong survive") versus a "helpless" orientation ("These people are victims and need our help"). The compromise is, yes, help may be needed but it is help in the form of education, job training and assistance, making jobs available to willing workers, day and pre-school care when needed for children, short-term assistance with food and housing, and coordinated services that provide support but do not take away dignity or make recipients into helpless victims of an unjust society.

As an example of the approach, take the principal of a tough inner-city high school who was dealing with the young, black male student who had gotten into trouble and been sent to her office who was discussed in Chapter 7. In my presence, she told him that despite his status and his problems of poverty and home life, he needed to take responsibility for his own actions, or else he was likely to end up out on the streets, a drug pusher or poor, or even dead. Although the response may seem harsh, it presented reality to the student and asked him to be responsible for his own behavior, while simultaneously indicating the supportive role that the school would play.

Thus, on the other side of providing support and assistance is developing the expectation that individuals will contribute to their own well-being and take responsibility for their own actions. For example, small loans to help people get started in business, take a necessary course, or gain a needed skill may be useful ways to start with a different assumption base. One concept that integrates the provision of human services is being developed, as will be discussed below, in Louisville, Kentucky.

One-Stop Shopping Concept

In Louisville, some integration between schools and human services agencies has already begun taking shape in the form of Family Resource Centers housed within the schools. These centers were mandated by the Kentucky Educational Reform Act (KERA) as one means of helping schools to improve their performance by ensuring that children come to school ready to learn. One individual involved with this program explains,

"We are focusing on family and youth services; it's the next stage. If it's done right, it could redesign how human services are delivered. This approach can move us away from the traditional segmented clients and problems approach to a collaboration in which agencies use resources for a *family*-centered approach, impacting what they can. You pull together some knowledgeable service providers.

"Think of how it works now, families getting multiple calls. One agency calls and wants to see you at ten, another at eleven, the phone was just pulled, you have no car and the kids are in detention and the electricity is turned off. Now you might be able to say to these people, 'You're not alone in this world.' The Family Resource Center is where a parent can go and the center can serve *all* the children and members of the family. Someone takes charge of the family. It's a holistic concept. If the school sees that the child is eligible for a free lunch, then the whole family can be served once the grant is received." This is the type of "break the mold" thinking that is needed for schools.

Family Resource Centers in Louisville are housed within the schools because children are supposed to go to school each day and because, as institutions, schools represent a fundamental and usually largely untapped community resource. They are also the institution through which most children pass and thus the most likely to be able to reach out, through the network of linkages, to other elements of society.

THE ROLE FOR PROFESSIONALS: TEACHER AND PRINCIPAL AS FACILITATORS

What will teachers and administrators do in the school designed as a network organization, loosely coupled with other social institutions? For one thing, they will better be able to teach, since their current concerns with social services, psychological counseling, values formation, feeding children, helping families overcome serious problems, safety and security, and the like will be handled by others in a way that begins to assure that these needs are adequately addressed and that responsibility for them is spread around.

Further, the requirements of teaching are also dramatically changing as the twenty-first century opens before us. Not only must teachers gain new skills in making the necessary linkages between schools and other institutions happen, skills of communication, new knowledge about other institutions, collaboration and coordination of activities, and listening to name only a few, but they must also re-energize and recharge their instructional methods to catch up to the demands of the new era. They will have to gain new skills and knowledge and communicate many of these same skills to their young charges. Technological sophistication will be demanded of graduates in the future, and therefore teachers will themselves have to gain technological skills. Teamwork, personal initiative and responsibility for learning, the ability to take appropriate risks, as well as content knowledge in traditional areas (the so-called basics) and emerging areas (international emphases, for example; or in computer, information, and other electronic technology) will all be required as new pedagogies are developed or as underused, but more participative approaches already in existence are implemented.

In this new world, the model that exists at the school level, one of linking teachers and administrators to a wide network of family and institutions that share responsibility will have to be replicated within the school. Classrooms and student activities will look quite different if students are made to assume responsibility for their learning and teachers become facilitators and coaches, helping and supporting students to learn, but not "teaching" in the traditional sense of dumping facts, figures, and knowledge from teachers' into students' heads. In this new classroom environment, teaching approaches that emphasize collaborative as well as individual learning, that focus on the student as learner rather than the teacher as instructor, will be needed if the model that is being demonstrated organizationally is to actually play out in the daily lives of students in schools.

Many of these approaches place the teacher, as well as the manager (principal), into the role not of expert, lecturer, or controller in the classroom, but into a relatively new role of *facilitator* of students' learning. As many managers today are having to learn to be coaches, mentors, or facilitators of employee learning, rather than supervisors, so teachers will need to assume these new teaching roles, which place the emphasis on learning and not teaching; concurrently, the facilitator role places responsibility for *learning* on the student rather than for teaching on the teacher.

To gain the skills necessary to operate in this changed teaching environment, teachers will need to ask for and receive training in the new skills and pedagogies this facilitative approach requires. Clearly, training or education can be an important point of leverage for system change because once a critical mass of teachers become knowledgeable in these techniques, they will become advocates for change. An appropriate time for such education might be during summers or vacations, especially if teachers can be financially supported or paid as part of their regular salaries for participating in such workshops, seminars, and courses. The school year is unlikely to be lengthened in the near term, although this would be desirable simply to allow the U.S. educational system to operate on a level playing field with other advanced nations with reasonably successful educational systems, like Japan or Germany.

Thus, teachers will need to develop local political agendas to seek additional financial support for the crucial training and education they need to work in the twenty-first century environment. Some of this training might be supplied through collaboration with local employers who are providing related or the same type of training to employees. In some school-business partnerships already established, such as Procter & Gamble's partnership with Cincinnati schools, corporate training sessions are made available to relatively large groups of teachers and administrators. When room is available in individual sessions, the company occasionally includes teachers or administrators in training sessions.

In general, however, both teachers and school administrators will need to seek public funds for intensive, rigorous training, supplied by the best colleges, universities, and corporate training departments. Far from the typical staff development of schools (frequently known as "in-services," or workshops that run for an hour or two with no expectations that there will be any follow-up), this training needs to be paid for as part of the teacher's annual contracted duties. Goals focused on implementation of the new learning need to be set, with high expectations that the learning will be put into practice, developed, and maintained through appropriate reward systems. Accountability systems, which follow up on how well training has been implemented, can be designed cooperatively by teachers, administrators, and trainers and built into the administration of training programs.

In a truly collaborative system, a process for setting these goals would be established. Not only would teachers and principals be involved in this process, but also parents, community representatives, local business leaders, representatives of government and the other organizations that are linked in the network to schools would all have input into the setting and achievement of appropriate goals expectations for citizenship, productive working lives, and contribution back to their communities that schools would establish for their students. This involvement by an array of stakeholders would provide a sound base of support for schools because it would increase understanding of the needs and realities on all sides.

Political agendas such as those needed to convince the public that training funds are a necessary adjunct to school improvement are a far cry from the typical adversarial union-management relationships that now exist, in which union leaders try to protect teachers from being overworked or having more responsibilities added to their plates.

Schools of the twenty-first century can work only if teachers demand real professionalism, professionalism that stresses constant learning and retraining of the sort that all professions now find they must undergo. Schools can succeed only if teachers themselves are willing to face a future of constant change and development, rather than a static and stable status quo. Teachers will probably have to work not necessarily harder but smarter in this environment, because there will be demands on them to upgrade their own learning and skills.

This need to work smarter, to deploy talents and resources to advantage, and to tap into the resources of others through the linkages that have been described will place significant demands upon teachers. But these demands are no more and no less than the types of demands that are already being placed upon employees in organizations of all sorts. The pressures of restructuring, resource constraints, and increased competition are forcing people in all domains to do more with less. Teachers may even be able to simplify their jobs, in one sense, if they are primarily expected to teach rather than to also add responsibilities of parenting, social work, health services, and discipline and safety. By involving all of the relevant stakeholders directly in developing the goals and expectations of schools and by having them actively participate in evaluation processes, observing daily activities, and sharing of the responsibilities for achieving some of those outcomes when they are within a particular group or organization's domain, schools can build an active support network in the community.

Schools might make linkages to the businesses that can offer other kinds of training and insight into the way the world of work actually operates today. Many teachers would benefit from formalized linkages with business organizations, such as paid summer or vacation internships in which they do real work for the company, but also are exposed to what happens at work daily. Shadowing experiences with managers and other workers could also prove useful. As in the case of some Rochester, New York, teachers serving internships in corporations, company executives and managers might find themselves pleasantly surprised at the talents of the teachers brought in for temporary or project-based work. Such relationships have the long-term potential to benefit both parties: teachers from the knowledge of the world of work and exposure to business; businesspeople in terms of the respect that they gain for the very real talents of teachers. Again, depending on the diagnosed needs of the community, these programs can be developed holistically based on the kinds of goals that the community seeks in improving its schools and the schools' relationships to key external constituencies.

UNIONS: RETHINKING INTERNAL SCHOOL RELATIONSHIPS

Believe it or not, one of the most restrictive constraints upon schools, in terms of their responding more effectively to community and student needs, tends to be the contracts negotiated by those whose services support education. Custodial contracts, in particular, pose severe problems when a principal or PTA decides that it wants to open the school at night so that it can be used by residents in local communities, so that other services can be offered using school facilities during off-school hours, or so that children can have a safe haven from the streets before or after school or on weekends.

All too frequently these contracts specify that all overtime work must be paid double time and that at least two custodians must be present for functions in the school. As an example, the PTA in my son's school wanted to work with a local neighborhood association to present a history of the neighborhood. The neighborhood group hoped to bring in citizens of all ages, with and without children, as well as members of the PTA, to listen to this history and to charge the minimal fee of one dollar. Unfortunately, because the event was scheduled for an evening and required chair set ups, it also required two custodians present at a cost of about $150 for the three-hour period the school was to be opened. Since attendance was not expected to be that high, the custodial cost almost prohibited the event from being held, except for the contribution of the PTA to cover half the expense. Unfortunately, most schools face similar expenses in their efforts to become more open to the community or even to put school facilities to better use during off-school hours.

A creative solution for this problem would involve a systematic rethinking of the custodial relationship to the whole of education's purpose and as a consequence, the restructuring of the hours of coverage to include events that go beyond the traditional scope of the custodians' responsibility. Custodians' union representatives might be expected to object to the diminishment of overtime that might be implied in such an arrangement. But there is a better way to think about this relationship. Instead of reducing the work of custodians, such arrangements might actually, in the medium to longer term, provide more custodial jobs, more union jobs, because if schools were kept open for community events, then there would be greater need for custodial work in general. So while it is true that overtime pay might be less frequent, more people might be hired to cover the greater number of hours and increased workload that would result. Unions might benefit from more members, the school might obtain additional resources from use of its facilities, students and their families might gain from the presence of more opportunities for play, provision of necessary services, and care. Members of the community would benefit from the availability of local meeting space and good auditorium facilities at reasonable cost, and would also become familiar with the school and its students through increased interaction. The school, in turn, would benefit from improved relations with the community and with a community better informed about school activities from the simple expedient of seeing what's happening in the schools once in a while. The better-informed community members, representing families with school-age children to be sure, but also including younger people with no children as well as singles and families whose children have grown and left home, might be far more willing to support the schools and children with whom they are now more familiar.

EDUCATIONAL POLICY MAKERS AND UNIVERSITIES

There is tremendous organizational inertia in the relationship that exists now between the Departments of Education at the federal and state levels, teachers' unions, and schools. Changing any of these relationships requires adopting a very different perspective than the typically adversarial and "checking on" mentality that now exists. But even the U.S. Department of Education has shifted its focus away from its traditional activities toward sponsoring community-based investigation of the needs of education, a thrust that began during the Bush Administration and has continued into the Clinton Administration. Recent efforts of the U.S. Department of Education to improve education have focused on community-building and collaboration instead of merely monitoring grants to the disadvantaged. Although progress toward actually achieving the six national education goals has been termed "wholly inadequate,"[5] significant learning is taking place about the need for high standards and high expectations in schools.

From the analysis in this book, we can conclude that such community-based approaches to school change have far more long-term potential for success, however, than do the programmatic and curricular fixes that are generally applied. Indeed, one reason that so little progress has been made is that for the most part, the reality is that little has been changed in schools in the past decade and that what has changed has mainly had little to do with real restructuring of schools, their relationships, the pedagogies, or the responsibilities of teachers and students. People have tended to think in terms of simplistic, single-dimension solutions rather than change the system itself: more rigorous testing as if testing alone could change performance, more guards at the door to increase safety as if that would quell the violence in some students' lives, or a return-to-basics teaching without changing teaching methodologies to involve students more fully in their learning, as examples.

The community-based and more systemic approaches now being tried in some towns and cities require time, trust, and hard work to bring about real changes. They require the kind of change process discussed earlier, including questioning of assumptions about what good teaching is, what the students are capable of learning, and how they learn. They demand participation by all of those who are affected by the outcomes of education: students, parents, businesses, other institutions in the community. They will not be short-term solutions and policy makers at the community, state, and federal levels have only just begun to realize the implications of these types of systemic changes.

Saying this, however, does not let policy makers off the hook. Setting high expectations for education in general is as important as it is for individual students, but goals have to be clearly defined and achievable. The new recognition is that expectations alone are not enough. Setting national standards, which the National Education Goals Panel began to do finally in 1993, is an essential element of this process of both building expectations and determining what needs to be done.[6] Although the standards will be voluntary once created, they do set both a standard of performance and a set of high expectations for schools and children to achieve. Once the expectations are set and goals are made clear—and policy makers are in a position to set both—then real rethinking of the strategies for achieving those goals is needed. Ultimately, it will be up to policy makers, in conjunction with legislators, town and city councilors, mayors, and school personnel to establish the important, interactive and participative processes that are needed and to advocate for and, in the end, find the resources, financial, managerial, and time resources, to set in motion a process of change.

Policy makers at all levels need to recognize that the changes will not be easy or necessarily cheap: schools have gotten into their current conditions as a result of many years of thinking that they could bear burdens that they were not set up to bear. They have been asked to achieve goals they were never set up to achieve, goals of equal education for all, despite differing circumstances of birth and social condition.[7] Establishing a system in which those burdens can be more appropriately shared is, in fact, the role of policy makers and finding the resources school and other personnel will need to understand the necessary changes to meet community needs is the responsibility of policy makers in education. They, like school personnel, will need to become advocates in the public arena for the types of resources that are necessary fiscally, they need to become better able to articulate the needs of schools and the problems that school officials face so that a recalcitrant public is exposed to much more real dialogue about why schools are performing the way that they are. Only then can realistic decisions be made by the voting public; only when the problems are better understood through dialogue, interaction, and honesty on both sides can responsibility be better distributed.

Perhaps the most critical role that policy makers at all levels have is establishing goals and standards regarding what students should learn. The national education goals were an important first step, but as has been pointed out, they do not really speak to issues about the curriculum, as the voluntary national goals are far more likely to do. At some level, whether locally, statewide, or nationally, it becomes critical for standards to be established and, even if they are voluntary, for the expectations to be set that high goals will actually be met. These standards should and very likely will detail what students should know and in what topics they should know it, what students should be able to do, and how well they should do it, thus they represent a critical step in building better schools.

In this new network environment, teachers will be making linkages, too, to the universities and colleges providing education and asking them to provide the kind of education they will need to meet the demands upon them. In assuming their own share of the burden, colleges and universities will need to accept the responsibility for changing their own curricula to meet the real needs of the twenty-first-century teacher rather than holding on to archaic models of instruction. Colleges of education will, in this model, need to reach out themselves, making linkages to actual classrooms that go beyond student teaching, so that there is an on-going interaction between the research being done to inform teaching and the research and instruction that goes on in college.

TEXTBOOK AND OTHER PUBLISHERS

Textbook publishers, going after the easiest and fastest buck, also bear some responsibility for the "dumbing down" and homogenization of textbooks. With new technologies emerging that permit much more flexibility in the publication field, textbook publishers have opportunities to work closely with local or state school officials who determine what texts will be used in schools to reverse the trends toward simplistic, easy to understand but ultimately less-than-useful texts. There is tremendous opportunity here for publishers given the flexible technologies, if they can learn to work creatively with districts that are making textbook selections.

Indeed, publishers who maintain current strategies of standardized texts that delete any difficult, controversial, or in-depth materials may find themselves at a disadvantage with school districts that have surveyed their communities' needs and want to develop curricula that meet established national, statewide, or local standards. Far greater flexibility in the materials available to students may be demanded should those conditions arise than is currently needed and the new electronic publishing technologies will permit this flexibility in ways that are not yet fully understood.

VALUE SHAPERS

Values are shaped by families, of course, but also by the media in all its guises, and by institutions such as churches, civic, and political organizations. In the next chapter we will turn to the important role that employers and the economic system play with respect to the schools. In the final section of this chapter, we will explore briefly the linkages that might exist in communities with church and civic organizations and the media.

Church and Civic Organizations

Churches and civic organizations represent an important element of values development. The bully pulpit of politics or the church provides a forum for establishing public dialogue about values and about what is valued and how it is to be valued. Leaders might play a fundamental role in reforming education by becoming more knowledgeable about the problems and opportunities in education and using their bully pulpits to the advantage of establishing or ensuring the maintenance of an on-going dialogue about the value of education, and how good education is to be achieved. Issues of equity and fairness, opportunity, educational expectations and achievement are fair game for open forums and dialogues. Church and civic leaders can play a central role in making the linkages among community members that are necessary if the conversation about responsibility for education, problems of education, and actions needed is ever to be engaged. They provide a natural forum for bringing together members of the community, including teachers and school administrators, parents and students, political leaders, members of the business community, and representatives of other key organizations, such as health care institutions, social and human service agencies, and so on.

There are other kinds of activities that these organizations can play that might have a direct impact on schools by making the linkages between schools and some key external groups explicit. Churches might be able to help schools by organizing some of their membership to run before- and after-school programs for children, a solution that not only helps working parents, but also provides activities for individuals who may be bored and lonely, as well as providing an infrastructure that is now lacking for the children. Civic organizations like senior centers might organize volunteers to come into schools to read to children, mentor them, or just work with them on a regular basis.

Television and Other Media

Values are also shaped in important ways by the media, by advertisements that young people see, by the television shows they watch and the materials they read, by the billboards they see on the way to school or on the highways as they travel about, by the editorials parents may discuss, and in many other subtle and less subtle ways. In general, the messages from the media have tended to devalue rather than value the hard work necessary for education. As one example, consider the cartoon strip "Calvin and Hobbes," in which Calvin consistently is shown to hate school, not want to do his work, and in which his intransigence toward hard work and his dislike of his teachers plays an important, central role in what apparently makes the strip appealing. Yet are these the values that we, as a society, really wish to convey to our children about school?

What about the popularity of such shows as "Beavis and Butthead" or others that consistently downgrade the work of teachers and show children as successful when they avoid schoolwork or express negative attitudes? It is the pervasiveness of these negative attitudes toward education, combined with the criticism of many schools that is found in newspaper and magazine headlines that approach the problems of education with the simplistic solutions generally offered (a more rigorous test, school choice, or more recently charter schools) that creates part of the problems schools face. Children are exposed to the media regularly and the attitudes conveyed toward education are too frequently not supportive of the need for hard work or of a positive attitude toward educators.

The media in part reflects the opinion of individuals in society and in part shapes those opinions. Some television shows, for example, attempt to highlight positive aspects of education (e.g., Sesame Street or Reading Rainbow on public television). But if the media were to accept its responsibility for education and to think through the consequences of portraying the problems of education overly simplistically or constantly negatively, then more constructive approaches might be developed. Again, these constructive approaches need to be based on real, in-depth understanding of the problems of education and collaboration as a means of solving problems, so that everyone recognizes his or her part in the total system.

The next chapter will explore the important roles of employers, particularly businesses, in improving education. The final chapter will summarize the major conclusions reached in the analysis presented in this book.

NOTES

1. I thank Linda Braun, director of Families First and a professor at Wheelock College in Boston, for a helpful conversation that highlighted many of the ideas expressed in this section.

2. E.g., J. P. Comer (1984), "Home-School Relations as They Affect the Academic Success of Children," *Education and Urban Society* 16(3): 294–337.

3. See D. W. Osborne and T. Gaebler (1992), *Reinventing Government: How the Entrepreneurial Spirit is Transforming the Public Sector* (Reading, MA: Addison-Wesley).

4. For an in-depth analysis of individualism and communitarian strains in U.S. society see R. N. Bellah, R. Madsen, W. M. Sullivan, A. Swidler, and S. M. Tipton (1985), *Habits of the Heart: Individualism and Commitment in American Life* (New York: Harper & Row); and by the same authors (1991), *The Good Society* (New York: Alfred A. Knopf).

5. Report of the National Education Goals Panel (1993b), *Building a Nation of Learners* (Washington, D.C.: U.S. Department of Education).

6. See the Summary Guide by the National Education Goals Panel (1993a), *The National Education Goals Report: Building the Best*, Washington, D.C.: NEGP Communications.

7. See G. Wiggins (1993), "Accountability, Testing, and Schools: Toward Local Responsibility and Away from Change by Mandate," *Business Horizons* September–October: 13–23.

Chapter 10

Businesses and Other Employers Linked to Schools

In assessing the linkages that schools might make with other institutions, there is one type of institution that stands out as particularly important: the employer, particularly the business organization, whether large or small. As has been pointed out in earlier chapters, many businesses have become intensely involved in collaborative or partnership activities with schools since the issuance of *A Nation at Risk* in 1983. Yet far too many of these partnerships have worked only at the margins, doing little to effect real school restructuring. Others have been one-sided or one-dimensional forcing attention onto changes that the schools must make, rather than recognizing that employer practices are also subject to change in the *interaction* that necessarily exists between schools and employers when they recognize their inherent interdependence.

This chapter will explore some of the reciprocal linkages that, in a holistic conception of the system in which schools and employers are embedded, might enhance the potential for real school improvements. Achieving this potential requires new understanding of the roles of employers, particularly large businesses, but also smaller businesses and other organizations, both for-profit and not-for-profit, who employ individuals within communities.

ROLES AND RESPONSIBILITIES FOR EMPLOYERS, PARTICULARLY BUSINESSES[1]

Although we have come to think of business enterprises and other employers becoming "involved" in the schools through public-private partnerships and other forms of collaboration, we seldom think about the impact that business policies have on schools, on children, and on families in general. In the sections below, we will explore some of the roles that businesses can take and are taking with respect to helping the schools, and conversely, we will look a little bit inside of businesses to try to assess the ways in which businesses themselves may need to change if they are to meet their responsibilities toward school improvement. That is, as with families, and with human service and health institutions, the relationship and responsibilities for school improvement between businesses and schools are not one-sided. We will look first at the explicitly collaborative activities between businesses and schools in recent years. We will then explore businesses' family policies as yet another way of working out the relationships that actually do exist among schools, parents (employees), and their employers. A wide range of potential (and some actualized) roles for businesses and other economic or employer organizations will be explored.

Businesses have taken a number of positions with respect to schools, ranging from roles that assume the least interaction, involvement, and acceptance of responsibility to those that assume considerably more responsibility. Schools and businesses can view each other as independent institutions that maintain the separateness of their institutions despite periodic interaction. A second position is that the businesses can see themselves as institutional bridges between schools and work, with the employers serving as external change agents. Alternatively, businesses and other relevant groups can take an interinstitutional perspective in which they view themselves as equals collaborating in a process of systemic change in which all parties need to reshape their thinking and their behaviors, thereby creating a new institutional infrastructure. Finally, businesses can begin to view themselves as not only part of the solution but as part of the problem, and to reshape the ways in which they develop their own policies and practices so that they are more supportive of the efforts of schools and families. Each of these perspectives will be explored below.

INDEPENDENT INSTITUTIONS: BUSINESS AS RESOURCE PROVIDER

The primary role that business has historically assumed with respect to school is as provider of resources above and beyond those provided through the public policy process. These resources take two general forms, tangible and monetary resources, and human resources; giving resources is essentially a philanthropic gesture on the part of business and does not necessarily involve any long-term interaction or the development of on-going links between school and business. In effect, businesses give these resources to schools either as supplements to existing resources or for specific programs.

Although elements of such largess are found in more collaborative arrangements between schools and businesses, in its strictest sense the provision of resources keeps schools and businesses separate institutionally, although some interpersonal or short-term linkages may be formed. Much of this involvement has achieved changes only at the margins,[2] in part because these arrangements were never intended to reform schools, in part because they tend to be one-way relationships, and in part because partners have maintained a hands-off stance with respect to any significant internal school issues. Few partnerships or adopt-a-school partnerships have accomplished the systemic reform that schools, like businesses in the past decade and a half, must now undergo in their efforts to regain or build the ability to adequately educate their students.

Tangible and Monetary Resources

Throughout the twentieth century, the primary role of businesses with respect to schools (other than as employer of graduates) has been as the provider of resources above and beyond what the public was willing to provide, that is, marginal resources. Businesses have historically been called upon for donations, predominantly money, for equipment and supplies, for guest lecturers who can speak in classes and at graduations, and for support of specific school programs and activities (e.g., the band uniforms, or an after-school science program). All of the 133 companies listed in a *Fortune* magazine survey of how businesses contribute to schools made some financial or in-kind commitment to school improvement. In *Fortune*'s survey of business contributions, only two of the 133 companies listed contributed less than $100,000; thirty-two contributed between $100,000 and $499,999; twenty-two made contributions worth between $500,000 and $999,999; fifty-five contributions were between $1 million and $4,999,999; and twenty-two were over $5 million. Clearly, significant resources are being devoted to schools by at least these 133 businesses. Presumably many companies not included on this list also make monetary, equipment, and in-kind contributions in support of school programs.

Human Resources

Businesses can make other contributions in their roles as resource providers, specifically in donating the time and energy of employees deployed in the schools to supplement human resources. Many school officials interviewed for this research argued that the human resource is by far the most important resource that businesses have to provide schools, although this view is a fairly new one. Historically, the provision of human resources by businesses to schools was pretty much restricted to guest speakers, visiting executives and scientists, and similar activities that tended to be one-shot visits rather than an on-going relationship.

For example, human resources can be deployed from businesses to schools through visiting scientist, visiting lecturer, and visiting executive programs. Xerox Corporation, for example, has an extensive visiting scientist program in Rochester, New York, in which engineers and scientists, using extensive hands-on materials developed by Xerox to guide their curricular interventions, are granted release time from work to visit classrooms and demonstrate what scientists actually do. Xerox's underlying purpose in permitting release time to employees for this program is to develop a cadre of future scientists among the young people who experience the hands-on programs. Each of these initiatives and many other similar initiatives can be used by schools and employers to start making linkages and developing a shared understanding of the problems of education and the ways in which different institutions can work together.

In part because of the serious family changes noted earlier, many businesses have begun deploying human resources in cooperation with schools in new ways when schools are open to having outsiders come inside. Some of these programs, when structured properly do develop long-term, consistent, and systematically oriented relationships, but mainly between individuals. These individual relationships are important, in some cases essential, for children as well as providing many psychic benefits for the tutor or mentor, but they do not change the underlying structure of the school, nor do they have any intentions of doing so. The rationale for such initiatives is that one of the critical missing ingredients for many children is adult role models, who care enough to provide individual attention. One role that employees can take with individual and groups of students include structured tutoring relationships (as is happening, for example, in the Detroit Public Schools with tutors from some of the auto companies).

Mentoring relationships, when taken seriously as they are in Cincinnati, a city that has developed an extensive mentoring program, do involve long-term relationships between individual children and employees within various types of organizations and thus have some potential for system impact. Key to their success tends to be the development of an appropriate system of support surrounding the mentoring program, including training of mentors and communication with families, on-going mentor development, and maintenance of the formal relationship between the participating schools and businesses through regular contact among administrators and managers.[3]

In urban settings, there is sometimes a decided paucity of role models with whom students can identify or to whom they can look up. Such students may be very bright, but not really understand the opportunities that education can provide them. They may have poor attitudes toward school because they have, quite literally, never seen anyone going off to work on a daily basis or because they see no way out of their current situation. In some cities, Cincinnati and Pittsburgh, for example, many young people seldom if ever venture beyond the borders of their own neighborhoods. As one respondent indicated, "It is difficult to think about competing in a global economy when one never explores life further than a few blocks." Many children are the product of single-parent families with the result that frequently there are too few successful male role models for them. While mentors can never replace parental involvement with children, for children who have few role models or supportive adults in their world, they can provide a bridge to the adult world that is, in effect, life saving. But to really be successful, mentoring and on-going tutoring programs need to be designed with the students' needs in mind, based on an assessment of the needs of the children, with appropriate and systemically supplied support (education, training, on-going review and evaluation) for the adults involved, mentors and parents alike.

INSTITUTIONAL BRIDGE: BUSINESS AS EDUCATOR AND ADVOCATE

The mentoring, tutoring, and visiting lecturer initiatives discussed in the previous section are frequently corporate sponsored and represent a form of partnering to achieve linkages. These types of links establish a multi-nodal network of potentially helpful relationships essentially at the individual or one-to-one level. Another type of linkage schools can make is to form "bridges" between them with outside institutions, like businesses (or other major institutions and employers).[4] Businesses acting in supportive roles can enhance the performance of schools through using some of their own training and management resources to achieve systemic change within schools by improving management practice and by fostering the types of external pressures both on and on behalf of schools that public policy initiatives can generate. These roles linking employers and schools will be considered in detail below.

Since publication of *A Nation at Risk* in 1983, many business leaders have viewed their roles with respect to schools differently. Recognizing the need for change and improvement in school performance, some business leaders have shaped two predominant types of activities. In the first role, business itself becomes the educator; in the second role, business-people become advocates for schools or for change in schools. In both of these capacities, businesses serve as bridges between the world of school and the world of work, linking these institutions through their change agent effort.

Business as Educator

Historically, the separate operations of school and business personnel have fostered a general lack of interaction and trust. There is increasing recognition that education takes place not only in schools, but also in the home and in other types of organizations as well, such as museums, arts enterprises, cultural and community centers, and television to name only a few influences.[5] Business organizations have in many instances recognized that they potentially have an important role, properly developed, to play in the delivery of important elements of nonschool-based education.[6] Similarly, businesses have recognized that they may have to better communicate their own needs regarding employees to schools. Many business executives also believe that certain business practices will help schools improve their own performance. Thus, while school and business remain separate institutions in these bridging relationships, there is a recognition that each can inform the other in important ways that may have previously gone unrecognized if they establish an on-going basis of interaction, such as mutual training, management, or skills development programs. These programs mean that some links and some degree of the network have been established.

Business as educator performs three primary tasks: "world of work" education; staff development; and education about management tools and techniques for teachers and administrators. Reversing these roles, many teachers can offer skills development, basic education, such as reading, writing, and communication, and specialized seminars to individuals and groups in employer organizations where there are needs that cannot be readily met by corporate personnel. The exchange, that is, can go two ways. The advantage of such two-way exchanges is one of exposure. By having teachers exposed to businesspeople, the teachers become more knowledgeable and sophisticated about the demands that businesses place upon employees today. Similarly, by having businesspeople exposed to teachers, the businesspeople will become better acquainted with the talents of teachers and their skills in delivery of education.

Over time, with interaction, mutual trust and better appreciation of the difficulties that teachers and businesspeople face in their work lives can develop, leading to a deeper understanding and the potential for greater collaborative efforts to improve education in the future because it becomes recognized that the needs are mutual and not one-sided. In this chapter we will explore the ways some businesses have developed partnering activities that expand the network of the school well beyond school walls and begin some of this important interactive process.

World of Work

One of the more serious complaints about schools is that students perceive few links between what they are taught in school and the application of skills to the world of work. In part, this gap exists because the processes of industrialization and movement toward what has been termed a supersymbolic (or intensely knowledge-based) society[7] have made connections between school learning and actual work less direct than they were in the agricultural era (and even the industrial era where the gap first emerged). In part, the gap exists because students and even teachers infrequently contact the world of work; as a result, they understand few of its demands or the realities of how what they are learning relates to various elements of their future roles in society. In some cases, the gap exists because there may, in fact, be little relationship between what is taught and either work or citizenship activities; it is here where intensive and regular contact between teachers and businesspeople can provide both formal and informal incentives for change as each group comes to understand the other better. Many businesses are working with schools to close these gaps by allowing students, teachers, or both to experience the demands and content of the work world.

As means of closing this gap, some businesses arrange for students and/or teachers to visit worksites to see what is actually going on in the workplace so that better connections can be made between school and work in the students' minds. Others bring teachers into their operations through summer internships or programs that allow teachers to see what is actually happening in business. Similarly, some businesses provide summer and part-time jobs for students, sometimes complete with an assigned mentor. Still others provide training about the business world and try to teach students about the expectations that employers have of them, especially with regard to specific skills, such as communication and interpersonal skills, motivation and attitudes toward work, and personal traits. When these are one-shot programs, they are less useful from a system change perspective than when they are on-going, mutually involving efforts that require regular contact, conversations, and connections.

Internships are sometimes developed in which students are paired with workplace mentors who guide them through the rigors of workplace expectations and demands, help them over hurdles, and set high standards and expectations for their performance. Other times, such as John Hancock's HOPE (Hancock On Premises Education) program, businesses actually develop seminars for students to help them with resume-building and interviewing skills and to share with them the norms and expectations of the business world. Such techniques attempt to bridge the gap in knowledge, performance expectations, and skills that is perceived to exist between schools and employers.

Staff and Leadership Development

In addition to providing opportunities for students to learn about the world of work, many businesses are working to enhance school performance through staff development with three groups other than students: teachers, administrators, and policy and/or advisory groups. Such activities also form a bridge between schools and businesses. Too frequently, teachers are attempting to engage students' interest in learning without having themselves a clear understanding of workplace demands, norms, or needs. Some businesses have provided internships, summer work experience, and shadowing opportunities for teachers to provide them with a realistic view of business skills and demands. The most progressive firms also reverse the shadowing process to allow businesspeople contact with the world of teaching and school administration, frequently opening eyes to the complexities of the tasks that educators face.

Another way that some businesses, such as Procter & Gamble, have attempted to work with schools is by providing access to corporate employee and management development programs for teachers and administrators. Such programs can focus on skills such as team-building skills, time management, budgeting and accounting principles and procedures, supervisory and management skills, communication and presentation skills, and strategic planning. Sometimes corporate programs incorporate teachers into on-going management and employee development programs, which has the side benefit of bringing teachers face-to-face with businesspeople in action, to the standards that are expected of them, and to some of the norms of the corporate world. Other times, companies have donated their training programs, bringing in whole groups of teachers or administrators to be trained at once.

Management Expertise

The third bridging mechanism is provision of management tools and techniques by business managers to school personnel, especially those facing restructuring, site-based management, or pressures to use more professional management techniques. Many of the tools and techniques of budgeting, professional development, time management, strategic planning and thinking, accounting and finance, marketing or understanding constituency needs, and organizational change processes, while perhaps differently applied in schools, are very relevant to school improvement initiatives. Some of these management skills can be developed through training seminars provided by companies. Other times, business managers work with schools more directly to help staff develop these skills.

Many of the techniques that managers use to run companies can be successfully applied to school systems, despite the differences in goals, focus, time, and process orientations. Techniques of goal-setting and strategic planning, for example, are as relevant to schools attempting to restructure as they are to businesses. The goals that schools establish might differ from those of businesses, and schools might lack the clear, bottom-line measures of progress. Successful efforts to define "core values" for schools, establish clear goals, and figure out measurable ways of determining the extent to which those goals are being reached have, however, proved helpful to some restructuring schools. Business leaders can help school officials to learn how to adapt some of these strategic planning and other management tools to their own environments provided that they understand some of the important differences that exist between businesses and schools.

Further, few teachers yet understand the implications of a technology- and information-based world for their students[8] or how the nature of jobs is changing for graduates.[9] Businesses may have the ability to help teachers better understand the world that their students will face and, if their talents are used to provide skill-based training and relevant seminars and workshops to employees, businesspeople can gain a lot from more interaction with teachers as well.

BUSINESS AS ADVOCATE

Many progressive business leaders have assumed the role of advocate (as well as critic) for schools over the past decade, a role that also serves as a pressure point for change within schools coming from an external constituent. Business advocacy has taken place at four levels: national, state, community, and local school levels. For top-level executives involved in organizations such as the Business Roundtable (BRT), the Committee for Economic Development, or national education conferences, such as those sponsored in recent years by *Fortune*, advocacy has taken place at the national level and many business leaders have become articulate spokespeople for education or for reform of education. Advocacy has involved coming to terms with understanding what schools do, how and why they do it, and what the very real problems are that they face in modern America.

The BRT, for example, has issued strong policy guidelines and numerous reports about the status of the schools and what needs to be done. BRT also made a ten-year commitment to education at the national level, a commitment which is to be implemented by members at the state level, and that has received significant support from the National Alliance for Business. *Fortune*'s and others' education conferences as well as the policy-shaping reports issued by various national commissions have also helped shape the national dialogue about education and what needs to be done to improve it. Further, major commitments to educational improvement have been made by national business organizations such as the Chamber of Commerce, the Conference Board, the Committee for Economic Development, and the National Alliance of Business. These organizations have all helped to draw attention to the situations in which American schools find themselves locally, statewide, and nationally.

At the local level, many business leaders have become involved in school committees and school boards, thereby influencing funding allocations and general educational policy. They also lobby local government officials to increase (or decrease) funding for schools. Further, if they are parents, they are frequently involved in parent-teacher organizations and begin to influence what happens directly within their own children's schools.

Like the role of educator, the role of advocate serves as a link between societal expectations of schools, business needs, and schools themselves. In its capacity as advocate, business therefore serves as a change agent, attempting to foster changes inside schools by exerting external pressures for reform.

Better-informed businesspeople mean more significant advocacy is possible to help the schools. In this respect, educators have a responsibility to begin "educating" people outside of their walls about the real problems they face, the difficulties of dealing with undisciplined children who have no time for homework, and the need for mutual acceptance of responsibility. By ensuring that educators themselves have a common understanding and framing of the issues they face, and by working with business groups to discuss these issues in open forums and community settings, educators could do themselves a great service. Many businesspeople are still quite uninformed about the real nature of education's problems and may therefore have a tendency to "blame" the schools for failing. Only when they gain insight into the difficulties faced by educators—and when they realize that educators themselves are open to change and to useful suggestions—will they be able to take positive advocacy positions. This education about education is therefore a joint responsibility between schools and businesses. Educators have to be open enough to allow "outsiders" in to see their daily issues and concerns, to follow them around and gain insight into the problems. And businesspeople have to be willing to take the time to become educated about education, so that when they do try to influence public policy or make decisions related, as will be discussed below, to family policies, those decisions are well informed. Dialogue and on-going interaction is essential to this process. To some extent, engaging in this dialogue moves businesspeople and educators to a different perspective altogether: a perspective of collaboration and shared responsibility.

INTERINSTITUTIONAL PERSPECTIVE: BUSINESS AS EMPLOYER AND COLLABORATOR

A fundamental shift in thinking about the performance and responsibilities of schools takes place when institutions begin to rethink their own relationships to schools, their own roles in school performance, and how they need to relate to each other in a comprehensive *system* of influential factors that mutually affect student and school performance. This perspective can be called interinstitutional in that companies reconsider their roles as employers. The focus is on collaboration with schools and other relevant stakeholders as equal partners in a long-term process of social change. This perspective is the truly systemic one, for it provides for a "we are all in this together" approach to school restructuring that places responsibility mutually on schools *and* on employer partners.

The interinstitutional perspective shows up in two forms: business as employer and business as collaborator in systemic change. Interinstitutional relationships recognize the fundamental interpenetration[10] of social institutions in solving common problems. Adopting this perspective incorporates some of the activities in the independent institution (provision of resources, adopting schools, tutoring and mentoring relationships) as well as those occurring under the institutional bridge perspective. The emphasis, however, is on better understanding and reconstructing the *institutional infrastructure* that binds social institutions so that all can do their jobs better or at least differently.

Business as Employer

Business (or other employers, including government, small business, and nonprofits) practices have received relatively little attention in the school reform debate. Despite the lack of attention, business employment practices may be directly affected by the very problematic status of the family in the United States discussed in earlier chapters. As business leaders have begun to recognize that their practices affect the nature and availability of jobs that support families and that internal business practices affect the ability of parents to fulfill their parental and school-related responsibilities, some have begun making changes. There are three major arenas in which business's role as employer is important: provision of employment and economic opportunities, hiring practices, and development of family-related policies for employees.

Employment/Economic Opportunities

Providing jobs is one of the key roles that business plays as employer, yet the fundamental individualism that characterizes American business has, unlike much Japanese business enterprise, permitted businesses to shift resources, facilities, and jobs without consideration of the common good. Indeed, the federal public policy process itself has played little historical role in requesting businesses to consider the common good in business decisions, except (in some cases) at the state level. Thus, U.S. inner cities as well as other areas have been stripped of economic opportunities for relatively low-skilled residents as jobs have been outsourced to low-wage nations.

Where disinvestments, plant closings, outsourcings, and other forms of restructuring have occurred, the stability, cohesiveness, and tax bases of involved communities have been disrupted as jobs have been lost or changed. For example, the closing of automobile plants with relatively high-paying assembly line jobs in Detroit has left many youth in that city with no real hope of any economic opportunity if they stay in Detroit. Many jobs that are left have moved out to the suburbs. Companies have provided few new jobs to take the place of those lost. With few realistic economic opportunities open to them (combined with failing families that provide few socially positive role models for youth), it is little wonder that many inner-city youth are left, as one respondent indicated, "hopeless."

In addition, the very nature of the jobs provided and the kinds of skills those jobs require has shifted in recent years. Much of the so-called skills gap exists not because schools are providing particularly worse education than they did in the past, but rather because the types of jobs that are still available are demanding very different types and higher orders of skills and knowledge. As the economy moves into a knowledge-based economy, it becomes more imperative that skills provided in schools match with the upgraded needs of employers. Business decisions about location, sourcing, and training affect the availability and type of jobs in a given area, as well as the tax base, the amount of money citizens have to spend, and the general health of the community.

Hiring Practices

In the United States there have historically been few direct linkages between schools graduating entry-level workers and business enterprises. The reality has been that few students use schools to help them find jobs, few employers use grades, attendance, or other measures of student performance in hiring decisions, and high-school grades are only weakly correlated with early wages or entry to higher-status jobs.[11] In other developed nations, such as Japan, Germany, and the United Kingdom, there is much more explicit recognition of and attention to employers' roles in hiring recent school leave-takers, though these nations have evolved different systems for dealing with the transition between school and work, as noted above.

Seeing this gap suggests that some of the important things that businesses can do involve changing hiring practices so that those practices emphasize and support the importance and relevance of education. Simple things, such as asking for transcripts, checking grades, seeing that graduates have actually received diplomas before hiring them, would send an important message about the relevance of education to youth. For employers who hire part-time workers, similar practices might involve checking on grades and temporarily laying off students receiving failing grades or not meeting preset standards of academic performance. Such policies stress the value of education to students, its relevance and importance to employers, and highlight the relationship between working hard in school and future success in the workplace.

Family-Related Policies

Arguably, if companies truly wish to have a skilled future workforce, they need to reassess their own commitment to the family supports that are necessary to achieving a well-educated graduate. Corporate policies, wittingly or unwittingly, affect family life. Business practices affect the stability of employees' families, which in turn affects the state in which children attend schools. How much time parents have for their children and the extent to which parents encourage and support their children's educational attainments are important determinants of the degree to which the children themselves believe their education is important and how hard they work. The time available for parental support of education, in small and large ways, is partly a function, in turn, of corporate policies and the demands employers make on their employees. For example, many companies have fairly flexible policies for management-level employees who wish to take time off to deal with children's schools. Few, however, have extended such privileges to nonmanagers.

To overcome some of these gaps, companies could provide school-related "flextime" for all employees, by officially granting all employees a specified amount of time each year with which they can interact with their children's schools and encouraging such involvement. By encouraging employees to visit the children's classrooms, hold meetings with teachers and principals, attend school conferences, assemblies, and other events that show interest in the child's education, the company would send the message that what the school does is important and deserves to be supported by parents. Companies could also make investments in schools by permitting all employees with school-age children the equivalent of one personal day a year, to be used for school activities at the parent's discretion. Parents would then be able to attend two or three parent-teacher conferences, watch a play or assembly in which their child is performing, or help out with field day or field trips, as examples. They might spend an hour once a month helping out in the classroom and learning what is going on firsthand or use the time to spend a whole day aiding the teacher in some project.

More importantly, companies who are serious about improving education have to think about the demands placed on employees that affect family life. Strengthening families is fast becoming a societal issue of significant proportions (witness the Los Angeles riots). Businesses have an often unacknowledged and unrecognized but very important role to play in this arena. Consideration needs to be given to overtime demands, relocation requests, maternal- and paternal-leave policies, and time off for child care so that family members who are working have the flexibility they need to encourage youngsters with regard to their school activities. For example, parents need to be able to arrive home at a reasonable hour so that they have both time and energy enough to assure that a child's homework is done. A few progressive businesses are beginning programs at work that educate parents about appropriate ways to deal with schools, with homework, and with other educational matters as another way of emphasizing the importance of schools.

Collaborators in Systemic Change

Most progressive of all the initiatives to improve school performance are those based in comprehensive system change that intensively involve all of the relevant stakeholders. These collaborative alliances begin when key players from multiple sectors, typically including the schools, business, government, and possibly community service organizations, churches, the media, and others (depending on the local community structure) sit down at the same table and begin a dialogue focusing on how school performance can be improved. For communities where the dialogue is not "empty" but rather is substantive, new awareness about the nature of the problems schools face develops. As the dialogue continues, recognition that many of the problems of schools are, in fact, serious social problems rooted in economic, family, or value issues arises. As this happens, a subtle shift in thinking takes place: rather than blaming schools for their problems, participants in collaborative alliances begin to see that they are facing common problems and that solutions will require a united, collaborative effort, in which each of them changes the ways in which they relate to others.

Rather than being a multisystem orientation, successful collaborative alliances develop what can be termed an interinstitutional perspective. If the process works, collaborators become equal (or relatively equal in terms of the voice that participants have in the process of system change. Shifts in thinking at the local, state, and federal level are fueling this rethinking of the institutional infrastructure that binds schools, businesses, community organizations, and other agencies.

As has been discussed, one major shift has taken place in the early 1990s at the federal level, and it represents an archetype of what is beginning to happen at other levels. Apparently building on work done for the Hudson Institute, Workforce 2000,[12] combined with work done by the National Center for Education and the Economy, *America's Choice*,[13] among other major documents, the U.S. Department of Labor issued its Secretary's Commission on Achieving Necessary Skills (SCANS) report in 1991.[14] Termed the "missing link between business and schools" by *Business Week*,[15] the SCANS report identifies five competencies dealing with resources, interpersonal skills, information management, systems understanding, and use of technology, and a three-part foundation, consisting of basic skills, thinking skills, and personal qualities.

The promise of SCANS, in combination with the eight GOALS 2000: Educate America education goals mandated by Congress, is the potential to bring together two key government agencies in articulating a coherent vision for educational policy makers as well as business leaders. Whether the promise of these efforts will be realized, of course, is highly questionable as few monetary resources are being devoted to these efforts, at least at the federal level. They do arguably represent, however, a dramatic shift in thinking about the problems of the schools and need to be recognized as such.

Following issuance of SCANS, a number of key business organizations began incorporating the education goals and SCANS skills and competencies into their on-going educational agendas (or, in some cases, developing an educational agenda around them). Some of these organizations represent extensive networks of participants who can potentially be drawn into an educational agenda for their local areas. Key among these are the U.S. Chamber of Commerce and its many local affiliates, which has established broad goals for business involvement in education reform, The Conference Board, the National Association for Partners in Education, the Business Roundtable, and the National Alliance of Business.

The involvement of such networks in education holds a promise that national agendas can be translated down into local communities and that the shifts in thinking about schools that educated observers have made can be articulated locally in communities as well as at the state level. Recognizing that businesses, schools, and other institutions are all party to the common problem of education and that all need to take part in its solution is a first step toward long-term systemic change.

NOTES

1. Much of the thinking in this section is derived from S. A. Waddock, (1992a), "The Business Role in School Reform: From Feeling Good to System Change," *International Journal of Value-Based Management* 5(2): 105–126.

2. See T. Kolderie (1987), "Education That Works: The Right Role for Business," *Harvard Business Review* 65(5): 56–62.

3. P. M. Timpane and L. M. McNeill (1991). *Business Impact on Education and Child Development Reform* (New York: Committee for Economic Development).

4. To simplify exposition, the term "businesses" will be used to represent any employer or institution that might serve in these capacities.

5. See L. A. Cremin (1990), *Popular Education and Its Discontents* (New York: Harper & Row).

6. See Cremin (1990); and also his (1988), *American Education: The Metropolitan Experience, 1876–1980* (New York: Harper & Row).

7. See R. B. Reich (1991a), *The Work of Nations: Preparing Ourselves for Twenty-first Century Capitalism* (New York: Alfred A. Knopf).

8. S. M. Davis and W. H. Davidson (1991), *2020 Vision: Transform Your Business Today to Succeed in Tomorrow's Economy* (New York: Simon & Schuster).

9. S. Zuboff (1988), *In the Age of the Smart Machine: The Future of Work and Power* (New York: Basic Books).

10. L. E. Preston and J. E. Post (1975), *Private Management and Public Policy: The Principle of Public Responsibility* (Englewood Cliffs, NJ: Prentice-Hall).

11. There are numerous studies of this, including National Center for Educational Statistics (1983), "High School and Beyond: 1980 Senior Cohort First Follow-up," *Data File User's Manual*, Washington, D.C.; R. H. Meyer and D. A. Wise (1982), "High School Preparation and Early Labor Force Experience," in R. B. Freeman and D. A. Wise (eds.) *The Youth Labor Market Problem* (Chicago: University of Chicago Press), 277–347; J. Johnson and J. G. Bachman (1973), *The Transition from High School to Work* (Institute for Social Research. Ann Arbor: University of Michigan Press); all cited in J. E. Rosenbaum and T. Kariya (1989), "From High School to Work: Market and Institutional Mechanisms in Japan," *American Journal of Sociology* 94(6): 1334–1365.

12. W. B. Johnston and A. H. Packer (1987), Workforce 2000: Work and Workers for the Twenty-first Century (Indianapolis, IN: Hudson Institute).

13. National Center on Education and the Economy's Commission on the Skills of the American Workforce (1990), *America's Choice: High Skill or Low Wages!* (Rochester, NY: National Center on Education and the Economy).

14. Secretary's Commission on Achieving Necessary Skills (1992), *Learning a Living: A Blueprint for High Performance, A SCANS Report for America 2000*. Issued by the U.S. Department of Labor.

15. A. Bernstein (1992), "This is the Missing Link Between Business and Schools," *Business Week* April 20: 42–43.

Chapter 11 _____

Conclusions

So what have we learned about responsibility, networks of organizations sharing that responsibility, and the problems of education? It is clear by now that there *are* keys to improving American schools. But as we have seen there are no simplistic or single-faceted keys. Good schools are *part* of a total system of interactive forces and dynamics, individuals and institutions, goals and expectations that are linked together inextricably. To improve the schools, we need to deal with the system as a whole and not just small pieces of it. We have explored in detail the importance of family and community in leveraging improvement in schools. We have seen, though largely left to others to detail, the importance of fundamentally rethinking the ways in which education is delivered, both to meet the needs of current students and their families and to enable those students to meet the demands they will face in their nation, in their lives, and in their work. We have tried to look at the system and understand the interplay of forces and their impact on students and education and to outline the ways in which schools might restructure themselves into networks that spread the responsibility for education around, so that it can be appropriately shared in society.

Key elements of the system we have been exploring which may provide points of leverage for system change for the better include the following:

- strong communities that support family efforts to raise their children
- strong and supportive families that provide proper discipline, appropriate attitudes toward education, and support for children's educational achievement

- clear educational goals for individual children, for schools and school districts, and for the education system as a whole
- setting and maintaining high expectations for children, families, and communities that they will achieve the goals set and take on their appropriate responsibilities with respect to education
- recognition that education is a responsibility that must be shared by everyone in society
- organization of schools and other institutions into flexible networks that meet the local as well as national needs and standards
- provision of adequate resources for system change, for training, for educating all constituents about the importance and problems of education today, for dialogue and discussion in community forums, and for taking on and implementing the changed pedagogies, curriculum, and organizational structures (including new technologies) that will be needed in the future

Because of the general short-term orientation and "quick fix" attitude of many Americans, it is not entirely clear that the longer-term and more systemic approaches that are now being tested out will hold. Questions about whether there is enough patience to let these longer-term strategies play out abound, yet from the analysis we have seen in this book, short-term fixes of the programmatic or curriculum addition sort are unlikely to provide much real improvement. Indeed, that has been the experience over the past decade. Noble efforts to change the schools at the margins have been tried, while some of the more systemic approaches were being experimented with in some communities. But because the real problems in the system went largely unaddressed by the policies and initiatives, little really changed, as we saw in the early chapters of this book.

Only with the more community-based, participative approaches that involve everyone in taking on some of the burden for education will things really begin to change. The emergence of thinking about national standards, like the GOALS 2000, is a sign that progress is being made toward long-term solutions. Such long-term solutions are difficult; many false starts will be made, but good faith efforts do hold some degree of promise of real change.

Of course, none of these strategies of linking and sharing responsibility for education are short term in either their development or their impact. It takes time to establish and develop these relationships, especially the trust on which they are founded. And it also takes time to foster the types of changes in which people begin to change their attitudes, behaviors, and level of responsibility. Even when the right levers are found, it may be that no results will be immediately forthcoming. It takes time to establish goals nationally and locally and to have them promulgated, accepted, and implemented. It will take time to rethink our communities and the infrastructures that support them and to rebuild some of our lost connections to each other. But these connections are critical: they are connections of caring and of sharing responsibility.

Collaboration between schools and other institutions would expose more people to education, to children, and to the ways in which society has changed since World War II. Such linkages begin to rebuild through institutional mechanisms some of the community infrastructure that has been dissolving as families have hit troubled shores, women have returned to work, unemployment has taken its toll on some families, and poverty rates worsened or at best remained unabated. In effect, what is needed is to replace the lost networks of community with more formalized structures that rethink the very concept of community in a way that suits it to meet the needs of the twenty-first century. The twentieth century model is failing and barring a return to traditional values that seems currently unlikely, new mechanisms, such as the ones proposed in this book need to be devised to better link people within communities, provide them with a common sense of purpose, and a way to live their lives successfully despite the turbulence that surrounds us.

The road is long and arduous, but it is long past the time to travel down that road. Let us begin that journey together.

References

AFL-CIO. 1994. *The New American Workplace: A Labor Perspective*. Washington, D.C.: AFL-CIO.

Aldrich, H., and D. A. Whetten. 1981. Organization-sets, Action-sets, and Networks: Making the Most of Simplicity. In Nystrom and W. Starbuck (Eds.), *Handbook of Organizational Design*, vol. 1. Oxford: Oxford University Press.

Ansoff, H. 1. 1979. The Changing Shape of the Strategic Problem. *Journal of General Management* 4(4): 23–33.

Applebee, A. N., J. A. Langer, and I.U.S. Millis. 1989. *Crossroads in American Education*. Princeton, NJ: National Assessment of Educational Progress, Educational Testing Service.

Austom, D. R., and L. J. Lad. 1989. Issues Management Alliances: New Responses, New Values, and New Logics. In J. E. Post (Ed.), *Research in Corporate Social Performance and Policy*, vol. 11. Greenwich, CT: JAI Press.

Barrett, M. J. 1990. The Case for More School Days. *Atlantic* 266(6): 78–106.

Barth, R. S. 1991. *Improving Schools from Within: Teachers, Parents, and Principals Can Make the Difference*. San Francisco: Jossey-Bass.

Bartunek, J. M. 1988. The Dynamics of Personal and Organizational Reframing: Paradox and Transformation. In R. E. Quinn and K. S. Cameron (Eds.), *Toward a Theory of Change in Organization and Management*: 137–162. Cambridge, MA: Balinger.

Bellah, R. N., R. Madsen, W. M. Sullivan, A. Swidler, and S. M. Tipton. 1985. *Habits of the Heart: Individualism and Commitment in American Life*. New York: Harper & Row.

Bellah, R. N., R. Madsen, W. M. Sullivan, A. Swidler, and S. M. Tipton. 1991. *The Good Society*. New York: Alfred A. Knopf.

Benson, J. K. 1982. A Framework for Policy Analysis. In D. L. Rogel, D. A. Whetten, and associates (Eds.), *Interorganizational Coordination: Theory, Research, and Implementation*. Ames, Iowa: Iowa University Press.

Berger, S., M. L. Dertouzos, R. K. Lester, R. M. Solow, and L. C. Thurow. 1989. Toward a New Industrial America. *Scientific American* 260(6): 39–47.

Bernstein, A. 1992. This is the Missing Link Between Business and Schools. *Business Week* (April 20): 42–43.

Bird, F. E., and J. A. Waters. 1989. The Moral Muteness of Managers. *California Management Review* (Fall): 73–88.

Bloom, A. 1987. *The Closing of the American Mind.* New York: Simon & Schuster.

Boyd, W. L., and C. T. Kerchner. (Eds.). 1989. *The Politics of Excellence and Choice in Education: 1987 Yearbook of the Politics of Education Association.* New York: The Falmer Press.

Brodsy, M. 1989. International developments in apprenticeship. Monthly Labor Review (July): 40–41.

Callahan, R. E. 1962. *Education and the Cult of Efficiency*: 244–264. Chicago: The University of Chicago Press.

Carnegie Foundation for the Advancement of Teaching. 1992. *School Choice: A Special Report.* Princeton: Carnegie Foundation for the Advancement of Teaching.

Carnevale, A. P., and J. W. Johnston. 1989. *Training America: Strategies for the Nation.* Alexandria, VA: American Society for Training and Development and the National Center for Education and the Economy.

Chandler, A. D., Jr. 1962. *Strategy and Structure: Chapters in the History of the American Industrial Enterprise.* Cambridge, MA: The MIT Press.

Chubb, J. E., and T. M. Moe. 1988. No School is an Island: Politics, Markets, and Education. In W. L. Boyd and C. T. Kerchner. *The Politics of Excellence and Choice in Education: 1987 Yearbook of the Politics of Education Association*: 131–142. New York: The Falmer Press.

Chubb, J. E., and T. M. Moe. 1990. *Politics, Markets, and America's Schools.* Washington, D.C.: The Brookings Institution.

Clark, D. M. 1988. Has Business Missed the Boat on Educational Reform? *Business and Society Review* (Spring): 39–40.

Clendenin, J. L. 1989. For True Education Reform, Urgency and Patience. *Financier* (April): 30–34.

Cohen, S. S., and J. Zysman. 1987. *Why Manufacturing Matters: The Myth of the Post-Industrial Economy.* New York: Basic Books.

Cohen, S. S., and J. Zysman. 1989. Why Manufacturing Matters: The Myth of the Post-Industrial Economy. *California Management Review* 29(3): 9–26.

Comer, J. P. 1984. Home-School Relations as They Affect the Academic Success of Children. *Education and Urban Society* 16(3): 294–337.

Comer, J. P. 1987. Our National Dilemma: Building Quality Relationships. *EDRS*, November: 40.

Comer, J. P. 1988. Educating Poor Minority Children. *Scientific American* 259(5): 42–48.

Comer, J. P. 1989. Child Development and Education. *Journal of Negro Education* 58(2): 125–139.

Committee for Economic Development. 1985. *Investing In Our Children: Business and the Public Schools.* New York: Committee for Economic Development.

Committee for Economic Development. 1987. (revised 1989) *Children in Need: Investment Strategies of the Educationally Disadvantaged.* New York: Committee for Economic Development.

Committee for Economic Development. 1990. *An America That Works: The Life-Cycle Approach to a Competitive Work Force*. New York: Committee for Economic Development.

Committee for Economic Development. ca. 1992. *An Assessment of American Education: The View of Employers, Higher Educators, The Public, Recent Students, and Their Parents*. A Louis Harris Study. New York: Committee for Economic Development.

Committee for Economic Development. 1993. *Why Child Care Matters: Preparing Young Children for a More Productive America*. New York: Committee for Economic Development.

Cremin, L. A. 1970. *American Education: The Colonial Experience, 1607–1783*. New York: Harper & Row.

Cremin, L. A. 1980. *American Education. The National Experience, 1783–1876*. New York: Harper & Row.

Cremin, L. A. 1988. *American Education: The Metropolitan Experience, 1876–1980*. New York: Harper & Row.

Cremin, L. A. 1990. *Popular Education and Its Discontents*. New York: Harper & Row.

Crossen, C. 1990. Getting Down to Business. *The Wall Street Journal* February 9: R30.

Cummings, T. 1984. Transorganizational Development. In B. Staw and T. Cummings (Eds.), *Research in Organizational Behavior*, vol. 5. Greenwich, CT: JAI Press.

Davis, S. M. 1987. *Future Perfect*. Reading, MA: Addison-Wesley.

Davis, S. M., and W. H. Davidson. 1991. *2020 Vision: Transform Your Business Today to Succeed in Tomorrow's Economy*. New York: Simon & Schuster.

Derber, C. 1992. *Money, Murder, and the American Dream: Wilding from Wall Street to Main Street*. Boston: Faber and Faber.

Dertouzous, M. L., R. K. Lester, and R. M. Solow. 1989. *Made in America: Regaining the Production Edge*. Report of the MIT Commission on Industrial Productivity. Cambridge, MA: MIT Press.

Drucker, P. F. 1988. Management and the World's Work. *Harvard Business Review*, September–October: 65–76.

Drucker, P. F. 1989. *The New Realities: In Government and Politics / In Economics and Business / In Society and World View*. New York: Harper & Row.

Drucker, P. F. 1991. Japan: New Strategies for a New Reality. *The Wall Street Journal*, October 2.

Elbaum, B. 1989. Why Apprenticeship Persisted in Britain but not in the United States. *The Journal of Economic History* 49(2): 337–349.

Emery, F. E., and E. L. Trist. 1965. The Casual Texture of Organizational Environments. *Human Relations* 18: 21–31.

Finn, C. E., Jr. 1992. Up From Mediocrity: What Next in School Reform. *Policy Review* (Summer): 80–83.

Fosler, R. S. 1990. *The Business Role in State Education Reform*. New York: National Committee for Economic Development.

Freeman, E., and J. Liedtka. 1991. Corporate Social Responsibility: A Critical Approach. *Business Horizons*, July–August: 92–98.

Galagan, P. 1988. Joining Forces: Business and Education Take on Competitiveness. *Training and Development Journal* 42(7): 26–29.

Gardner, H. 1991. *The Unschooled Mind: How Children Think and How Schools Should Teach*. New York: Basic Books.

Gerlach, M. 1987. Business Alliances and the Strategy of the Japanese Firm. *California Management Review* (Fall): 126–142.

Goddard, R. W. 1989. The Crisis in Workplace Literacy. *Personnel Journal* (December): 73–81.

Goodlad, J. I. 1976. In J. S. Golub (Ed.), *Facing the Future: Issues in Education and Schooling*. New York: McGraw-Hill.

Gordon, S. 1991. *Prisoners of Men's Dreams: Striking Out for a New Feminine Future*. Boston: Little, Brown and Company.

Graham, P. A. 1992. *SOS: Sustain Our Schools*. New York: Hill & Wang.

Gray, B. 1985. Conditions Facilitating Interorganizational Collaboration. *Human Relations* 38(10): 911–936.

Gray, B. 1989. *Collaborating*. San Francisco: Jossey-Bass.

Halberstam, D. 1986. *The Reckoning*. New York: Avon Books.

Hamburg, D. A. 1992. *Today's Children: Creating a Future for a Generation in Crisis*. New York: Times Books.

Hamilton, S. F. 1990. Is There Life After High School? Developing Apprenticeships in America. *The Harvard Education Letter* 6(4): 39–43.

Hammer, M., and J. Champy. 1993. *Reengineering the Corporation: A Manifesto for Business Revolution*. New York: Harper Business.

Handy, C. 1990. *The Age of Unreason*. Boston: Harvard Business School Press.

Haney, W. 1984. Testing Reasoning and Reasoning About Testing. *Review of Education Research* 54(4): 597–654.

Hayes, R. H., and W. J. Abernathy. 1982. Managing Our Way to Economic Decline. *Harvard Business Review* 58(4): 58–73.

Hayes, R. H., and S. C. Wheelwright. 1984. *Restoring Our Competitive Edge: Competing through Manufacturing*. New York: John Wiley & Sons.

Hogan, D. 1992. School Organization and Student Achievement: A Review Essay. *Educational Theory* 42(1): 83–105.

Iannaccone, L. 1988. From Equity to Excellence: Political Context and Dynamics. In W. L. Boyd and C. T. Kerchner (Eds.), *The Politics of Excellence and Choice in Education: 1987*: 49–66. New York: The Falmer Press.

IBM. 1990. *Education Fact Sheet*. Armonk, NY: IBM Press.

Jallade, J. P. 1989. Recent Trends in Vocational Education and Training: An Overview. *European Journal of Education* 24(2): 103–125.

Johnson, J., and J. G. Bachman. 1973. *The Transition from High School to Work*, Institute for Social Research. Ann Arbor: University of Michigan Press.

Johnston, W. B., and A. H. Packer. 1987. *Workforce 2000: Work and Workers for the Twenty-first Century*. Indianapolis: Hudson Institute.

Jorde, T. M., and D. J. Teece. 1989. Competition and Cooperation: Striking the Right Balance. *California Management Review* 31(3): 25–37.

Kanter, R. M. 1989. *When Giants Learn to Dance*. New York: Simon & Schuster.

Katz, M. B. 1987. *Reconstructing American Education*. Boston: Presidents and Fellows of Harvard College.

Kolderie, T. 1987. Education That Works: The Right Role for Business. *Harvard Business Review* 65(5): 56–62.

Kotlowitz, A. 1991. *There Are No Children Here: The Story of Two Boys Growing Up in the Other America*. New York: Doubleday.

Kozol, J. 1985. *Illiterate America*. New York: New American Library (Plume).

Kozol, J. 1991. *Savage Inequalities: Children in America's Schools*. New York: Crown.

Leonard, H. B. 1992. *By Choice or By Chance? Tracking the Values in Massachusetts Public Spending*. Boston: Pioneer Institute for Public Policy Research.

Lerman, R. I., and H. Pouncy. 1990. The Compelling Case for Youth Apprenticeships. *The Public Interest* 101: 62–77.

Lodge, G. C. 1990. *Perestroika for America: Restructuring Business-Government Relations for World Competitiveness*. Cambridge, MA: Harvard Business School Press.

Lodge, G. C., and E. F. Vogel. 1987. *Ideology and National Competitiveness: An Analysis of Nine Countries*. Boston: Harvard Business School Press.

Magaziner, I., and M. Patinkin. 1989. *The Silent War: Inside the Global Business Battles Shaping America's Future*. New York: Random House.

Marshall, S. 1991. The Genesis and Evolution of Pre-Vocational Education: West Germany. *Oxford Review of Education* 17(1): 89–102.

Mauriel, J. J. 1989. *Strategic Leadership for Schools: Creating and Sustaining Productive Change*. San Francisco: Jossey-Bass.

McCann, J. E. 1983. Design Guidelines for Social Problem-solving Interventions. *Journal of Applied Behavioral Science* 19(2): 177–192.

Meyer, R. H., and D. A. Wise. 1982. High School Preparation and Early Labor Force Experience. In R. B. Freemand and D. A. Wise (Eds.) *The Youth Labor Market Problem*: 277–347. Chicago: University of Chicago Press.

Miles, R. E., and C. C. Snow. 1986a. Fit, Failure and the Hall of Fame. *California Management Review* 26(3): 10–28.

Miles, R. E., and C. C. Snow. 1986b. Network Organizations: New Concepts for New Forms. *California Management Review* 38(3): 62–73.

Mishel, L., and D. M. Frankel. 1992. *The State of Working America, 1990–91 Edition*. Armonk, NY: M. E. Sharpe Company (Economic Policy Institute).

Nadler, D. A., and M. L. Tushman. 1989. Organizational Frame Bending: Principles for Managing Reorientation. *Academy of Management Executive* 3(3): 194–204.

National Alliance of Business. 1989a. *The Compact Project: School-Business Partnerships for Improving Education*. Washington, D.C.: National Alliance of Business.

National Alliance of Business. 1989b. *Business Strategies that Work: A Planning Guide for Education Restructuring*. Washington, D.C.: National Alliance of Business.

National Alliance of Business. 1989c. *A Blueprint for Business on Restructuring Education*. Washington, D.C.: National Alliance of Business.

National Alliance of Business. 1989d. *America's Leaders Speak Out On Business-Education Partnerships*. Washington, D.C.: National Alliance of Business.

National Alliance of Business. ca. 1990a. *The Business Roundtable Participation Guide: A Primer for Business on Education*. New York: Business Roundtable.

National Alliance of Business. 1990b. *Business Strategies that Work: A Planning Guide for Education Restructuring*. Washington, D.C.: National Alliance of Business.

National Alliance of Business. 1991. *The Compact Project: Final Report*. Washington, D.C.: National Alliance of Business.

National Association of Partners in Education, Inc. 1991. *National School District Partnership Survey: Statistical Report 1991*. Alexandria, VA: National Association of Partners in Education, Inc.

National Center for Educational Statistics. 1983. High School and Beyond: 1980 Senior Cohort First Follow-up. *Data File User's Manual*. Washington, D.C.: U.S. Department of Education.

National Center for Education Statistics. 1991. *The Condition of Education 1991*, vol. 1. Washington, D.C.: U.S. Department of Education.

National Center for Education Statistics. 1992. *Digest of Education Statistics*. U.S. Department of Education, Office of Educational Research and Improvement.

National Center on Education and the Economy's Commission on the Skills of the American Workforce. 1990. *America's Choice: High Skill or Low Wages!* Rochester, NY: National Center on Education and the Economy.

National Commission on Excellence in Education. 1983. *A Nation at Risk: The Imperative for Educational Reform*. Washington, D.C.: U.S. Government Printing Office.

National Education Goals Panel. 1993a. *The National Education Goals Report: Building the Best*. Summary Guide. Washington, D.C.: NEGP Communications.

National Education Goals Panel. 1993b. *Building a Nation of Learners*. Washington, D.C.: U.S. Department of Education.

Ohmae, K. 1990. *The Borderless World: Power and Strategy in the Interlinked Economy*. New York: Harper Business.

Orton, J. D., and K. E. Weick. 1990. Loosely Coupled Systems: A Reconceptualization. *Academy of Management Review* 15(2): 203–223.

Osborne, D. W., and T. Gaebler. 1992. *Reinventing Government: How the Entrepreneurial Spirit is Transforming the Public Sector*. Reading, MA: Addison-Wesley.

Perkins, D. 1992. *Smart Schools: From Training Memories to Educating Minds*. New York: Free Press.

Peters, T. 1987. *Thriving on Chaos*. New York: Harper & Row.

Peters, T. 1988. Facing Up to the Need for a Management Revolution. *California Management Review* 30(2): 7–38.

Phillips, K. 1990. *The Politics of Rich and Poor: Wealth and the American Electorate in the Reagan Aftermath*. New York: Random House.

Poplin, M., and J. Weeres. 1992. *Voices From The Inside: A Report on Schooling from Inside the Classroom*. Claremont, CA: The Institute for Education in Transformation at the Claremont Graduate School.

Porter, M. E. 1990a. The Competitive Advantage of Nations. *Harvard Business Review* (March–April): 73–93.

Porter, M. E. 1990b. *The Competitive Advantage of Nations*. New York: Macmillan.

Postman, N. 1979. *Teaching as a Conserving Activity*. New York: Delacorte Press.

Postman, N. 1992. *Technopoly: The Surrender of Culture to Technology*. New York: Alfred A. Knopf.

Preston, L. E., & J. E. Post. 1975. *Private Management and Public Policy: The Principle of Public Responsibility*. Englewood Cliffs, NJ: Prentice-Hall.

Quinn, J. B. 1992. The Intelligent Enterprise: A New Paradigm. *Academy of Management Executive* 6(4): 48–63.

Rasell, M. E., and L. Mishel. 1990. *Shortchanging Education: How U.S. Spending on Grades K-12 Lags Behind Other Industrial Nations*. Briefing Paper. Washington, D.C.: Economic Policy Institute.

Reich, R. B. 1990. Who Is Us? *Harvard Business Review* (January–February): 53–64.

Reich, R. B. 1991a. *The Work of Nations: Preparing Ourselves for Twenty-first Century Capitalism*. New York: Alfred A. Knopf.

Reich, R. B. 1991b. Who Is Them? *Harvard Business Review* (March–April): 77–88.

Reich, R. B. 1983. *The Next American Frontier*. New York: Times Books.

Richards, C. 1990. What Western Europe's Job Training Systems Can Teach America. *Commerce Magazine*: 39–40.

Rosenbaum, J. E., and T. Kariya. 1989. From High School to Work: Market and Institutional Mechanisms in Japan. *American Journal of Sociology* 94(6): 1334–1365.

Russell, R. 1984. *The Institutional Background for the Transition from School to Working Life in the FRG*. Coombe Lodge Working Paper, Information Bank Number 1881. Blagdon, England.

Savas, E. S. 1987. Privatization. In S. P. Sethi and C. M. Falbe (Eds.), *Business and Society: Dimensions of Conflict and Cooperation*: 270–281. Lexington, MA: Lexington Books.

Scherer, F. M. 1980. *Industrial Market Structure and Economic Performance*, 2d ed., Chicago: Rand McNally.

Schor, J. 1991. *The Overworked American: The Unexpected Decline of Leisure*. New York: Basic Books.

Schoultz, C. O. 1986. Reading Between the Lines: The High Cost of Ignorance. *Training and Development Journal* (September): 44–47.

Secretary's Commission on Achieving Necessary Skills. 1992. *Learning a Living: A Blueprint for High Performance, A SCANS Report for America 2000*. Washington, D.C.: U.S. Department of Labor.

Senge, P. M. 1991. *The Fifth Discipline: The Art and Practice of the Learning Organization*. New York: Doubleday.

Sizer, T. R. 1992. *Horace's School: Redesigning the American High School*. Boston: Houghton Mifflin Company.

Starr, M. K. (Ed.). 1988. *Global Competitiveness: Getting the U.S. Back on Track*. New York: W. W. Norton.

Steele, S. 1990. *The Content of Our Character*. New York: St. Martin's Press.

Stevenson, H. W., C. Chen, and S.-Y. Lee. 1993. Mathematics Achievement of Chinese, Japanese, and American Children: Ten Years Later. *Science*, 259: 53–58.

Stevenson, H. W., S.-Y. Lee, and J. W. Stigler. 1986. Mathematics Achievement of Chinese, Japanese, and American Children. *Science* 231: 693.

Stone, M. 1983. The Plague of Illiteracy. *U.S. News and World Report* (February 21): 90.

Stone, N. 1991. Does Business Have Any Business in Education? *Harvard Business Review*, March–April.

Sykes, C. 1992. *A Nation of Victims: The Decay of the American Character*. New York: St. Martin's Press.

Teece, D. J. 1987. *The Competitive Challenge: Strategies for Industrial Innovation and Renewal*. Cambridge, MA: Ballinger.

Timpane, P. M., and L. M. McNeill. 1991. *Business Impact on Education and Child Development Reform.* New York: Committee for Economic Development.

Toffler, A. 1990. *Powershift: Knowledge, Wealth, and Violence at the Edge of the Twenty-first Century.* New York: Bantam Books.

Towers Perrin and Hudson Institute. 1990. *Workforce 2000: Competing in a Seller's Market: Is Corporate America Prepared?* Indianapolis: Hudson Institute.

Troy, K. 1986. *Meeting Human Needs: Corporate Programs and Partnerships.* From The Conference Board Corporate Relations Program. New York: The Conference Board, Inc.

United States Department of Education. 1991. *America 2000: An Education Strategy— National Goals of President Bush and Governors.* Washington, D.C.: U.S. Department of Education.

Useem, M. 1989. *Liberal Education and The Corporation: The Hiring and Advancement of College Graduates.* New York: A. de Gruyten.

Van Scotter, R. D. 1991. *Public Schooling in America: A Reference Handbook.* Santa Barbara, CA: ABC-CLIO.

Vice, D. G. 1990. Business and Education in Canada. *Business in the Contemporary World* Autumn: 52–57.

Waddock, S. A. 1986. Public-Private Partnership as Product and Process. In J. E. Post (Ed.), *Research in Corporate Social Performance and Policy,* vol. 7. Greenwich, CT: JAI Press.

Waddock, S. A. 1988. Building Successful Social Partnerships. *Sloan Management Review* 29(4): 17–23.

Waddock, S. A. 1989a. Understanding Social Partnerships: An Evolutionary Model of Partnership Organizations. *Administration and Society* 21(1): 78–100.

Waddock, S. A. 1989b. How Job Training Can Work for Everyone. *Business and Society Review* (Fall): 64–68.

Waddock, S. A. 1991a. A Typology of Social Partnership Organizations. *Administration and Society* 22(4): 480–515.

Waddock, S. A. 1991b. The Centrality of Social Issues in Management: A Macrosystems Perspective. In K. Paul (Ed.), *Contemporary Issues in Business and Society in the United States and Abroad.* Lewiston, NY: Edwin Mellen Press.

Waddock, S. A. 1992a. The Business Role in School Reform: From Feeling Good to System Change. *The International Journal of Value-Based Management* 5(2): 105–126.

Waddock, S. A. 1992b. The National Alliance of Business Compact Project: Business Involvement in Public Education. In J. E. Post (Ed.), *Research in Corporate Social Performance and Policy* 13: 31–82. Greenwich, CT: JAI Press.

Waddock, S. A. 1993a. Lessons from the National Alliance of Business Compact Project: Business and Public Education Reform. *Human Relations* 46(7): 849–879.

Waddock, S. A. 1993b. The Spider's Web: Influences on School Performance. *Business Horizons,* September–October: 39–48.

Waddock, S. A. 1993c. The Fractal Organization or Alliances, Networks, and Fragments: How Organizations Adapt to Chaos. Presented at the 1993 Academy of Management Annual Meeting, Atlanta, GA.

Waddock, S. A. 1994. *Collaboration for Systemic Reform in Education: The Fourth Wave.* New York: The Conference Board.

Waddock, S. A., and J. E. Post. 1991. Social Entrepreneurs and Catalytic Change. *Public Administration Review* 51(5): 393–401.

Waterman, R. H., Jr. 1987. *The Renewal Factor*. New York: Bantam Books.

Watts, G. 1992. Interview by author at The National Center on Educational Innovation of the National Education Association, Washington, D.C.

Weick, K. E. 1976. Educational Organizations as Loosely Coupled Systems. *Administrative Science Quarterly* 21(1): 1–11, 19.

Whetten, D. A. 1987. Interorganizational Relations. In J. W. Lorsch (Ed.), *Handbook of Organizational Behavior*: 238–253. Englewood Cliffs, NJ: Prentice-Hall.

The White House. 1991a. *Remarks by the President at the Presentation of the National Education Strategy, 1991*. Washington, D.C.: Press Secretary.

The White House. 1991b. *America 2000: The President's Education Strategy*. Fact Sheet. Washington, D.C.: Press Secretary.

Wiggins, G. 1993. Accountability, Testing, and Schools: Toward Local Responsibility and Away from Change by Mandate. *Business Horizons* September–October: 13–23.

Wolff, S. B., and G. C. Leader. 1993. *Business and the Public Schools: The Potential for a Partnership Based on Total Quality Management*. Boston: Boston University, Human Resource Policy Institute.

Woodring, P. 1983. *The Persistent Problems of Education*. Bloomington, IN: Phi Delta Kappa Educational Foundation.

Zuboff, S. 1988. *In the Age of the Smart Machine: The Future of Work and Power*. New York: Basic Books.

Index

About the Author

SANDRA A. WADDOCK is Associate Professor at Boston College's Carroll School of Management, where she teaches Strategic Management and Social Issues in Management. She is widely published on the topics of public-private partnerships, corporate social performance, corporate community involvement, and business involvement in education. She has completed a major study on business involvement in systemic education reform for the Conference Board.